CULTURE, RELIGION, AND THE SACRED SELF

A Critical Introduction
to the Anthropological Study
of Religion

Jacob Pandian
California State University, Fullerton

Prentice Hall, Englewood Cliffs, New Jersey 07632

Library of Congress Cataloging-in-Publication Data

Pandian, Jacob.
    Culture, religion, and the sacred self : a critical introduction
to the anthropological study of religion / Jacob Pandian.
        p.   cm.
    Includes bibliographical references.
    ISBN 0-13-194226-3
    1. Ethology—Religious aspects. 2. Religion—Study and teaching.
3. Religion—Study and teaching.--History. I. Title.
BL256.P36 1991
306.6—dc20   89-77876
                                                        CIP

Editorial/production supervision: Cyndy Lyle Rymer
Cover design: Ben Santora
Manufacturing buyer: Ed O'Dougherty

Printed in the United States of America
10 9 8 7 6 5 4 3

ISBN 0-13-194226-3

Prentice-Hall International (UK) Limited, *London*
Prentice-Hall of Australia Pty. Limited, *Sydney*
Prentice-Hall Canada Inc., *Toronto*
Prentice-Hall Hispanoamericana, S.A., *Mexico*
Prentice-Hall of India Private Limited, *New Delhi*
Prentice-Hall of Japan, Inc., *Tokyo*
Simon & Schuster Asia Pte. Ltd., *Singapore*
Editora Prentice-Hall do Brasil, Ltda., *Rio de Janeiro*

This book is dedicated to my mother, the late Rathnam Ammal of Trivandrum, India; and to my wife, Dr. Susan Parman, and our daughter, Gigi Pandian.

Contents

Preface

This book offers a comprehensive discussion of the objectives and scope of the anthropological study of religion and provides an interpretation of the relationship between religion and the cultural formulations of the self. I review the relevant anthropological theories of religion and present a comparative, cross-cultural analysis of the nature of shamanism, religious movements, myth, and ritual. I hope that readers will find this book a useful guide to understanding how and why cultural conceptions of supernatural beings/powers and the cultural formulations of the self are interconnected. I also hope that this book will help readers to become acquainted with the wide range of anthropological studies of religion and will thereby facilitate the evaluation of different anthropological approaches to the study of religion.

In some ways, this book may be viewed as a theoretical discourse on the anthropological study of "self." The anthropological study of self differs from the psychological study of self in its investigation of the nature of the cultural or symbolic self: Through such a study, we gain an understanding of universal "religious" features in the cultural construction of human identity; also, in anthropological analysis, we examine the cultural formulations of the self in relation to the consequences of such formulations for the maintenance of particular cultural traditions (including political, economic, religious, and other activities that have significance for a group). We may identify this approach to the study of self as "semiotic" in the sense that we are involved in the analysis of how the symbols of the self are related (syntactics), what the symbols signify or mean (semantics), and how the symbols are used (pragmatics). Religion, I suggest, is a cultural activity that is linked with the creation and maintenance of certain kinds of self-conceptions. Religion transforms biological (natural) human identity into supernatural human identity through semiotic structures: Symbols of self (representations of who am I and what am I) are connected with symbols of the supernatural or sacred other (gods, goddesses, spirits, etc.); conceptions of self acquire meaning as sacred through the reference of self to its connectedness with the sacred other; and the symbols of the sacred self are deployed in affirming or explaining various aspects of human life (as such aspects are defined as valid in a given cultural tradition).

Many chapters of this book can be read as separate "essays" or "papers." The fundamental unity of the book stems from the use of a semiotically oriented "culture and self" framework for the study of religion, and from the interpretation of shamanism, priesthood, religious movements, myth, and ritual as cultural activities that pertain to the creation and maintenance of the cultural or symbolic self as sacred (supernatural). I suggest that the concepts of shamanism and priesthood can be used to identify two types of cultural phenomena pertaining to the creation and maintenance of the sacred self. One type refers to the affirmation of the sacredness (supernaturalness) of the cultural self as it occurs (in times of crisis and anxiety) through a ritual merger between the symbols of the self and symbols of the sacred other (gods, goddesses, spiritual powers, etc.). The other type refers to the affirmation of the sacredness (supernaturalness) of the cultural self as it occurs (in everyday social life) through the symbolic enactments of mythological charters. The former type of sacred self has been identified in this book as the "shamanistic self" and the latter type as the "priestly self."

The chapters of this book are organized into five major units of discourse. Part One introduces the reader to the anthropological discourse on culture, religion, and self; discusses the central premises of the book; and reviews how anthropologists have defined and classified religious phenomena. Part Two summarizes significant theoretical contributions in the anthropological study of religion; it includes chapters on the historical development of the study of religion, and reviews and compares particular approaches (psychological, sociological, linguistic, and phenomenological) to the anthropology of religion; it also presents a theoretical formulation for the study of the relationship between culture, self, and religion. Part Three offers an extensive description and comprehensive discussion of shamanism, priesthood, and religious movements. Part Four examines some relevant theoretical studies on myth and ritual and includes examples and interpretations of different types of myth and ritual. Part Five raises some questions about the relevance of the anthropological study of religion; offers some thoughts on the unnecessary, counterproductive opposition between science and religion; and suggests that our understanding of religion will be enhanced by synthesizing the contributions of the anthropology of religion and the history of religion. Each of the five units is organized internally as a coherent whole, in terms of the designated topic of discussion, so that a reader can select any unit and acquire an understanding of the data and discussion contained in it. The reader can, in fact, study each unit independent of the others.

I thank Dr. Don A. Schweitzer, dean of the School of Humanities and Social Sciences, California State University at Fullerton, for his support of this project. I also thank Dr. James J. Preston, SUNY—Oneonta, and Dr. Luther P. Gerlach, University of Minnesota, for their helpful reviews of the manuscript. Columbia University Press gave permission to quote from the book *Totems and Teachers: Perspectives on the History of Anthropology* edited by Sydel Silverman (© 1981).

I could not have completed this book without the confidence and love of my wife, Professor Susan Parman. Our daughter, Gigi, gave me enthusiastic support and help throughout the writing of this book. I am grateful to them.

Jacob Pandian
Department of Anthropology, California State University at Fullerton

PART ONE
INTRODUCTION:
CULTURE, SELF, AND RELIGION

CHAPTER ONE
Objectives and Scope of This Book

THE OBJECTIVES OF THIS BOOK

A main objective of this book is to formulate an anthropological approach to the study of religion, conceptualizing and analyzing the relationship between religion and the self. I analyze and interpret the different kinds of relationship that exist between the symbols of the self (representations of and meanings associated with identity images such as "who am I" and "what am I") and the symbols of the sacred other (representations of and meanings associated with supernatural beings and powers).

Besides formulating a particular theoretical and methodological approach to the study of religion, this book also presents a detailed discussion of the distinctive features of the anthropological perspective, the anthropology of religion, and anthropological theories of religion. It also provides descriptions and interpretations of religious phenomena that are anthropologically delineated as shamanism, priesthood, religious movements, myth, and ritual.

In a broad, theoretical sense, this book's goal is to promote the study of religion within a semiotic framework of culture and self. It is generally acknowledged that the anthropological study of religion combines the insights and findings of several disciplines, including linguistics, history, psychology, philosophy, and sociology. *My orientation to the anthropological study of religion is that it is particularly aligned with history and linguistics in its commitment to reveal and interpret both the unconscious (or underlying) and conscious (or surface) aspects of cultural reality.* Anthropology, linguistics, and history are inseparable in the foregoing commitment: These disciplines decode the unconscious, reversible structures of culture as well as interpret the patterns of conscious, irreversible expressions of particular cultural traditions.

In a general, philosophical sense, the anthropological study of religion is dependent on the existence of free inquiry and critical thinking. The teaching of the anthropology of religion may be viewed as a barometer of a society's commitment to the high ideals of liberal arts and social science education in academia. In the anthropological study of religion, we analyze our cherished and sanctified assumptions of culture and self, and, as a result, we raise questions about how we define ourselves as human beings. The anthropologist does not uphold or condemn any particular religious self-conception to be true or false but is committed to exploring the relationship of culture, religion, and the self; in other words, the anthropological orientation promotes *methodological relativism* to analyze and understand why and how the cultural formulations of the relationships between (and among) the symbols of self and the symbols of supernatural beings/powers are coherent and meaningful to those who use them.

THE THESIS OF THIS STUDY

> Men alone have the faculty of conceiving the ideal, of adding something to the real. . . . [T]he sacred is that something added to and above the real. (Durkheim 1915: 469)
>
> [Human beings put themselves] in the place of the generalized other, which represents the organized responses of all the members of the group. (Mead 1934: 163)
>
> The role of culture in human life implies that men must be concerned . . . with the *meaning* of their experience, that is, not merely with whether a given experience gratifies a wish or fills a need or contrariwise involves pain or deprivation, but also with the *fit* between the *expectations* of experience. . . . (Parsons 1972: 91)
>
> [The Bororos, members of a tribe by that name in Brazil] go beyond even Durkheim and Comte and consider that human life should itself be regarded as a department of culture. To say, therefore, that death is either natural or unnatural is meaningless. In fact and law alike, death is both *natural* and *anti-cultural*. (Levi-Strauss 1968: 219)

Human beings acquire their humanness by becoming symbols to themselves and others; they exist as subject and object, and as self and other, in an interactional relationship in a world of symbols that involves taking the role of the other and organizing thoughts and feelings in a culturally coherent and appropriate manner. Cultural coherence and appropriateness are achieved by learning to deploy the public symbols that constitute a culture or way of life. *Culture* refers to "the forms of things that people have in mind, their models for perceiving, relating and otherwise interpreting them" (Goodenough 1957: 167), but as Geertz (1973) has forcefully argued, *culture* cannot be defined in psychological terms: "[C]ulture consists of socially established structures of meaning" embodied in symbols, and "culture is public because meaning is" (Geertz 1973: 12). Stated differently, human interaction is cultural interaction, and meaning is a culturally constituted reality.

The identity of any object, event, or person derives from the meanings associated with and conveyed through its representations or symbols. Cultures everywhere have symbols of the self that convey the characteristics and meanings of human identity, and cultures everywhere have symbols that convey the characteristics and meanings of supernatural identity; in other words, symbols that signify "who am I" or "what am I" and "who or what is supernatural" are universal. However, a symbol's representation of an object, event, or person is an arbitrary association of meanings that is shared conventionally; an individual has to learn the characteristics and meanings that are associated with the human and supernatural identities in specific cultural contexts, that is, within the boundaries of a particular cultural configuration. Thus, we find great variation in how human and supernatural identities are symbolized.

I suggest in this book that the roots of religion are in symbolizing human identity as having "super-natural" characteristics, that is, in having qualities that are not confined to the physical/natural world. Symbolization of human identity as having supernatural characteristics is most often linked with or related to symbols or representations of supernatural beings and powers, and occasionally with pantheistic ideas about how the human mind is an aspect of the universal mind. My study examines the nature of the relationship between cultural representations of supernatural beings and powers (which I denote as *symbols of the sacred other*, or the *symbolic sacred other*) and cultural representations of human identity (which I denote as *symbols of the self*, or the *symbolic self*). I describe and interpret how the relationship between the representations of supernatural and human identities acquire different significations in the cultural formulations of shamanism and priesthood, and I analyze how these formulations are constituted, maintained, evaluated, and dramatized in the domains of myth and ritual.

The thesis advanced in this book is as follows: Symbols of the self (the symbolic self) signify the characteristics and meanings of what it is to be human. Symbols of the sacred other signify the existence and characteristics of supernatural beings, entities, and powers, and they connote the linkages between the symbolic self and the sacred other. I delineate "religion" as a concept to identify cultural phenomena pertaining to the production and maintenance of the *symbolic self as sacred or supernatural*. The formulation or production of the symbols of the sacred self occur in two modalities, with variations that result when these two modalities combine in different ways: (1) through contact, resulting in partial or complete union between the symbols of the sacred other and the self, and (2) through positive or negative identification with the symbols of the sacred other. The first modality constitutes what I will characterize as the *shamanistic sacred self*; the second type can be identified as the *priestly sacred self*. These are "ideal type" constructs.

The creation of the self as sacred is an ongoing cultural process that occurs in socialization of children and in various "secular," social domains in which the symbols of supernatural beings and powers are deployed, but the significance of symbolizing the self as sacred in relation to the representation of the sacred other (symbols of supernatural beings and powers) is more pronounced in the operation of shamanism and priesthood, as well as in the domains of myth and ritual. The study of religious movements can reveal clearly the constitution and reconstitution of the sacred self and can shed light on the nature and significance of the different types of sacred selves (shamanistic and priestly selves) in different cultural contexts.

The shamanistic self is a type of symbolic coherence and integration that manifests in cultural arenas in which a resolution of stress (arising from unpredictable events, sickness, life passages, etc.) occurs; thus, ritual contexts such as divination, healing and initiation, and religious movements in their early stages are "ideal" laboratories for the study of the nature and meaning of the shamanistic self.

The priestly self is a type of symbolic coherence that manifests in everyday life patterns of thought and behavior in which human beings validate social order and social conventions with reference to the symbols of the sacred other.

THE COMPARATIVE, CROSS-CULTURAL STUDY OF RELIGION: THE ANTHROPOLOGY OF RELIGION

In later chapters I review the contributions of leading anthropologists, sociologists, psychologists, and historians of religion who have explained the origin and function of religion, and I relate their theories to the perspective taken in this book. In this section I describe the distinctive features of the anthropological perspective and discuss the cultural study of religion.

Every discipline has its own paradigmatic framework that justifies or validates the theoretical approaches and methods used to explain phenomena. The phenomena studied by anthropology are humankind and the creations of humankind, a definition of subject matter that by itself is obviously too broad to retain disciplinary integrity; there are many other disciplines that study humankind and the creations of humankind. However, anthropology is distinct in that its primary data are from "other" (i.e., non-Western) cultures, and anthropologists explain humankind and the creations of humankind holistically and comparatively from a naturalistic, cross-cultural perspective. Anthropologists want to understand the past, present, and future of humankind as well as to explain or interpret the nature of institutions and the similarities and differences in cultures. The central concept of anthropology is culture, a nonbiological, nonpsychological reality that is created by and that governs and guides human behavior.

The *anthropology of religion* is a comparative, cross-cultural study of religion that takes into account biological, social, psychological, and historical factors in describing and theorizing about religion as part of culture. Anthropologists frequently use the theoretical formulations and studies of sociologists, psychologists, historians, and philosophers, just as these branches of knowledge use anthropological findings, but their focus and areas of inquiry are different.

The *sociology of religion* studies the functions and functional interrelatedness of religion and other institutions as well as the processes of religious institutionalization and religious organizations in urban or socially elaborate societies.

The *history of religion* is primarily concerned with the study of world religions as well as the study of the historical development and phenomenological structure of religious ideas in different parts of the world. Mircea Eliade (1969:70–71) looks at the scope of the history of religion as assimilating "culturally the spiritual universes" of all peoples without reducing them to other phenomena.

In the *psychology of religion,* psychologists often study the relationship between personality structure and religious beliefs. William James (1937:31–32) theorized about the "feelings, acts and experiences of individual men in their solitude . . . in relation to whatsoever they consider the divine." Sigmund Freud theorized about the relationship between neurosis and religion, and many psychologists study the personality configuration of religious leaders and their followers.

The *philosophy of religion* is a field of inquiry devoted to the examination of the validity and logical coherence of various religious systems, as well as the theories that explain religion.

In the *anthropology of religion,* the scholar is not concerned with proving or disproving the validity of religious beliefs and practices. Anthropologists investigate the nature of religion, viewing religion as a cultural or social phenomenon. Although anthropologists have described a variety of religious systems, most of their descriptions have been of the religious customs of non-Western, nonliterate peoples. As a result, the anthropological study of religion is often viewed as the study of "primitive" religion. There has been a shift in recent times, and anthropologists such as Victor Turner (1969, 1974), Clifford Geertz (1969, 1973), and Edmund Leach (1982) have promoted an eclectic approach, combining different fields of inquiry, and have studied "world religions" of literate societies.

Many factors have contributed to the anthropological focus on "primitive" religion:

1. *Historical accidents and disciplinary territoriality:* As the various disciplines became established, sociologists studied their own urban societies, historians studied the past of literate societies, and anthropologists studied the nonliterate, other peoples.

2. *Anthropology's claim of universality:* Because it takes "humankind" as its focus, anthropology is assumed to have the capacity to reveal the basic, elemental structures of phenomena. Primitive cultures are considered good laboratories for such studies.

3. *Anthropology's concern with underlying principles:* It is assumed that anthropologists explore the "unconscious" principles that underlie culture—in contrast with historians and sociologists, who discuss and explain the explicit events and processes that occur in societies.

4. *Cross-cultural objectivity:* Many anthropologists believe that in the study of "other" cultures, they can be less emotionally involved and more objective.

5. *Anthropology's traditional focus on small-scale "island" societies:* Anthropologists have often been reluctant to discuss "great" religions such as Christianity, Judaism, and Islam because these religions often have multiple interpretations with elaborate theological scholarship, and the study of these religions often evokes emotional responses or attacks that make analysis very difficult.

The anthropological study of religion often involves descriptions and formulations of different "types" of religious practitioners, religious movements, myths, and rituals. The compilation of ethnographic source materials known as the *Human Relations Area Files* is commonly used to test hypotheses about the association of religious beliefs or rituals with political or economic phenomena, or with modes of child-rearing. Anthropological inquiry includes cross-cultural studies of the use of drugs in religious ritual, the occurrence of possession, the role of the prophet, the function of witchcraft and divination, the relationship between social structure and eschatological beliefs, and so on.

The most widely known correlational study on religion by an anthropologist is that of Guy E. Swanson, who compared several societies to relate religious beliefs and social structure. Swanson (1962) theorized that conceptions of spiritual beings and religious practices corresponded to and were modeled after particular social and political institutions. He formulated several statements of relationships between specific types of religious beliefs/behavior and social or political organizations and tested for their occurrence in several societies. Swanson found supporting data for the following hypotheses:

1.   "Witchcraft tends to be prevalent when people must interact with one another on important matters in the absence of legitimized social controls and arrangements." (Swanson 1962: 151)

2.   "Cumulative scores which combine the number of sovereign groups in a society with the presence of unlegitimized contacts, the size of the units of settlement, and the presence of sovereign kinship groups are related . . . to indicators of a belief in the immanence of the soul." (Swanson 1962: 135–136)

3.   "Reincarnation is positively and significantly related to a settlement pattern of neighborhoods, nomadic bands, extended family compounds, and other small, but continuing units." (Swanson 1962: 120)

4.   "There is a positive and significant relationship between the presence in a society of sovereign kinship groups other than the nuclear family and a belief that ancestral spirits are active in human affairs." (Swanson 1962: 108)

5.   "Societies with social classes are significantly more likely than others to possess a belief in superior gods." (Swanson 1962: 96)

6.   "The number of superior deities is positively and significantly related to the number of specialties of a type compatible with the nature of a society's ultimately sovereign organization." (Swanson 1962: 96)

7.   "Monotheism is positively related to the presence of a hierarchy of three or more sovereign groups in a society." (Swanson 1962: 81)

8.   "Supernatural sanctions for interpersonal relations are most likely to appear in societies in which there are interpersonal differences according to wealth." (Swanson 1962: 174)

9.   "Societies with matri-families or unlegitimated contacts with aliens are less likely to possess . . . supernatural sanctions for interpersonal relations. . . ." (Swanson 1962: 174)

In order to examine the validity of the theoretical proposition that religious beliefs derive from socialization practices, that supernatural beings are projections of parental images, and that rituals are similar to the enactments of child–parent interactions, Spiro and D'Andrade (1967) formulated several hypotheses, relating social and religious variables, and found supporting evidence in a majority of societies to suggest that social factors determine or cause religious factors. The following hypotheses were supported:

1. "The greater the initial satisfaction of dependence, the greater the degree to which supernatural nurturance is contingent upon compulsive ritual." (Spiro and D'Andrade 1967: 199)

2. "The greater the initial satisfaction of the oral drive, the greater the degree to which supernatural nurturance is contingent upon the employment of compulsive ritual." (Spiro and D'Andrade 1967: 200)

3. "The greater the socialization anxiety of dependence, the greater the degree to which supernatural nurturance is contingent upon propitiatory ritual." (Spiro and D'Andrade 1967: 200)

4. "The lower the socialization of dependence, the greater the degree to which supernatural nurturance is noncontingent." (Spiro and D'Andrade 1967: 200)

5. "The greater the socialization anxiety of all behavior systems, the greater the degree to which supernatural punishment is contingent upon disobedience of supernatural demands." (Spiro and D'Andrade 1967: 201)

Contemporary studies in the anthropology of religion have been less concerned with categorizing types of religious phenomena than with studying the role of religious symbols and meanings in human action; ethnographic monographs provide detailed descriptions of the symbolic, religious classifications that exist in different cultures. Contemporary anthropologists such as Victor Turner, E. E. Evans-Pritchard, Mary Douglas, Edmund Leach, Clifford Geertz, and others have contributed extensively to the understanding of meaning embedded in religious phenomena through symbolic analysis. Levi-Strauss's structural analysis of myth has stimulated scholars in different fields and has generated various theories and interpretations of mind and culture. The anthropological study of religion— whether it is based on the earlier evolutionary/functionalist/typological approach or on the contemporary symbolic/structuralist/phenomenological approach—contributes significantly to our understanding of the nature of culture, society, and the mind.

THE ANTHROPOLOGICAL PROBLEM
OF DEFINING RELIGION

As I mentioned earlier, I use the term *religion* to designate cultural phenomena pertaining to the creation and maintenance of the self as sacred or supernatural. Religious phenomena such as shamanism, witchcraft, priesthood, myth, and ritual are involved in different ways in the creation and maintenance of "sacred human identity."

The foregoing definition may appear odd to some readers because the concepts of religion and sacred have acquired specific meanings in the interpretations of Christianity in Western scholarship. These concepts developed out of the Roman discourse on worship. The Greeks, who are usually credited with giving us our most ancient Western concepts, did not have a word to represent all the different types of beliefs and rituals associated with supernaturalism. Herodotus, the Greek historian-anthropologist, described Egyptian and Persian myths and rituals and referred to the similarities and differences in how gods were conceptualized and worshipped; but the word *religion*, as it denotes a certain type of relationship between human beings and supernatural reality, was formulated first in the Roman tradition and was elaborated upon by the church fathers of the medieval period.

The word *religion* is a derivative of two Latin words: *religio*, which meant piety (as well as reverence, devotion, consciousness, etc.), and *religure*, which meant to bind or fasten together. The early church fathers, medieval scholastics and philosophers, and modern philosophers and social scientists of Western civilization contributed to the development of various Western culture-specific meanings that we associate with the concepts of religion and sacred; as a result, when we use these terms, they often refer to specific Western customs, and we link the concepts of religion and the sacred with morality, to suggest that they designate holiness or godliness, and to dichotomize religion and magic; but in many cultural traditions, there is no necessary connection between religion and morality, and the dichotomy between religion and magic is seldom made.

In order to illustrate the ethnoepistemology of the concept of religion I give here the definition from the *Oxford Dictionary of English Etymology* (1966):

> *religion:* state of life (as of monks) bound by vows and a rule; religious order or rule; system of faith in and worship of a divine power; recognition of a divine being to whom worship is due. –(O)F. *religion*=Pr., Sp. *religion*, It. *religione*– L. *religio*(n-), obligation (as of an oath), bond between man and the gods, scrupulousness, scruple(s), reverence for the gods; religious (monastic) life;

by Cicero ('De natura deorum') derived from *relegere* gather together, peruse, but elsewhere connected by him with the idea of obligation (e.g. *religione obstringere*) and more prob. to be derived (as by Servius, Lactantius, and Augustine) from *religare* bind fast, f. re-RE-7+*ligare* bind; see LIGATURE, -ION. So religious bound by monastic vows; imbued with religion; pert. to religion; sb. as pl. monks, etc.—OF *religious* (mod. -IEUX) -L. *religiosus*. religio-SITY. -L.; in more recent use perh. after F.

In a paper titled "Religion: Problems of Definition and Explanation," Spiro (1966: 87) points out:

> An examination of the endemic definitional controversies concerning religion leads to the conclusion that they are not so much controversies over the meaning either of the term "religion" or of the concept which it expresses, as they are jurisdictional disputes over the phenomenon or the range of phenomena which are considered to constitute legitimately the empirical referent of the term.

Spiro notes that anthropologists have an "obsession with universality" and that we should recognize the fact that "universality is a creation of definition." In defining religion, should the definition be such that it presupposes the existence of religion in all cultures? In other words, is the "cultural universality" of religion an invention of scholars who define religion in such a way that religion is made a universal? Issues such as whether people everywhere believe in god or spiritual beings (which Edward Tylor used as the defining criterion of religion) are debatable because there are "religions," such as certain forms of Buddhism, that do not include such beliefs. Emile Durkheim made the concept of "sacred" the central defining feature of religion in order to avoid the question of whether every group believes in gods or spirits.

Kluckhohn (1979: v–vi) in the foreword to the *Reader in Comparative Religion* (Lessa and Vogt 1979) suggests that tool-making, language, and religion are the three characteristics that distinguish humans from other animals. According to him, "The universality of religion [in the broadest sense] suggests that it corresponds to some deep and probably inescapable human needs." But as Norbeck (1974: 7) correctly points out,

> . . . no clearly defined biological wellspring of religion is evident unless it is the human capacity and proclivity to create culture, to interpret the universe, and to formulate that interpretation in such a way as to make life and perpetuation of the human species possible.

We should be careful in invoking "needs" to explain phenomena because in discussing humankind we must distinguish between and among biological, social, psychological, historical, and cultural needs. Can human beings function biologically, psychologically, or socially without religion? Are "needs" biologically, socially, or culturally generated in the individual? Does "needs" refer to the existence of beliefs in "supernatural" beings and powers, or to the existence of conceptions about ultimate goals, concerns, and values of life? If the needs have to do with the "ultimate," then political ideologies may also be viewed as "religions."

The problems of defining and explaining phenomena are disciplinary problems. The psychologist may define and explain the same "religious phenomena" differently from the anthropologist. The disciplines are concerned with establishing knowledge about phenomena with their distinctive perspectives, asking different questions about the same phenomena.

Anthropologists have long used a combination of Edward Tylor's (1873) narrow but open-ended definition of religion as "the belief in Spiritual Beings" (animism) and Emile Durkheim's (1915) sociological definition of religion as "a system of beliefs and practices relative to sacred things." However, the concern in contemporary anthropology with the study of symbol and meaning has led many anthropologists to concentrate on the semantics and pragmatics of religious symbols (i.e., what they mean and how they are used).

Following is a selection of anthropological definitions of religion, a critique, and my own definition.

A religion is a unified system of beliefs and practices relative to sacred things, that is to say, things set apart and forbidden—beliefs and practices which unite into one single moral community called a Church, all those who adhere to them. (Durkheim 1915)

Religion is a system of ideas, attitudes, creeds and acts of supernaturalism. (Norbeck 1961)

Religion is a set of symbolic forms and acts which relate to man to the ultimate conditions of his existence. (Bellah 1964)

Religion is a set of rituals, rationalized by myth, which mobilizes supernatural powers for the purpose of achieving or preventing transformation of state in man and nature. (Wallace 1966)

Religion is an institution consisting of culturally patterned interaction with culturally patterned superhuman beings. (Spiro 1966)

Religion is a system of symbols which acts to establish powerful, pervasive, and long-lasting moods and motivations in men by formulating conceptions of a general order of existence and clothing these conceptions with such an aura of factuality that the moods and motivations seem uniquely realistic. (Geertz 1966)

[Religion refers to a]ll explicit and implicit notions and ideas, accepted as true, which relate to a reality which cannot be verified empirically. (Van Baal 1971)

Religion is a system of symbols orienting action with reference to ultimate needs and to a higher order reality. . . . Religion is ideology and the system of symbols and institutions in which it is shared and communicated. (Feuchtwang 1984)

Durkheim's definition of religion is simultaneously too broad and too narrow. It is too broad because it is possible to include political totems or other objects (which evoke adoration and fear and are separated from the mundane, phenomenal world of everyday experience). It is too narrow because his identification of the moral community or the church as the foundation for the maintenance and application of the sacred leaves out the beliefs and practices of supernatural beings, events, and powers that may not be rooted in the moral conventions of a group. For example, his definition would exclude the beliefs and practices commonly referred to as "magical." Durkheim considered magic to be "antisocial" and maintained that the unity of the moral community has priority over individual activities that may be contrary to the collective will of the community. Such a distinction between religion and magic raises questions about the foundation and the function of magic and creates an unnecessary disjunction between the individual and society.

Norbeck and Wallace identify beliefs and practices associated with supernaturalism in their definitions of religion. Whereas Norbeck does not define what supernaturalism is, Wallace provides an explanation of supernaturalism in terms of how it is maintained and how it functions. To Wallace, religion is linked with ritual, a mammalian characteristic that involves stereotypic, repetitive acts of communication and is linked with mythic explanations of ritual behavior. In other words, religion cannot exist without ritual and myth, and religion uses ritual and myth to achieve or prevent certain goals. Wallace says that the objective of religion is to transform man and nature. This definition of religion enables us to analyze religious phenomena with reference to specific states of transformation.

The definitions of Bellah and Feuchtwang refer to religion as concerned with questions about the ultimate needs and conditions of humankind. Bellah identifies the symbolic forms and acts that relate humans to those questions, and Feuchtwang identifies the ideological, symbolic, and institutional factors that sustain or deal with those questions.

Spiro makes it clear that *religion* refers to a type of interaction that cultures create, and that this interaction relates human beings and superhuman beings within an institutional framework that we identify as religion. Van Baal defines religion as an empirically unverifiable reality that is maintained by believers. Both Spiro and Van Baal suggest in their definitions that religion refers to a set of norms that govern the relationship between humankind and the culturally created superordinary reality.

The function of religious symbols, according to Geertz, is to provide believers with a cognitive and emotional configuration that affirms the existence of order. Because human experiences often undermine conceptions of order, humans need symbols which show that there is no basic contradiction between the experiences of disorder and the existence of order; without these symbols, human life becomes intolerable, and cultural continuity becomes untenable. Every cultural tradition has symbols that function to synthesize disorder and order, known and unknown, continuity and discontinuity.

THE SYMBOLIC UNIVERSES
OF HUMANKIND

All human beings belong to the species *Homo sapiens sapiens,* and no scientific evidence links genetic characteristics with cultural characteristics. Thus differences between cultures in domains such as religion must be explained with reference to how humans function as meaning-creating, language-using animals, and with reference to the historically created and maintained cultural or symbol-configurations. Human beings share a common psychobiological heritage and confront common universal "problems." Differences in cultural configurations may be viewed as products of different solutions to similar universal problems, and as elaborations of particular cultural representations that also serve as vehicles for the formulation of group boundaries.

The term *culture* has been defined in a number of different ways. The term acquired significance in the Western intellectual tradition during the eighteenth century when the empiricist epistemology provided the foundation for explaining knowledge as an acquired reality. Anthropologists today agree that culture may be explained as a nongenetic, extra-somatic aspect of humankind, although various disputes exist on defining the relationship between culture and mind as well as in establishing the primacy of genetic, psychological, or cultural aspects for explaining certain types of human behavior. Also, there are philosophical debates centering on the validity of rationalist and empiricist discourse on culture, and scholars disagree on whether culture should be studied as a separate reality having its own laws, different from physical, biological, and psychological laws, or whether culture should be studied as the product of the operation of genetic, psychological, or social processes.

Marvin Harris (1979) has suggested that it is necessary to recognize two contrasting ways in which culture is analyzed. In an approach that may be described as "cultural materialism," culture can be conceptualized with the metaphor of the organism. The anthropologist is concerned with explaining cultural adaptations to environment and cultural development as well as a culture's internal, institutional adaptations. Institutions such as religion can be explained as an adaptation to other institutions that have more importance or significance for the material survival of culture.

In a second approach, which may be characterized as "cultural idealism," culture can be conceptualized with the linguistic metaphor, and the anthropologist focuses on the study of the interconnectedness of symbols in terms of their communication of meaning.

The frameworks of cultural materialism and cultural idealism are appropriate for formulating different questions about culture, and their differences should not be viewed as a breakdown in the anthropological unity in the study of culture. No one would disagree that humans create, transmit, and live in cultural or symbolic universes that are made up of interconnected symbols that communicate knowledge and meaning. Language is the vehicle for such communication, and human beings have to "make sense" of their experiences with the aid of symbols. Some anthropologists theorize about the organization and development of symbolic forms in causal or systemic terms, whereas others seek to discover the existence of logical correspondences or patterns of relationship in the creation and maintenance of cultural forms.

James Lett (1987) suggests that cultural materialism and cultural idealism are two paradigms that must complement cultural research. Cultural materialism is a framework that is useful in analyzing the origin and maintenance of cultural factors that contribute to the survival of individuals, and cultural idealist frameworks such as symbolic anthropology are important in studying how human beings achieve symbolic identification and integration. Robert Ulin (1988) distinguishes between instrumental and communicative rationalities of cultural systems and argues that communicative systems are best understood through interpretive or hermeneutic analysis.

Despite the fact that anthropology attempts to be a nonreductionistic, holistic discipline that analyzes the interrelationships of biological, sociological, psychological, and cultural/historical factors in formulating theories of human behavior, it is the discourse on culture that provides the discipline with its theoretical and methodological unity, and it is in defining and analyzing the nature of culture from a comparative perspective that the discipline has an edge over other disciplines that deal with human behavior. Of course, anthropology is conceptualized differently in various countries. When continental scholars use the term *anthropology*, they mean the study of the physical characteristics and biological evolution of humankind. The study of human social relationships is referred to as comparative sociology or social anthropology, and the comparative study of culture is the subject of ethnology, semiology, or psychology. In the United States, scholars have, for the most part, tried to maintain the holistic integrity of anthropology by linking linguistics, cultural anthropology, biological anthropology, and archaeology with the thematic reference to culture, and by distinguishing anthropological research with reference to ethnographies (holistic descriptions of cultural traditions), cross-cultural analysis, and the comparative perspective.

CULTURE AND SELF

Until recently, the concept of the self had no prominent place in the study of culture by anthropologists. Within the Western intellectual traditions, the self, originally a theological/philosophical formulation—as unique character, essential quality, self-reflective individuality, locus of identity, the I-that-is/acts/reacts—was subdivided into functions that were redistributed among reductionist academic specialties. Anthropologists used the concept of the self to discuss the social identity of individuals with reference to social prerogatives and obligations associated with status positions, and therefore the concept was often used in discussing ethnic identity. This restricted usage narrowed the scope of the concept of the self that could be used for a general understanding of the relationship between culture and human behavior. As Wallace (1966: 139) points out: "In a more general psychological sense, a person's identity is the whole set of images of self which over a given span of time that person maintains."

In a recent book, Marsella, DeVos, and Hsu (1985: ix) celebrate the return of the self as a central concept for an understanding of culture and human behavior:

> After almost seven decades, there has been a resurgence of interest in the concept of self. At the turn of the century, the self was a major tenet in many theories of human behavior.
>
> Today, social scientists, philosophers, and even theoretical physicists are increasingly invoking the self as an explanatory concept for understanding complex human behavior.

No one would dispute the fact that people who live in different cultural universes differ in how they represent the self. Often the symbols of the sacred other play a crucial role in defining the boundaries of the symbols of the self and their characteristics. To illustrate this fact, following are two examples of contrasting representations of the self.

> The western concept of the self is to a large part influenced by a monotheistic tradition in western thought which may lead to a more individualistic perception of the world. Experience is considered either true or false. There are dichotomous definitions rather than the more amorphous diverseness of thought which attends polytheism. Monotheistic normative systems are more narrowly bipolar and may enforce the necessity for judgments about

qualities of existence which are also directed toward the self. These bi-polarities are positively and negatively judgmental, such as good versus bad, beautiful versus ugly, love versus lust, God versus Satan, etc. (Marsella et al. 1985: 13)

There are some difficulties encountered by the westerner who searches for consistency in behavior related to Indian notions of self. If one believes in the single true "self" as immaterial, actual behavior, materially governed, is ephemeral, conventional, relative. As Bharati points out, an individual can be a Marxian, a fascist, and a Hindu at the same time, since these various manifestations of thought emanating from the material self are partial, situational, needing no reconciliation since they are all less than the true self. (Marsella et al. 1985: 11)

In my book *Anthropology and the Western Tradition* (Pandian 1985) I discuss the Judeo-Christian orientation of dichotomizing the symbol of the self into the "true self" (which is linked with divine representations of the holy other) and the "untrue self" (which is linked with monstrous representations of the unholy other). I also discuss how human characteristics that could not be represented in the symbol of the Judeo-Christian divine being (the sacred other) were excluded from the representation of the self and were relegated to the symbols of the self of non-Christians. The non-Christian or non-Western "others" were viewed as the repository of all that was excluded from the representation of the Judeo-Christian self.

The relevance of the symbolic self-concept in the study of culture has not been fully understood in anthropology for various reasons. Because of anthropology's preoccupation with the discovery of the relationships and types of institutional structures and the search to discover "unconscious" principles or structures that determine human activities, anthropologists tend to relegate the actor's intentionality and motivation, and the actor's meanings, to a secondary or peripheral level of analysis. I take the view that it is necessary to take into account the paradigmatic and syntagmatic principles of culture, as well as how people make use of what they know of the principles in their conscious representations of intentions, motivations, and explanations when they interact with others. People have to use the symbols of "who they are" or "what they are" and know how to interpret these symbols to conceptualize their experience in a culturally appropriate way in relation to how they conceive of themselves and others. A culture is maintained because there are people who use these symbols or representations and can represent and interact with one another with similar significations of interpretations of reality and meaning, or shared significances. Thus, it is imperative that we know how people are able to interpret, predict, and evaluate the behavior of one another. In other words, we must know how culture is recreated in its use by the actors.

CHAPTER TWO
Anthropological Classification of Religious Phenomena

THE OBJECTIVE OF THIS CHAPTER

This chapter introduces the reader to the theoretical and methodological assumptions that underlie the delineation of religious phenomena in different categories and provides an overview or synopsis of the range and scope of the anthropological study of religion. Parts III and IV develop in greater detail many of the topics presented in this chapter and introduce additional data on and discussion of contemporary anthropological studies on religion. This chapter includes data on supernatural power, supernatural beings, totemism, taboo, and "magic" that are not repeated in other chapters. However, many other chapters refer to such beliefs and practices either in relation to the theoretical contributions of particular scholars or in relation to the perspective of this book. I describe and discuss in detail shamanism and religious movements in Chapters 11 and 12, and I present several examples as well as an interpretive analysis of different kinds of myths and rituals in Chapters 13 through 18. Thus the reader who wishes to know more about shamanism, religious movements, myths, and rituals before delving into the study of the development of anthropological ideas on religion (in Part II) can combine the following two sections with Chapters 13 and 14, the next section with Chapters 15, 16, 17, and 18, and the final two sections with Chapters 11 and 12.

THE STUDY OF SACRED POWER
AND SACRED BEINGS

In his book *The Threshold of Religion* (1909), the British philosopher-turned-anthropologist R.R. Marett (1866–1943) explained the origin of religion as a product of primitive man's inability to explain rationally the experience of sacred power. Marett theorized that primitive man must have responded in fear and awe to the manifestation of this power; religion originates, according to him, in a feeling about the existence of impersonal sacred power. Marett identified the belief in this power as *animatism* and viewed animatism as the earliest or most primitive stage in the development of religion. In the eighteenth century, the Scottish philosopher David Hume had advanced a similar view of the origin of religion. Robert Lowie (1883–1957), the American anthropologist, in his book *Primitive Religion* (1924) wrote that "religion is verily a universal feature of human culture, not because all societies foster a belief in spirits, but because all recognize in some form or other awe-inspiring, extraordinary manifestations of reality."

Beliefs and practices associated with sacred power occur all over the world. The most widely known symbol of sacred power is the Oceanic term *mana*. In Melanesia *mana* is an attribute of inanimate objects, individuals, ghosts, and spirits, and individual success is often attributed to *mana*. In Polynesia, *mana* is associated with particular objects and individuals in terms of their having greater or lesser sacred power, and chiefs are seen as embodiments of *mana*. Geertz, in his book *Islam Observed* (1969), provides a detailed discussion of the sacred power known as *baraka* and offers an interpretation of its use by the Islamic holy men (*marabouts*) in the maintenance of *maraboutism* (the cult of the holy men) in Morocco. Lowie (1924) describes the significance of the sacred power known as *maxpe* in relation to the ritual of vision quest among the Crow Indians. Other symbols of sacred power are *wakan* (among Siouan Indian tribes), *manitou* (among Algonquin-speaking tribes), *buha* (among the Shoshone), and *kami*. The use of objects with sacred power, such as the cross and the swastika, is widespread. (See Norbeck 1961: 37–51.)

The American anthropologist Ruth Benedict (1887–1948) made a substantial contribution to the study of religion by analyzing "vision quest" among the Plains Indians and by postulating that religious themes underlie emotional configurations. She theorized about the difference between the representations of impersonal sacred power and personalized sacred beings, a model that was later elaborated upon by Edward Norbeck in his book *Religion in Primitive Society* (1961). Norbeck (1961: 37) notes:

> Benedict draws a distinction between impersonal and personified conceptions as being based upon analogies, on the one hand, with properties of

objects, such as color and weight, and, on the other, with attributes of human beings—will, desires, emotions, and intentions.

Ethnographic data indicate that symbols of impersonal sacred power are often associated with symbols of sacred beings. This association is particularly prominent in native American cultures, and often a combination of the representations of impersonal power and sacred beings occurs in the enactment of rituals linked with witchcraft and sorcery, divination, healing, and vision quest. For example, Jorgensen (1972) in his study *The Sun Dance Religion* describes how the Ute and Shoshone Indians combine conceptions of sacred power (*puwa* or *pokha*), acquisition of sacred power, vision quest, shamanism, and healing rituals. Sun Dance is performed to affirm and acquire sacred power; the Utes and Shoshones believe that impersonal sacred power exists everywhere and that this power is deposited in large amounts in certain beings such as "god" or "that man" and in objects such as sun, moon, and fire. The dancer pursues power through the synthesis or fusion of the dry-hot and wet-cool attributes (or forces) of the sacred power. The dancer may experience a vision of his encounter with the spirits, including the Buffalo spirit, from whom he learns the use and meaning of sacred power and becomes a shaman. Although the pursuit of power is an individual quest, the use of power must serve the needs and well-being of the group.

Beliefs and practices associated with symbols of gods and goddesses, spirits, ghosts, and tricksters are common. In some societies a sharp distinction is made between various types of gods, and sometimes they are ranked. The attributes of the gods may change contextually, with goddesses subordinated or given primacy. Gods may be represented as self-created, all-powerful, or limited in power. Occasionally, a god is symbolized as omnipotent and omniscient, and as the creator god. Some creator gods (identified as otiose gods) are represented as being far removed from human affairs and concerned only with world harmony. These gods are seldom worshipped. Gods who participate in human affairs are propitiated, supplicated, and worshipped with or without the aid of priests. Trickster gods, such as the coyote of the Winnebago Indians (Radin 1956), are sacred beings who do not seek to help human beings but inadvertently contribute to the welfare of people.

Hindu societies may be used to describe and discuss the creations and uses of personalized sacred beings. Babb (1975) in his book *The Divine Hierarchy* provides a detailed description of the various deities who are part of the sacred texts that have universal significance for the Hindus, and the various deities who are significant for only particular individuals, groups, villages or regions. The great gods Siva and Vishnu (and Vishnu's incarnations) are associated with elaborate myths and rituals that affirm and dramatize the worldviews and ethos of the Hindu tradition. Often many other deities (godlings, goddesses, spirits) are linked to the great gods, and specific gods and goddesses represent only particular aspects of human life and are objects of specific rituals or cults.

Beliefs and practices associated with life after death vary considerably from culture to culture. For example, Hindu and Christian eschatologies differ markedly in conceptualizing the reasons for human suffering in this world, and in conceptualizing what happens after death. To the devout Christian, eternal rewards await the faithful follower of Christ; to the devout Hindu, the ultimate realization of life is in not being born again.

Beliefs and practices associated with ghosts, or spirits of the dead, are common in most cultures. Some spirits are feared and avoided, but others are worshipped to secure their help. Two basic types may be distinguished: spirits that involve themselves in the everyday concerns and welfare of the society and thus are propitiated for aid, and those that are propitiated to prevent harm. Spirits may incorporate benign and malevolent qualities and may be linked with the maintenance of social control. In some societies individuals strive to avoid contact with the spirits of the dead (as among Blackfoot Indians), and in other societies individuals strive to have close contact with the spirits of the ancestors (as among the Lugbara or the Chinese). Occasionally, dead ancestors are worshipped as ancestor gods, and elaborate ceremonies are performed. The worship of saints in the Roman Catholic Christian tradition may be viewed as a variety of spirit worship.

Goddesses often serve as fertility symbols and as symbols that combine contrasting benign and malevolent qualities. Goddesses are vital components of the Hindu religious experience. They are also central elements in the Roman Catholic religious orientation as well as in many other religious traditions.

A recent anthology on mother worship (Preston 1982) deals with the question of why mother-goddess worship is common. Freeman (1982), in his introduction to the anthology, asks: Are certain beliefs, themes and institutions associated with mother goddess universal? What are the foundations of these universal forms? Do all societies use the forms in a similar manner? Is mother worship derived from a deep biopsychological bond between infant and mother? Does the female body serve as a metaphor, or do the parts and functions of the body such as breast, womb, vagina, menstruation, and birthing serve as models to conceptualize various experiences relating humans to nature? Preston (1982: 335–36) identifies ten symbolic associations in mother-goddess representation: (1) fertility of crops and humans, (2) child-bearing and nurturance, (3) expression of ambivalence, (4) protection from natural disasters, (5) mediation between human and divine, (6) justice, (7) ethnic identity, (8) healing, (9) spiritual purity, and (10) punishment.

THE STUDY OF MYTH AND TOTEMISM

The word *myth* is derived from the Greek work *mythos*, which is defined in Webster's *Seventh New Collegiate Dictionary* as "a pattern of beliefs expressing often symbolically the characteristics or prevalent attitudes in a group or culture." The same dictionary defines *myth* as a "traditional story of ostensibly historical events that serves to unfold part of the world view of a people or explain a practice, belief, or natural phenomenon; parable, allegory; a person or thing having only an imaginary or unverifiable existence; an ill-founded belief held uncritically especially by an interested group." From an anthropological point of view, whether the belief is ill founded or not, it has meaning for the believers to sustain or validate their cultural reality.

Lessa and Vogt (1972: 249) hold that "The term 'myth' at best serves as a unifying concept which enables anthropologists to talk about etiological narratives and other forms which, for the society involved, make up a body of 'assumed knowledge' about the universe, the natural and supernatural worlds, and man's place in the totality." Anthropologists have for the most part studied myth by delineating certain religious narratives as myths and have asked questions such as (1) Why do myths of a particular kind exist in different societies, or why do certain kinds of myths recur? (2) What is the relationship between myth and ritual? (3) What is the relationship between myth and society? (4) Do myths reveal unconscious processes or workings of the mind? (5) Are myths distortions of historical events? (6) What are the functions of myths? (7) Are myths expressions of common human experiences of suffering, death, and so on?

In contemporary anthropology, the two dominant approaches in the study of myth are structuralism and symbolic analysis. Structuralist analysis of myth is closely identified with the work of the French anthropologist Claude Levi-Strauss, who has argued in several essays and in his multivolume study of myth that myth is a language which communicates messages to help the receivers cope with the contradictions of cultural life. The leading exponent of symbolic/interpretive approach are Clifford Geertz (1969, 1973, 1983) and Victor Turner (1961, 1962, 1967, 1969, 1973, 1974, 1978), who have written extensively to interpret mythic and ritual symbols, cultural archetypes of religiosity, and particular religious traditions.

The study of "totemism" has had an interesting history in the development of anthropology as a discipline. In the late eighteenth century, a fur trader named J. Long noted in his book *Voyages and Travels of an Indian Interpreter and Trader* (1791) that the Ojibwa Indians of Canada had individual and group *totams*, an Ojibwa word meaning guardian spirits in the form of animals, and that these animals were not killed or eaten. By the late nineteenth century, similar phenomena—that is, reverential identification of groups with animals and plants—were recorded from different parts of the world, and evolutionary anthropologists, particularly the Scottish anthropologist John F. McLennan, explained totemism as the most primitive, primordial type of religion and a type of kinship group identification.

In a critique of the late-nineteenth-century study of totemism, Roger C. Poole (1969: 18) suggests that speculation on the nature of totemism began with McLennan's articles in the *Fortnightly Review* for 1869–70.

> McLennan's search for the "origins" of totemism, and his belief that "the ancient nations came, in prehistoric times, through the totem stage, having animals and plants, and the heavenly bodies conceived as animals, for gods before the anthropomorphic gods appeared" affected a generation of scholars. . . . (Poole 1969: 18)

The problem with the late-nineteenth- and early twentieth-century theories of totemism was that scholars held onto their preconceived notions about totemism even when the data clearly suggested that different types of beliefs and practices had been erroneously lumped together as totemism.

William Robertson Smith's study (1889) of Semitic religions produced data which indicated that the "totemic animal" symbolically represented the clan and that the ritual consumption of the animal affirmed and strengthened the unity of the clan. He found in "totemic ritual" the semantic foundation for Hebrew orientations toward sacrifice and a particular type of relationship between man and God, and for the Christian orientation toward wine and bread (symbolic substitutes for the blood and flesh of Jesus Christ, the totem) to attain communal, internal fellowship.

James Frazer (1854–1941), who became an authority on totemism (he published an authoritative article on the subject and published a four-volume treatise entitled *Totemism and Exogamy* in 1910), was influenced by the views of his fellow Scots McLennan and Robertson Smith. Frazer changed his theories to fit the data on totemism and declared that totemism was both a religion (a primitive system of worshipping animals, plants, and inanimate objects) and a system of kinship classification (identifying individuals and groups as having descended from a lineal nonhuman ancestor). Originally, Frazer theorized that the eating of the totemic animal was prohibited and that clan exogamy was a fundamental principle of totemism. Later, he indicated that the ban on eating totemic animals was for the clan that was believed to be descended from the animal and not for the whole tribe, and that totemism may in fact be linked with a way of increasing the food supply (a view later echoed in slightly modified manner by Bronislaw Malinowski and A.R. Radcliffe-Brown).

Both Emile Durkheim (1858–1917) and Sigmund Freud (1856–1939) looked upon totemism as a central, crucial principle of culture; and both of these great thinkers used the theoretical insights of William Robertson Smith to arrive at two different kinds of formulations (sociological and psychological, respectively) concerning the importance and meaning of totemism.

Durkheim saw in "Australian totemism" an example of the most basic, elementary from of religious life. The Australians had sacred pieces of wood or polished stones with engravings or designs (*churinga*) that signified the sacred knowledge of the group. Durkheim theorized that the designs were totemic representations that affirmed the values of the society, and that the rituals associated with *churinga* were in fact ritual affirmation of the values; the carvings on *churinga* symbolized the social components and relationships.

Freud concluded that the ritual of sacrificing and eating an animal was an expression of a deep, underlying psychic resolution of guilt, tension, and anxiety that humans experience in their psychosexual development; the ritual sacrifice of the "totemic animal" and the "totemic feast" were substitutes or surrogates for the symbolic killing and worshipping of the father. Central to Freud's analysis is his assumption that ritual behavior of primitive peoples (in general) and neurotic behavior of individuals (in particular) have a common psychological foundation in unresolved, unconscious conflicts and fear. He saw in primitive and neurotic behavior a laboratory for the study of archaic, infantile, raw psychological processes that mark the beginnings of civilization: The primitive man, the child, and the neurotic had not yet acquired, or were incapable of using, the sophisticated disguises and canopies of the civilized man; the repressed sexual (and other) desires were expressed and enacted in ritual and the fantasy world of the primitive, the neurotic, and the child.

It is interesting that Claude Levi-Strauss (b. 1908), who was greatly influenced by the theoretical formulations of Durkheim and Freud, dismissed the various theories of totemism as illusory. Although Levi-Strauss borrowed from Durkheim the idea of symbolic classification and from Freud the idea that primitive culture was a window into the unconscious mental and cultural structures, it was clear to Levi-Strauss that both Durkheim and Freud had erred in assuming that totemism was a primitive form of worship. Levi-Strauss does not draw a parallel between primitive mentality and neurosis or infantile fantasies but instead focuses on revealing how the untamed or "savage" mind operates universally. He concludes that totemism is a way of thinking about parallels in the relationship between natural and social categories and that this kind of thinking is scientific insofar as it is based on concrete sensory experiences and imaginative analogies. The untamed mind everywhere—the past and the present, the primitive and the civilized—constructs social or group models of relationship (often based on nature). The study of this kind of classification reveals how the mind structures reality; and through the analysis of how the mind constructs classifications and typologies we gain an understanding of the structure of collective mentality. In this regard, Levi-Strauss differs considerably from Freud despite the fact that both attempt to penetrate the cultural layers to understand the unconscious mental processes, and both have used data on primitive cultures with the assumption that the primitive human is somehow a laboratory for the analysis of the collective mind in its natural state. Levi-Strauss finds in communication theory and the methodology of structural linguistics the key to open the door to the collective mind.

Freud links incest taboo and totemism, finding them both rooted in guilt; but Levi-Strauss sees incest taboo as a classificatory device to guarantee the exchange of women between groups to promote cooperation. Freud argues that the taboo against sex among siblings and between children and their parents came into being as a result of a psychological resolution of sexual drives, aggression, guilt, and remorse, and thus incest taboo is the foundation for the development of moral and social codes. In a recent book, provocatively titled *The Red Lamp of Incest*, Robin Fox (1980) raises questions about the universality and social function of the incest taboo and notes that the linkage between moral/social codes and the incest taboo in industrial-urban societies requires more anthropological research.

THE STUDY OF MAGIC, RITUAL, AND TABOO

The nature of "magic" has been a major topic of theoretical debate among anthropologists; many anthropologists distinguish between magic and religion. Evolutionary anthropologists viewed magic as an expression of the earliest mental and cultural development. Evolutionary anthropologists such as James Frazer declared that magic was "pseudo-science" and formulated a theory that explained why and how the primitive mind made erroneous cause-and-effect associations. Functionalists such as Bronislaw Malinowski declared that although both magic and religion had a common epistemological foundation in the acceptance of a supernatural reality, magic was a "practical art" that met specific individual needs, and religion was a complex cultural system that affirmed social values. According to him, magic "is always the affirmation of man's power to cause certain definite effects by a definite spell or rite. In religion, we have a whole world of supernatural faith. . . ." (Malinowski 1954: 88). The American comparative sociologist William Goode, in his book *Religion Among the Primitives* (1951: 52–55), has identified the ideal-typical features of magic: (1) specificity of goal, (2) manipulative attitude, (3) professional-client relationship, (4) meeting individual ends, (5) patron-customer ties, (6) success and error methods or techniques, (7) less emotion, (8) nonfixed timing, (9) potential for being anti-social, and (10) instrumental goals. Many contemporary anthropologists do not make a clear-cut distinction between magic and religion, and prefer to use the term "magico-religious," but as the recent anthologies on religion indicate, the distinction is still popular (see Middleton 1965; Lehman and Myers 1985).

From the perspective of ethology, ritual is a type of communication that is adaptive because it helps to reduce anxiety through an effective, quick transmission of signals. The American anthropologist Anthony Wallace combines ethnological and psychological perspectives to explain the relationship between ritual and religion.

> Ritual may be defined as stereotyped communication, solitary or interpersonal, which reduces anxiety, prepares the organism to act, and (in social rituals) coordinates the preparation for action among several organisms, and which does all this more quickly and reliably than can be accomplished (given the characteristics of the organisms and the circumstance) by nonstereotyped, informational communication. (Wallace 1966: 236).

Ethologists identify species-specific ritual behavior and theorize about the adaptive significance of such behavior. Individual organisms engaging in such behavior communicate to themselves (auto-communicative) and to others (allo-communicative) messages that help reduce anxiety. Wallace (1966) views this role of ritual as the foundation for religious ritual and argues that ritual is a preexisting biological trait used for religious purposes. He argues that "The primary phenomenon of religion is ritual. Ritual is religion in action; it is the cutting edge of the tool. Belief serves to explain, to rationalize, to interpret and direct the energy of ritual performance" (Wallace 1966: 102). The goal of ritual is to achieve "transformations of state in human beings or nature"; rituals seek to restore equilibrium of either the individual or nature. Myth provides the theoretical underpinning in that it legitimizes ritual by accounting for the existence of supernatural powers and explaining successes and failures. We may also recall his definition of religion as "a set of rituals, rationalized by myth, which mobilizes supernatural powers for the purpose of achieving or preventing transformations of state in man and nature" (Wallace 1966: 107).

Ethological and positivistic/functionalist interpretation of human ritual is unsatisfying to many anthropologists because the components of human ritual are multivocal symbols rather than mere biological or social enactments; and because ritual symbols are constituted as coherent systems that can be manipulated differently in different contexts, we need to understand the definition and delineation of the domains in which ritual symbols are deployed. Rituals constitute one human way of organizing and communicating information that is part of the cultural tradition of a group. As Leach (1966) notes, rituals communicate information and organ ize information in a condensed way. He points out that in ritual, "the verbal part and the behavioral part are not separable" and that ritual has "a great variety of alternative meanings implicit in the same category sets." Leach (1966: 403) points out that "For the ethologist, ritual is adaptive repetitive behavior which is characteristic of a whole species; for the anthropologist, ritual is occasional behavior by particular members of a single culture."

In his seminal paper on myth and ritual, Clyde Kluckhohn (1905–1960) theorized that it is necessary to study the adaptive or adjustive functions of myth and ritual in their historical/social contexts. In this respect, he anticipated the contemporary discourse on myth and ritual. The following quotes illustrate his views.

> The specific adaptive and adjustive responses performed by myth and ritual will be differently phrased in different societies according to the historical experience of these societies (including the specific opportunities they have had for borrowing from other cultures), in accord with prevalent configurations of other aspects of the culture, and with reference to pressures exerted by other societies and by the physical and biological environment. But the general nature of the adaptive and adjustive responses performed by myth and ritual appears very much the same in all human groups. Hence, although the relative importance of myth and of ritual does vary greatly, the two tend universally to be associated.

> For myth and ritual have a common psychological basis. Ritual is an obsessive repetitive activity—often a symbolic dramatization of the fundamental "needs" of the society, whether "economic," "biological," "social," or "sexual." Mythology is the rationalization of these same needs, whether they are all expressed in overt ceremonial or not. Someone has said "every culture has a type conflict and a type solution." Ceremonials tend to portray a symbolic resolvement of the conflicts which external environment, historical experience, and selective distribution of personality types have caused to be characteristic in the society. Because different conflict situations characterize different societies, the "needs" which are typical in one society may be the "needs" of only deviant individuals in another society. And the institutionalized gratifications (of which rituals and myths are prominent examples) of culturally recognized needs vary greatly from society to society. (Kluckhohn 1942: 78–79).

The British social anthropologist A.R. Radcliffe-Brown (1881–1955) in his essay "Taboo" (1939) raised the question of how ritual prohibitions and ritual avoidances symbolize social relationships and order, and another social anthropologist, Mary Douglas (1966, 1979), theorized that pollution taboos function to maintain order. In her view, taboos serve to establish boundaries and help avoid chaos, with the identification of order with holiness and ambiguities with impurity and disorder. In an essay on food taboos of the Jews ("The Abominations of Leviticus"), Douglass (1966) argues that the animals excluded from food are those that do not fit into any classificatory model. She notes:

By rule of avoidance holiness was given a physical expression in every encounter with the animal kingdom and at every meal. Observance of the
dietary rules would thus have been a meaningful part of the great liturgical
act of recognition and worship which culminated in the sacrifice in the Temple. (Douglas 1966: 57)

Any discourse on the caste system of India will point to the existence
of various types of taboos and their links to different kinds of individuals
and groups. Individuals and groups are generally conceptualized as participating in ritual pollution to a greater or lesser degree with reference to
gender, occupation, and birth (ascribed) status. Males are considered to be
less polluting than females; certain occupations are more polluting than
others, and individuals can be polluted temporarily (by coming into contact with ritually polluting objects such as blood); performance of purificatory rituals will remove such a pollution, but individuals born as
members of ritually impure caste groups are permanently polluted; only
through the purification of caste groups, as a whole, with the incorporation
of food taboos (such as not eating meat and not consuming alcohol) can an
individual discard the ritually impure status.

It is possible that beliefs and rituals associated with taboos such as
ritual prohibitions and avoidances foster their being used to classify human
groups in hierarchical arrangements. Apart from the Hindu caste system,
in which such as association is quite obvious, the association of taboos with
class or group boundaries can be seen in Polynesian societies, in Japan, as
well as in many Mediterranean societies. It can also be stated that in societies in which there are many ritual prohibitions and avoidances, there
are likely to be many food taboos and social segregations (as in India); and
that in societies in which there are few principles of ritual prohibitions and
avoidances, there are very few food taboos and very few ascriptive principles of social ranking (as in China).

THE STUDY OF RELIGIOUS SPECIALISTS

In every society, certain individuals are identified as having a special relationship with the sacred knowledge of the culture. These individuals may
or may not commune directly with the sacred beings and may or may not
become possessed by sacred beings and sacred power. Such individuals
may officiate over rituals and may interpret myths, and they are often
associated with established religious orders and conventions of the society,
but they may also become creators of new religious orientations or religious movements.

In distinguishing religious practitioners, we must remember that
most terms of identification are derived from their use by anthropologists

and other scholars. For example, the word *shaman* (derived from the Tungus language of Siberia) has acquired the connotation of a religious practitioner who communes with sacred beings and powers and functions as a diviner and healer, and shamanism has been viewed (erroneously, in my view) as the primordial or archaic form of religion; the shaman has been idealized (by a few anthropologists) as a heroic figure with esoteric knowledge of a non-ordinary or "separate" reality.

Terms such as *witch doctor, warlock, witch, sorcerer, sorceress,* and *medicine man* (which derive from European cultural categories) generally have connotations that link them to the category of shaman.

Anthropologists generally use the term *priest* to identify full-time religious practitioners who serve as the custodians of the sacred lore of a society—in contrast to the shaman, who is defined as a part-time religious practitioner whose authority derives from the ability to have communion with sacred beings and powers. Individuals such as mystics, prophets, and seers are often considered to be closer to the shaman than to the priest.

In order to sensitize the reader to the problem of how native, cultural categories of European societies often distort the anthropological discourse on the existence of similar and different types of religious practitioners, I present below a few definitions (from the *Random House Dictionary*) of terms used to identify religious practitioners:

> *Priest:* one whose office it is to perform religious rites, and especially to make sacrificial offerings; a person ordained to the sacerdotal or pastoral office; clergyman; minister; in hierarchical churches, a clergyman of the order next below that of bishop; a minister of any religion.
>
> *Priestess:* a girl or woman who officiates in sacred rites, especially of a pagan religion.
>
> *Prophet:* a person who speaks for God or a deity, or by divine inspiration; (in the Old Testament) a person chosen to speak for God and to guide the people of Israel; one of a band of ecstatic visionaries claiming divine inspiration and, according to popular belief, possessing magical powers; a person who practices divination; one of a class of persons in the early church, next in order after the apostles, recognized as inspired to utter special revelations and predictions; the Prophet, Muhammad, the founder of Islam; a person regarded as, or claiming to be, an inspired teacher or leader; a person who foretells or predicts what is to come; a spokesman or proclaimer of some doctrine, cause, or the like.
>
> *Mystic:* spiritually significant or symbolic, as the dove used in religious art to symbolize the Holy Ghost; of the nature of or pertaining to mysteries known only to the initiated; of occult character, power, or significance; of obscure or mysterious character or significance; of or pertaining to mystics or mysticism; a person initiated into mysteries; a person who claims to attain, or believes in the possibility of attaining, insight into mysteries transcending ordinary human knowledge, as by immediate intuition in a state of spiritual ecstasy.
>
> *Seer:* a person who sees; observer; a person who prophesies future events; prophet; a person who is endowed with profound moral and spiritual insight

or knowledge; a wise man or sage who possesses intuitive powers; a person who is reputed to have special powers of divination, as a crystal-gazer, palmist, etc.

Sorcerer: a person who is supposed to exercise supernatural powers through the aid of evil spirits; black magician; wizard.

Warlock: a man aided by the Devil in practicing magic arts; sorcerer; fortuneteller or conjurer.

Witch: a person, especially a woman, who professes or is supposed to practice magic, especially black magic; sorceress; an ugly or malignant woman; one who uses a divining rod; dowser.

Wizard: one who professes to practice magic; a magician or sorcerer.

It is interesting that Europe has so many native cultural categories to distinguish religious practitioners. (The Eskimo, in contrast, have several categories to identify varieties of snow but very few to identify varieties of religious practitioners.) Most cultures do not make a distinction between witch and sorcerer, and in most cultures the person whom we would identify as the shaman would also be the sorcerer, prophet, seer, mystic, warlock, or wizard. However, anthropologists generally distinguish between witch and sorcerer, denoting the former as someone (male or female) who is born with the power to harm people. The witch is invariably evil, and in some African societies witches are believed to possess an evil substance, an evil spirit, or animal in the body. Anthropologists point out that, in contrast with witchcraft, sorcery is a learned technique and that the sorcerer can perform evil or good deeds with or without the assistance of spirits. The witch can cause death and destruction by his or her presence or thought processes, but the sorcerer will use a knowledge system to bring about changes in persons.

THE STUDY OF RELIGIOUS MOVEMENTS

Religious movements constitute a category of religious change. Anthropologists have investigated the cultural conditions that foster the emergence of religious movements and have also studied the role of prophets in the creation and successful or unsuccessful development of religious movements (or, in the perspective of this book, the role of prophets as reformulators of the sacred self and the sacred other). Non-Western prophets of different types emerged in most situations of cultural contact between the West and the non-West. Many of these prophets adopted Christian-messianic orientations, and others sought to revive their traditional religious orientations. Some prophets were successful, and others were not.

Anthropologists recognize different types of religious movements but have also shown that there is a similar processual structure in the cultural conditions that necessitate the emergence of prophets and in the development of new cultural paradigms and configurations. The American cultural anthropologist Anthony F.C. Wallace (1956, 1966, 1969) formulated the concept of "revitalization movements" to identify and illustrate the processual structure of religious movements. Ralph Linton's (1943) typology of "nativistic movements," which illustrated the combination of revivalistic and perpetuative orientations with irrational and rational ideologies, can be used to classify religious movements into magical-revivalistic, magical-perpetuative, rational-revivalistic, and rational-perpetuative movements. David Aberle (1966) classified religious movements as either transformative movements (that seek to change society and nature) or redemptive movements (that seek to bring about an inner harmony and self-acceptance) and explains that religious movements arise when there is a discrepancy between legitimate expectations and actual conditions ("relative deprivation"). In a later chapter, I present a comprehensive discussion of religious movements and review various approaches to the study of religious movements.

Several anthropologists have pointed out that religious movements constitute phenomena that reveal the nature of the development and function of religion. The study of religious movements shows that religion plays a crucial role in establishing and maintaining a way of life. Christianity and Islam began as religious movements, became established religions, and in turn provided the paradigmatic foundation for the development of religious movements that became different types of Christianity and Islam. Historians and sociologists have written extensively on the development of these movements and religions in Europe, and anthropologists have studied the impact of these religions in the cultures of the New World, Oceania, Africa, and Asia.

In this chapter I have introduced the reader to some of the major concerns in the anthropological study of religion and have discussed the problems associated with the classification of religious phenomena. This chapter also served the purpose of defining certain terms that are used in anthropology and has provided brief summaries of the topics that will be examined in great detail in Parts III, IV, and V of this book.

In Part II, I review and discuss certain anthropological theories of religion to illustrate the continuities and changes in the anthropological study of religion.

PART TWO
CONTINUITY AND CHANGE IN THE ANTHROPOLOGICAL STUDY OF RELIGION

CHAPTER THREE
Foundations of the Anthropological Discourse on Religion in the Western Tradition

THE HISTORICAL ROOTS OF THE ANTHROPOLOGY OF RELIGION

In Chapters 1 and 2, I outlined the goals of the anthropology of religion and pointed out that anthropologists have tried to understand the nature of religion, delineating it as part of culture, and have asked questions about what accounts for the similarities and differences in religious phenomena. Although such inquiries can occur only in social/political contexts that foster free inquiry and critical analysis of beliefs and practices in naturalistic or nonreligious terms, the resulting analysis is not free of prevailing prejudices and cultural assumptions.

Modern anthropology began in the Western tradition during the late Renaissance (sixteenth and seventeenth centuries) in association with the rise of modern science but continued to reflect many medieval Judeo-Christian cultural assumptions about humankind and human history. In the eighteenth century, the systematic formulation of an empiricist epistemology provided a philosophical foundation for the study of beliefs and practices (i.e., culture) as nongenetic, socially acquired reality; and despite their belief in the superiority of Western beliefs and customs, many writers promoted a tolerance for cultural differences (Harris 1968). Theories of psychic unity and the natural history of the mind, and speculations about the evolution of social institutions such as religion, became common. However, in the nineteenth century, particularly during the second half, a biological worldview loomed large in Western consciousness, and raciocultural histories of humankind continued to be popular in the twentieth century. Specific theoretical approaches such as institutional and structural analysis (nurtured for a long time in the French-Scottish-English intellectual tradition) and the interpretive-cultural analysis of the German intellectual tradition became important in anthropological discourse of the twentieth century.

Prior to the emergence of modern anthropology in the late Renaissance, anthropological discourse on religion in Western civilization was an aspect of the philosophical discourse on humankind. Many ancient Greek and Roman philosophers analyzed naturalistically their beliefs and practices and engaged in interpreting how beliefs in certain kinds of deities emerged. For example, the Greek philosopher Xenophanes of Colophon (c. 570 B.C.–c. 480 B.C.) declared:

> Yea, and if oxen and horses and lions had hands, and could paint with their hands, and provide works of art, as men do, horses would paint the forms of gods like horses, and oxen like oxen, and make their bodies into the image of several kinds.

> The Ethiopians make their gods black and mule-nosed; the Thracians say theirs have blue eyes and red hair. (quoted in Malefijt 1968: 149)

According to Aristotle (quoted in Evans-Pritchard 1965: 49),

> . . . all people say that the gods also had a king because they themselves had kings formerly or now; for men create gods after their own image, not only with regard to form; but also with regard to their manner of life.

The Greek historian of customs Herodotus of Halicarnassus (c. 480 B.C.–c. 425 B.C.) discovered and wrote about the existence of functional parallels in the attributes of various deities found among different peoples he visited. The Sicilian philosopher Euhemerus (c. 330 B.C.–c. 260 B.C.) theorized that gods were originally dead ancestors and heroes of great distinction who had historically acquired veneration and significance as objects of worship. Romans such as Marcus Cicero (106 B.C.–43 B.C.) and Julius Caesar (c. 100 B.C.–44 B.C.), and Greek geographers such as Strabo (c. 63 B.C.–A.D. 21) theorized about or described religious customs of different peoples.

The ideas of "projection," "function," and "symbolic representation" were implicit in Greco-Roman writings about gods and spirits, but it is rare to find such theorizing about supernatural beings and powers between the fifth and sixteenth centuries A.D. Descriptions of alien religions were common, however, particularly after the twelfth century A.D. when Europe increased its trade and contacts with the Mongols, Turks, Arabs, Chinese, and others.

As I have argued elsewhere (Pandian 1985), modern anthropology was epistemologically linked with the Judeo-Christian tradition. The anthropological perspective on religion that emerged after the discovery of the New World combined naturalistic views about the physical world and the Judeo-Christian assumptions of the universal history of humankind, the Christian taxonomy of the Great Chain of Being, the idea of the chosen people, and other theological assumptions. The discovery of the New World generated fresh questions about the true nature of humanity in relation to the scriptural references that "man was created in the image of God." If humans were created in the image of God, did God have the image of Europeans and if so, how was it possible to account for the existence of non-European-looking humans? Did God create humankind once or more than once? The issue of monogenesis versus polygenesis became a central concern in anthropological discourse, and the classification of humankind a problem in the Western intellectual tradition. Margaret Hodgen (1964) points out that this problem was resolved during the late Renaissance by locating "savages" (non-Western peoples in general, and native Americans and native Africans in particular) between humans and animals on the Great Chain of Being. It was believed that God could not leave gaps in Creation, and that the savage, as not fully human, had a definite, preordained place in God's creations.

The comparative method was used to justify the perceived inferiority of non-Western peoples. The customs of non-Western peoples were viewed as analogous to the customs of the ancient Western past (for example, the religious customs of the Iroquois Indians were compared to those of the ancient Greeks—both pagans, as opposed to Christians). Western beliefs and practices such as monotheism and monogamy were seen as culminations of a progression toward truth.

It is interesting to guess what the history of the anthropology of religion would have been if the ancient Greeks and Romans had established political/economic dominance in the New World. The descriptions of alien religious customs that followed discovery of the New World in the late fifteenth century were meant to depict and denounce these customs as superstitious or satanic. The "universal histories" that were written in the Western tradition after the fifteenth century were similar to the universal histories written during the Middle Ages in the sense that both were written primarily to explain the history of God's plan (or God's plan in history) and how it unfolded through events in which Christians participated to glorify the kingdom of God.

In the eighteenth century, many Western scholars offered naturalistic (i.e., nonreligious) explanations of religion, possibly influenced by the empiricist epistemology and deistic beliefs of that period. The writings of David Hume (1711–1776), Francois de Voltaire (1694–1778), and Johann Herder (1744–1803) were important precursors to nineteenth century anthropological discourse on the "natural history" of religion and to the study of religion as part of culture. The French Jesuit priest Joseph Francois Lafitau (1681–1746), who served as a missionary among the Iroquois, compared the religious customs of the Iroquois and the Greeks and theorized that monotheism was the original religion of humankind. Whereas theologically inclined Western scholars viewed nonmonotheistic religions as degenerated forms of monotheism, non–theologically inclined scholars viewed monotheism as an evolutionary culmination of the progressive development of religion, a view that became dominant in anthropological discourse of the nineteenth century.

A discussion of some of the representative anthropological theories of religion in the nineteenth and early twentieth centuries will clarify the theoretical formulation of religion offered in this book. Anthropological explanations of religion differ in how they conceptualize religious phenomena, and yet there is a thread of continuity. The theories discussed in Chapters 5 through 9, and especially Chapters 8 and 9 ("Structural-symbolic Analysis of Religion" and "Phenomenological-symbolic Analysis of Religion"), lay the foundation for the theoretical formulation that I present in Chapter 10 ("The Semiotics of the Sacred Self").

NINETEENTH- AND EARLY-TWENTIETH-CENTURY ANTHROPOLOGICAL DISCOURSE ON THE EVOLUTION OF RELIGION

Nineteenth- and early-twentieth-century scholars focused on cognitive, emotive, linguistic, social, or cultural aspects in their theoretical formulations of religion, but their formulations were within the evolutionary framework. They were, for the most part, armchair anthropologists who wondered how primitives or savages would conceptualize various psychological and social phenomena without a scientific understanding of such phenomena. These scholars believed that the comparative method of grouping and classifying religious phenomena would enable them to understand the origin and development of religion because it showed logically how or why certain kinds of religious phenomena occurred at certain levels of mental or cultural development.

Scholars such as Edward Tylor (1832–1917) and James Frazer (1854–1941) distinguished between magic and religion but said that they were both based on a lack of scientific knowledge about life, visions, sleep, trance, dreams, sickness, death, and so on. To them, primitive humans had an erroneous understanding of psychological experiences and mental states and fallacious assumptions about the relationship between mind and objects.

In the evolutionist framework of scholars such as Tylor and Frazer, magic preceded religion. Magic was an infantile, pseudo-scientific worldview which operated on the assumption that it was possible to control or influence nature by coercing supernatural entities, whereas religious worship was a more mature development based on the realization that supplication and propitiation of supernatural entities were more adequate or appropriate. Religion was an intermediate stage that prepared the way for the emergence of the adult scientific worldview. Science was the culmination of mental development, manifesting the maturity of the human mind, and most scholars believed that a true scientific worldview would make it unnecessary to have either magic or religion.

Evolutionary thinkers failed to realize that a magician's or shaman's manipulation of the symbols of the sacred other was based on a rather accurate psychological understanding of stimulus and response to produce certain kinds of mental states rather than on a fallacious understanding of the relationships among objects or of the relationship between mental and physical phenomena.

It is likely that many thinkers were apprehensive about a revival of interest in spiritualist or psychic phenomena during the Victorian and Edwardian ages of Europe. The writer Arthur Conan Doyle and the biologist Alfred Wallace were among those who explored psychic phenomena, and scholars like Edward Tylor probably viewed such involvement as a threat to science and to human progress and happiness. It is interesting to note that Marvin Harris, the American anthropologist, has voiced a similar concern and apprehension in his denouncement of recent intellectual efforts to idealize paranormal phenomena and to glorify the shaman (Ortner 1984).

THE "FATHERS" OF PSYCHOLOGICAL, SOCIOLOGICAL, AND INTERPRETIVE APPROACHES TO THE STUDY OF RELIGION IN ANTHROPOLOGY

The theories of Edward Tylor (1832–1917) and James Frazer (1854–1941) as well as the theories of Auguste Comte (1798–1857), Herbert Spencer (1820–1903), Robert R. Marett (1866–1943), and Max Muller (1823–1900) can be classified as psychological theories that explain religion in terms of psychogenic processes (Evans-Pritchard 1965). Comte theorized that mental development occurred in three stages and that phenomena such as fetishism (worshipping objects believed to possess power) and polytheism (worship of many gods), had their origin in the first, theological stage of the mind. Progressive development of the mind led to the emergence of the metaphysical stage, which was followed by the scientific or positivistic stage. Spencer's theory was similar to Tylor's (discussed later) but differed in its emphasis on the worship of ancestral ghosts. Spencer's theory may be called *euhemerism*, named after the Sicilian philosopher Euhemerus (c. 330 B.C.–260 B.C.), who believed that religion was based on the deification and worship of dead heroes. Marett theorized that the earliest form of religion was characterized by feelings about supernatural power permeating the universe, an emotional orientation of the primitives that he characterized as animatism. Robert Codrington (1891), a missionary, described beliefs and practices associated with *mana* (a power or force residing in objects, spirits, etc., that could be captured and controlled for personal use) in Melanesia, and Robert Marett (1909) argued that primitive humans must have had an emotional involvement with objects that were believed to possess great supernatural power. Max Muller's (1870) theory of religion is frequently referred to as the linguistic or anthropomorphic theory of religion because he formulated the view that primitive humans were incapable of abstract, linguistic representation of phenomena in general and that physical phenomena such as the sun and moon as well as various human experiences were personified and given concrete form and qualities in early stages of linguistic development.

Another scholar whose ideas will be discussed in detail later is Sigmund Freud (1856–1939). Freud holds a unique position in the anthropological study of religion, although many of his specific conclusions about the nature and function of religion are dismissed by many anthropologists as the irrelevant speculations of a great mind caught in conflicting personal and cultural prejudices as it tried to pursue a total commitment to naturalism and the scientific inquiry of all phenomena.

Freud's contribution to the study of religion is in his development of the idea of projection, which has had a lasting impact on anthropological theorizing about religion, particularly in the "culture and personality" perspective of American anthropology (now called psychological anthropology). Freud shared with Tylor and others of the late nineteenth century the view that religion was an infantile, irrational phenomenon that would be eliminated from culture with the full development of rationality and science, but he also made use of Smith's seminal writings on totemism (beliefs and rituals that dramatize affinity between human groups and animals, plants, or objects) and explained the origin of religion by linking the helplessness of childhood, representation of authority figures to seek protection, neurotic hostilities and guilt in familial relationships, and psychosexual development.

An alternative to psychogenic theories was presented by a few French and Scottish scholars who examined the social foundation and function of religion. Prominent among them in the late nineteenth and early twentieth centuries were W. Robertson Smith (1846–1894) and Emile Durkheim (1858–1917), who explained the origin of religion with reference to social or sociogenic processes. To them, the beginning and maintenance of religion were in the conception of group identity and in the affirmation, through ritual, of social categories, values, and solidarity. Rather than focusing on individual psychology, these scholars used the framework of what we would identify today as social psychology. As the ideas of Smith and Durkheim have relevance for an understanding of the perspective taken in this book, I will mention them briefly here and will present a comprehensive interpretation of their views later.

Smith and Durkheim assumed that magic, as an individual-oriented, manipulative effort to achieve instrumental goals, came into existence after the formation of the social level of human existence with the representation of group-oriented religious beliefs and rituals that sanctified the consensus, goals, and values of the community. Magic, in their view, was antisocial. I disagree with this view because I consider the magical orientation a form of symbolic integration in certain contexts and domains of human existence. As Marcel Mauss (1975: 19) notes, magical beliefs and practices are also rooted in society and are collective representations just as religious beliefs and practices are. Durkheim, in his efforts to combat psychological and biological reductionism, which were prevalent during his time, took the position that categories of thought and human behavior could not be explained as products of psychological processes and that human thought and action were derived from social categories. Through such a theoretical formulation, Durkheim contributed to the development of the discipline of sociology and the relativistic study of religion, knowledge, and institutions as social facts.

Brian Morris in his book *Anthropological Studies of Religion: An Introductory Text* (1987) presents a comprehensive discussion of the theoretical formulations of German scholars such as Immanuel Kant (1724–1804), G.F.W. Hegel (1770–1831), Karl Marx (1818–1883), Friedrich Nietzsche (1844–1900), Max Weber (1864–1920), and Carl Jung (1875–1961) and also provides a detailed analysis of the German cultural context in which the positivistic approach to "cultural" or "human" sciences was rejected in favor of the historical-interpretive-phenomenological approach. It is conceivable that the revived interest in the study of German scholarship may be related to general anthropological interest in the study of symbol and meaning and in using the interpretive model as an alternative to the natural science model in the study of cultural systems. In a later chapter I discuss the theoretical contributions of Max Weber, the German sociologist, who is perhaps the most important link between positivist/mechanistic and interpretive/ phenomenological approaches in the anthropological study of religion. I will also discuss the phenomenological approach of Carl Jung.

Max Weber's treatise *The Protestant Ethic and the Spirit of Capitalism* (1930) has been frequently cited in anthropological textbooks on religion as a significant challenge to Marxist interpretation of history and the economic-deterministic model of change. It appears to me that such a citation does injustice to both Marx and Weber. Weber promoted a particular type of sociological research, combining historical scholarship with an empathetic understanding *(Verstehen)* of the motivations and intentionalities of goal-oriented actions of individuals. Weber called this "interpretive sociology," and his sociology became an alternative approach to Durkheim's group-oriented sociology. To Weber, the individual is the unit of sociological analysis, and it is necessary to study how individuals engage in meaningful behavior; the meaning systems embedded in the religious formulations of the self are significant aspects of human action. The protestant formulations of the self had, in Weber's view, certain consequences for rational economic action, and Weber showed, through historical scholarship, that societies which promoted the protestant conception of the self exceeded in the economic and industrial output more than the nonprotestant societies. Weber's views became important in American sociology through the writings of Talcott Parsons (1902–1986). In contemporary American cultural anthropology, the views of Weber and Parsons are evident in the "interpretive anthropology" of Clifford Geertz.

CHAPTER FOUR
Religion and Magical Thinking: Early Formulations

THE SYMBOLIC INTEGRATION
OF INTRA-PSYCHIC PROCESSES

As I pointed out earlier, there is a long history of explaining beliefs in sacred powers or beings as projective models that are based on actual experiences. Some scholars identify experiences such as dreams and altered states of consciousness as the foundation for the formulation of sacred beliefs; scholarly studies of this kind are often grouped as cognitivist psychological theories of religion. Other scholars identify emotional reactions to stimuli that cause fear or awe as the locus of sacred formulations, and such studies are grouped as emotionalist psychological theories of religion. Both types of theories focus on the analysis of intra-psychic processes for explaining religion, as opposed to the sociogenic or sociological theories of religion that focus on the analysis of social processes for explaining religion. (See Norbeck 1961; Evans-Pritchard 1965; Malefijt 1968).

In the study of the symbolic representations of intra-psychic processes, scholars such as Edward Tylor and James Frazer note that human beings in their primitive stages of mental and cultural development had erroneous or false understanding of their mental states: Symbolic representations such as spirits, ghosts, and supernatural power could not have been formulated if there had been scientific understanding of how the mind works.

The foregoing type of explanation is misleading: It suggests that we can go back in time and become a primitive philosopher or psychologist and theorize about our experiences from the vantage point of a primitive philosopher or psychologist; it also suggests that a false or pseudo-scientific explanation is the foundation of primitive religion, which is magical in its orientation.

The equation of primitive religion with magical thinking connotes that primitive religion, at its archaic level, was not linked with conceptions of morality or social order. The linkage, in this equation, occurred later, at a more advanced level of the mind, when it was realized that magic was futile and that the supplication and worship of the sacred powers or beings were much more effective.

Because of the foregoing assumption, the dichotomy between magic and religion acquired anthropological significance as corresponding to the dichotomy between "primitive" and "civilized" humanity. In a later section of this chapter I discuss the factors that contributed to the formulation of the dichotomy. It never occurred to the psychological-evolutionary scholars of the eighteenth, nineteenth, and twentieth centuries that the symbolic representation of intra-psychic processes as sacred may have been and may continue to be one way of achieving and maintaining symbolic integration or coherence of the self, particularly in contexts of stress and anxiety in any type of society, "primitive" or "civilized."

ANIMISTIC THEORY OF THE UNIVERSE AND THE UNIVERSE OF SPIRITUAL BEINGS

Edward Tylor (1832–1917), who was associated with Oxford University and is generally called the "father" of academic anthropology, made a significant contribution to the study of religion. The second volume of his treatise *Primitive Culture* (published in 1871 and titled *Religion in Primitive Culture*) was devoted to a detailed discussion of the underlying principles that governed the "laws" of religious development. This second volume, in combination with the first volume, called *The Origins of Culture,* provided the discipline of anthropology with a standard text on cultural evolution, just as Charles Darwin's study *The Origin of Species* (1859) provided the discipline of biology with a standard text on biological evolution. The following quotations are from Tylor's 1873 edition of *Religion in Primitive Culture,* which was reprinted by Harper Torchbooks in 1957.

Tylor defines religion as "the belief in Spiritual Beings" (1957: 8) and explains how such a belief came into being. He suggests that the belief in spiritual beings constitutes a philosophical perspective of the primitive human, a spiritualist perspective of the universe that he identifies as animism. The animistic theory of the universe, according to Tylor, is a product of primitive humans' intellectualizing about various states of human existence such as wakefulness and sleep, life and death, visions, trance, and good health and sickness. Primitive humans concluded that a second self must exist, and they speculated about the nature of the second self, its existence after death, its powers, and so on. These speculations led to the belief in an apparitional-soul, a ghost soul, and ultimately to "the actual conception of the personal soul or spirit among the lower races."

> What the doctrine of the soul is among the lower races may be explained in stating the animistic theory of its development. It seems as though thinking men, as yet at a low level of culture, were deeply impressed by two groups of biological problems. In the first place, what is it that makes the difference between a living body and a dead one; what causes waking, sleep, trance, disease, death? In the second place, what are those human shapes which appear in dreams and visions? Looking at these two groups of phenomena, the ancient savage philosophers probably made their first step by the obvious inference that every man has two things belonging to him, namely, a life and a phantom. These two are evidently in close connexion with the body, the life as enabling it to feel and think and act, the phantom as being its image or second self; both, also, are perceived as being its image or second self; both, also, are perceived to be things separable from the body, the life as able to go away and leave it insensible or dead, the phantom as appearing to people at a distance from it. (Tylor 1957: 12)

Tylor's theory is sometimes referred to as the "dream-theory of religion," the "ghost-theory of religion," or the "soul-theory of religion." Tylor describes, at length, how the belief in souls later developed into various other doctrines such as the doctrine of continuance (the abodes of souls and spirits), the doctrine of embodiment (the actions of souls and spirits), the doctrine of possession, and the doctrine of fetishism (objects with soul or spiritual power); and how polytheism and monotheism developed with the conceptualization of some spirits as gods and some gods as more powerful, ultimately leading to the concept of one powerful god. (See Van Baal 1971 and Skorupsky 1983 for a critique of Tylor's theory.)

It is possible to interpret Tylor's idea of the second self as being similar to what I identify as the symbols of the sacred self, and to interpret the idea of spiritual beings as corresponding to the idea of the symbols of the sacred other. Symbols of self are representations or formulations about human identity. By using Tylor's reasoning, we can say that the "second self" is a representation of the sacred because it defies space and time and becomes an "objective," public, cultural representation that can become identified as the symbol of the sacred other. The symbol of the sacred other fuses the known and the unknown and is, in turn, used to represent the "first self" as sacred.

SYMPATHETIC MAGIC
AND FALLACIOUS SCIENCE

James Frazer (1854–1941) was a classical scholar and a compiler of ethnographic information. Long associated with Cambridge University, he wrote extensively on a variety of subjects, but he is best remembered for the twelve-volume treatise on religious phenomena called *The Golden Bough: A Study in Magic and Religion,* published from 1911 to 1915. Frazer organizes ethnographic data within an evolutionary framework and makes a sharp distinction between magic and religion. For Tylor, the distinction between magic and religion is an analytic distinction: Both magic and religion are part of the animistic philosophy, although the magical orientation has precedence over the religious orientation. For Frazer, magic and religion belong to two different kinds of supernaturalism; the former is pseudo-science, based on the magician's or shaman's logic, which erroneously associates ideas of similarity and contiguity in formulating theories of relationship between objects and events.

> If we analyze the principles of thought on which magic is based, they will probably be found to resolve themselves into two: first, that like produces like, or that an effect resembles its cause; and, second, that things which have once been in contact with each other continue to act on each other at a distance after the physical contact has been severed. The former principle may be called the "Law of Similarity," the latter the "Law of Contact or Contagion." From the first of these principles, namely the Law of Similarity, the magician infers that he can produce any effect he desires merely by imitating it: from the second he infers that whatever he does to a material object will affect equally the person with whom the object was once in contact, whether it formed part of his body or not. Charms based on the Law of Similarity may be called "Homeopathic or Imitative Magic." Charms based on the Law of Contact or Contagion may be called "Contagious Magic." To denote the first of these branches of magic the term Homeopathic is perhaps preferable, for the alternative term Imitative or Mimetic suggests, if it does not imply, a conscious agent who imitates, thereby limiting the scope of magic too narrowly. For the same principles which the magician applies in the practice of his art are implicitly believed by him to regulate the operations of inanimate nature; in other words, he tacitly assumes that the Laws of Similarity and Contact are of universal application and are not limited to human actions. In short, magic is a spurious system of natural law as well as a fallacious guide of conduct; it is a false science as well as an abortive art. (Frazer 1911: 52)

Frazer's theory of magic has heuristic value for an understanding of certain kinds of associations that are made in the representation of the sacred other and the sacred self, but as Leach (1976: 29) has correctly pointed out, Frazer "assumed that the magician's mistake is to confuse expressive acts with technical acts," although "what the magician usually does is to interpret an index as a signal, after the fashion of Pavlov's dog." Magicians or shamans may believe that they caused certain events or transformations to occur through their knowledge of associating certain ideas or objects, and the proof of the validity of this knowledge comes from what happens to the people. For example, "voodoo death" occurs through imitative or contagious magic, and people are cured by the "removal" of alien substances or the retrieval of the "lost soul" or exorcism. Unless there are cultural assumptions that support a magical or shamanistic worldview, people do not die or get cured through these means.

The actions of the shaman must be interpreted not as an erroneous application of cause-and-effect relationships (Frazer's "pseudo-science") but as methods of constructing the symbols of the sacred self. The sorcerer or shaman promotes a merger of the symbols of the self and supernatural reality by using techniques such as rhythmic drumming, drugs, and physical and mental deprivations. The existence of the sacred reality is proved by the shaman's success in effecting this merger, and therefore the techniques to achieve the merger become the crucial aspects of shamanism. Once the merger is achieved, the symbols of the self function as sacred and are endowed with a coherent system of knowledge and meaning as it pertains to the symbols of the sacred other that are deployed. As long as the symbol of the self and the symbol of the sacred other are in communion, the logic of the symbol of the sacred other operates to produce the intended results expected or anticipated by the shaman.

THE MAGUS

It is very likely that if the anthropological study of religion had begun and developed in a non-Western cultural tradition, the dichotomy between magic and religion would not have had much theoretical significance, and scholars might not have viewed magical beliefs and practices as a primitive type of supernaturalism based on a fallacious theory of cause-and-effect relationships.

The word *magic* is a cognate of the Persian concept of *magus*. The magus was the priest of Zoroastrianism, endowed with supernatural powers and skills in interpreting the nature of the relationship between the stars and worldly or human events (astrology). The *magi,* according to the Bible, were able to visit with the infant Jesus because of their ability to know what the star signified (Matthew 2: 1–12). The Greek word *magike* and the Latin word *magika* (from the Persian *magus* and the Greek *magos*) referred to a variety of practices such as necromancy, sorcery, witchcraft, wizardry, and so on that were explained during the Middle Ages and the Renaissance as evil, Satanic, or occult beliefs and practices of the "pagan" world.

Christianity, as a state religion after the fourth century A.D., gradually succeeded in suppressing many of the ancient Greco-Roman myths and rituals as well as the various mystery cults and oracles but did not completely eliminate them. These "pagan" beliefs and practices became associated with the concept of magic, and magic was seen as a threat to the moral/political order that had been established by Christianity. Margaret

A. Murray's (1921) thesis that the pagan beliefs and practices continued to coexist in Western Europe (with Christianity) as a "witch cult" is plausible: Whether we agree with her interpretations totally or in part, the wealth of historical data she presents in the book *The Witch-Cult in Western Europe* suggests that alternative religious perspectives existed in Europe, often challenging the Roman Catholic interpretations of the nature of humans and the universe. (It may also be argued that the "magical" beliefs and practices had no historical link with the pagan world but were part of the religious Christian tradition of Europe and were functional in the rural areas.)

Because of the foregoing intellectual heritage of the West, scholars frequently assumed that magic and magical thinking belonged to a different class of phenomena from religion and religious worship. Magic was believed to be an inferior, antisocial activity that belonged to the pagan world—as opposed to religion, which was explained as an advancement in mental and cultural development. Scholars for the most part failed to recognize that what they identified as magic and magical thinking were an integral part of any religious belief and ritual as well.

In Western, Christian scholarship, descriptions of non-Christian religious beliefs and practices were primarily used to make a contrast between the magical, pagan world and the religious, Christian world. "Magical," "pagan" beliefs and practices were viewed as inherently evil, despite references to the dichotomy between "white" and "black" magic (when such a distinction is made, the former is identified as "good" and linked with conceptions of "exorcism" that have been part of the religious orientations of many Christian denominations).

From the ethnographic accounts of religious beliefs and practices it is clear that in most societies some sacred beliefs and practices have evil connotations, but it is not possible to delineate some as religious and others as magical. Such beliefs combine with cultural formulations of witchcraft, sorcery, health, sickness, and death and constitute a coherent symbolic system. For the believer, they are symbolic realities that affirm one another, providing explanations and answers. The creation of symbolic realities is not an expression of magical thinking or primitive mentality. As Stanley Diamond (1972: xxi–xxii) points out, "Even while creating their myths and ceremonials, their meanings and their insights, primitive people are aware of the reality that they mold."

CHAPTER FIVE
Religion and Collective Thinking: Early Formulations

THE SYMBOLIC INTEGRATION OF SOCIETY

The empiricist epistemology of John Locke (1632–1704) provided social philosophers with a model of knowledge that enabled them to conceptualize customs, institutions, and so on as acquired realities. This perspective posed a problem for anthropologically oriented scholars. If social reality was the product of individual experience, then how could individuals communicate and share in a common system of beliefs and practices? If, on the other hand, social reality was made possible because of the existence of the psychic unity of the mind or common structures of cognition, why do human beings have multiple social realities?

The classical sociological answer to the foregoing question was formulated by the French social philosopher Emile Durkheim, who theorized that the categories of cognition were themselves acquired. In this formulation, human rationality itself has an external locus, that is, in society. The internalization of society-specific rationality enables individuals to communicate their experiences to one another in a meaningful manner. The study of human behavior, therefore, involves the study of the social representations or the collective conscience of a group, and the analysis of society involves the delineation of the relationships of social facts.

In the following sections I review the contributions of W. Robertson Smith and Emile Durkheim, who provided the theoretical and methodological foundation for the study of the sacred representations of society. Also, I discuss briefly the contributions of the French social philosopher Lucien Levy-Bruhl. Writing at about the same time when Durkheim's views were gaining acceptance, Levy-Bruhl came under attack for suggesting that "natives" (i.e., non-Western peoples) differed from Europeans in manifesting primitive or prelogical mentality; he argued that the collective representations of non-Western society differed in kind from those of Western society, and that as a result there was a qualitative difference between Western and non-Western ways of thinking.

CLAN AND TRIBAL IDENTITY

It is not surprising that the two scholars who initiated the scientific study of the social foundations of religion were connected with the priesthood. W. Robertson Smith (1721–1793), the son of a minister, was himself an ordained minister of the Free Church of Scotland (a position he was forced to relinquish because of reactions against his historical and hermeneutical analysis of the Bible); and Emile Durkheim (1858–1917) was the son of a head rabbi in France and had initially planned to become a rabbi himself.

Smith, a professor of Semitic languages and religions, was closely connected with the intellectual circles of Britain and the continent. His contributions to anthropological thought were primarily in the study of Semitic ritual and in theorizing about totemism, sacrifice, and kinship. His influential books were *The Prophets of Israel* (1882) and *The Religion of the Semites* (1889).

Smith points out that an individual acquires his or her beliefs as a member of society and perceives the world through social categories, and that through ritual the members of a society strengthen their bonds with God and among themselves. The strengthening of the bond with God through ritual sacrifice of the totemic animal is the same as strengthening kinship bonds because the totem represents group or tribal identity, and in consuming the totemic animal the members of a tribe dramatize their unity with God. As the religious and group identities are the same, beliefs about the origin of the group and the origin of totemic worship are the same; God is the representation of the group's origin as well as the representation of the values of the group. Beidelman (1974: 66–67) is correct in noting that "Smith's single greatest contribution to social research was his emphasis upon the social basis of belief and values." As we will see later, Smith's originality and insights had a profound impact on Emile Durkheim and Sigmund Freud. The following quotes, from Smith's *The Religion of the*

Semites (first published in 1889), give a brief overview of the scope of his analysis of religion.

> Religion did not exist for the saving of souls but for the preservation and welfare of society, and in all that was necessary to this end every man had to take his part, or break with the domestic and political community to which he belonged. (1972: 29)
>
> It is only in times of social dissolution, as in the last age of the small Semitic states, when men and their gods were alike powerless before the advance of the Assyrians, that magical superstitions based on mere terror, or rites designed to conciliate alien gods, invade the sphere of tribal or national religion. In better times the religion of the tribe or state has nothing in common with the private and foreign superstitions or magical rites that savage terror may dictate to the individual. Religion is not an arbitrary relation of the individual man to a supernatural power, it is a relation of all the members of a community to a power that has the good of the community at heart and protects its law and moral order. (1972: 55)

Smith makes a distinction between magic and religion, viewing the former as antisocial, just as Durkheim does. But this distinction is derived from Smith's interpretation of the function of what he defines as religion: Religion serves the group, upholds social order, and enables the group to function as a moral community; magic, from Smith's point of view, is superstition that frightens and terrorizes.

COLLECTIVE REPRESENTATIONS AND THE APOTHEOSIS OF SOCIETY

Emile Durkheim's contributions to the study of religion are widely recognized and used within the disciplines of sociology and social/cultural anthropology. His writings provide us with the theoretical and methodological foundation for the analysis of the relationship between and among social facts, and for the study of symbols as collective or public representations of sentiments, values, and worldviews as well the social principles or categories of thought. The study of symbols in this manner, an approach sometimes identified as Durkheimian social psychology, is a central theme of this book.

Durkheim's study of religion is essentially a study of the social foundations of knowledge. In this respect, and in the analysis of the function of totemic representations and rituals associated with such representations, Durkheim was much influenced by Smith. This was an intellectual debt that Durkheim himself acknowledges in his book *The Elementary Forms of the Religious Life* (1915). Several scholars have made references to Durkheim's intellectual affinity to Smith. Beidelman (1974: 67) notes that Smith's sociology of knowledge influenced Durkheim. Douglas (1966: 20–21) states that "Durkheim adopted in its entirety Robertson Smith's definition of primitive religion as the established church which expresses community values. . . ." But Durkheim puts forth an elaborate sociological theory of religion and by explaining religious worship as none other than the worship of society renders society and religion interdependent facts of human life. As Douglas (1966: 20–21) points out, Durkheim does not follow Smith completely in all respects.

Durkheim rejects psychological and utilitarian theories of religion that reduce religious phenomena to irrational or rational psychological states and does not subscribe to the view that progress in scientific understanding of the world would lead to a decline in the role of religion. He therefore disagrees with Tylor's view of religious origin: For Tylor, religion originates in the deification of erroneous interpretations of mental states; for Durkheim, religion is the apotheosis of society—its sacred values, sentiments, worldview, and principles or categories:

> Religious representations are collective representations which express collective realities; the rites are a manner of acting which take rise in the midst of the assembled groups and which are destined to excite, maintain or recreate certain mental states in these groups. So if the categories are of religious origin, they ought to participate in this nature common to all religious facts; they too should be social affairs and the product of collective thought. At least—for in the actual condition of our knowledge of these matters, one should be careful to avoid all radical and exclusive statements—it is allowable to suppose that they are rich in social elements. (Durkheim 1915: 22)

In another profound statement on the human condition, Durkheim has this to say:

> Thus the collective ideal which religion expresses is far from being due to a vague innate power of the individual, but it is rather at the school of collective life that the individual has learned to idealize. It is in assimilating the ideals elaborated by society that he has become capable of conceiving the ideal. It is society which, by leading him within its sphere of action, has made him acquire the need of raising himself above the world of experience and has at the same time furnished him with the means of conceiving another. For society has constructed this new world in constructing itself, since it is society which this expresses. Thus both with the individual and in the group, the faculty of idealizing has nothing mysterious about it. It is not a sort of luxury which a man could get along without, but a condition of his very existence. He could not be a social being, that is to say, he could not be a man, if he had not acquired it. It is true that in incarnating themselves to individuals, collective ideals tend to individualize themselves. Each understands them after his own fashion and marks them with his own stamp; he suppresses certain elements and adds others. Thus the personal ideal disengages itself from the social ideal in proportion as the individual personality develops itself and becomes an autonomous source of action. But if we wish to understand this

aptitude, so singular in appearance, of living outside of reality, it is enough to connect it with the social conditions upon which it depends. (Durkheim 1915: 470–471)

Durkheim (1915: 57–63) applies his considerable analytic skills and mastery of facts to distinguish magic and religion. Like Smith, he holds that "magic is opposed to religion, as the individual to social," and goes on to identify magic as that which seeks "technical and utilitarian ends," profanes "holy things," "performs the contrary of the religious ceremony," and so on, and he comes to the following conclusion:

> There is no Church of magic. Between the magician and the individuals who consult him, as between these individuals themselves, there are no lasting bonds which make them members of the same moral community, comparable to that formed by the believers in the same god or the observers of the same cult. The magician has a clientele and not a Church, and it is very possible that his clients have no other relations between each other, or even do not know each other; even the relations which they have with him are generally accidental and transient; they are just like those of a sick man with his physician. The official and public character with which he is sometimes invested changes nothing in this situation; the fact that he works openly does not unite him more regularly or more durably to those who have recourse to his services. (Durkheim 1915: 60)

Durkheim's arguments are convincing up to a point; magicians manipulate, are often antisocial recluses, often create terror by their appearance and actions, have specific instrumental goals, and so on. But we must ask the same questions about the epistemological foundation of such magical or shamanistic behaviors that Durkheim would ask about religious behaviors. As Durkheim's student (and nephew) Marcel Mauss (1975: 18–19) noted, magic is also a social act.

> Magic and magical rites, as a whole, are traditional facts. Actions which are never repeated cannot be called magical. If the whole community does not believe in the efficacy of a group of actions, they cannot be magical. The form of the ritual is eminently transmissible and this is sanctioned by public opinion. It follows from this that strictly individual actions, such as the private superstitions of gamblers, cannot be called magical. (See O'Keefe [1982] for a "social theory of magic.")

The problem of whether magic is antisocial arises when we assume that there is an intrinsic, necessary relationship between religion and morality. Tylor does not assume this relationship; his theory of religion is based on the notion that the spiritual beings of primitive humans are the projection or representation of non-ordinary mental states. *Durkheim, however, assumes the existence of an intrinsic relationship between religion and morality because his theory of religion is based on the notion that "sacred things" are representations of social conventions.*

THE MYSTICAL DIMENSION
OF COLLECTIVE MENTALITY

Lucien Levy-Bruhl (1857–1939), the French philosopher-sociologist, wrote extensively on the nature of collective representations in several books such as *Primitive Mentality* (English translation 1923) and *How Natives Think* (English translation 1925). He speculated, on the basis of available ethnographic data, that primitive cultures (as opposed to European cultures) were characterized by the existence of collective representations or formulations that did not make logical discriminations in the approximation of reality or experiences. Instead, he argued, primitive representations fostered the blurring of contradictions and promoted mystical participation with nature. Levy-Bruhl said that both magic and religion ("magico-religious" phenomena) originated from mystical participation.

In his theoretical formulations, he suggested that there is a qualitative difference between how the "natives" and Europeans think: The former's social categories of thought render it impossible to engage in naturalistic investigation of phenomena, and, as a result, advancement in scientific knowledge cannot occur. The dichotomies in the following list illustrate Levy-Bruhl's speculation:

> Primitive Mind/Civilized Mind
> Prelogical Mind/Logical Discriminations
> Mystical Participation/Rational Approximation of Reality and Experience
> Magico-religious Worldview/Scientific Worldview

The following quote is from his book *How Natives Think* (1925: 386):

> . . . the mentality of primitive peoples is essentially mystic and prelogical in character; that it takes a different direction from our own—that is, that its collective representations are regulated by the law of participation and are consequently indifferent to the law of contradiction, and united, the one to the other, by connections and preconnections which prove disconcerting to our reason.

> It throws light, too, upon our own mental activity. It leads us to recognize that the rational unity of the thinking being, which is taken for granted by most philosophers, is a *desideratum*, not a fact. Even among peoples like ourselves, ideas and relations between ideas governed by the law of participation are far from having disappeared. They exist, more or less independently, more or less impaired, but yet ineradicable, side by side with those subject to the laws of reasoning. Understanding, properly so called, tends towards logical unity and proclaims its necessity; but as a matter of fact our mental activity is both rational and irrational. The prelogical and the mystic are co-existent with the logical.

Despite his use of concepts such as prelogical or primitive mentality, Levy-Bruhl's theories were not biological or racial formulations of inferior mentality, contrary to the theories of most late-nineteenth- and early-twentieth-century scholars in Europe and the United States; like Emile Durkheim, he was opposed to biological theories of social or cultural facts. He simply failed to realize that all cultures, whether primitive or European, have a nonscientific or nontechnological dimension. He also erroneously implied that in primitive cultures there was no clear demarcation between subjective and objective realities, and that in primitive culture a clear distinction between natural and supernatural realities was not made (cf. Cazeneuve 1972: 1–23).

CHAPTER SIX
Religion and Motivations: Early Formulations

UNCONSCIOUS AND CONSCIOUS MOTIVATIONS

In this chapter I discuss the theories of Sigmund Freud, Max Weber, and Carl Jung, who contributed much to the analysis of unconscious and conscious motivations in human action.

Freud perceived neurotic and religious behavior to be a manifestation of repressed desires and guilt. Freud's approach to the analysis of unconscious motivations led to the development of psychoanalytic psychology, which is concerned with how the experiences of childhood shape the adult personality. Within anthropology, Freud's contributions influenced the field of "culture and personality," in particular research on basic personality structure conducted by the psychoanalyst Abram Kardiner and the anthropologists Cora Dubois, Ralph Linton, James West, and others. These researchers assumed that economic and family conditions (called "primary institutions") had a direct impact on child-rearing and thus shaped the basic personality structure of members of the society. The frustrations associated with these primary institutions (such as the inability of a child to nurse during the oral stage of psychosexual development because the mother spent most of the day working in the gardens) contributed to the formation of a "projective system"; this in turn influenced the "secondary institutions" of a society—which included religion.

Weber argued that religious beliefs fostered conscious self-interests and rational actions that contributed to the achievement of economic and/or political goals. Weber's analysis of conscious motivations led to the development of "methodological individualism" and qualitative or interpretive sociology. Within anthropology, Weber influenced the American cultural anthropologist Clifford Geertz, who identifies his orientation as interpretive or hermeneutic anthropology.

Jung's analysis of the unconscious and symbols contributed to a view of myths and religious symbols as revealing the primordial archetypes of unity; his perspective has been influential among the followers of "human potential" and "new age" movements.

German philosophical-sociological scholarship of the nineteenth and early twentieth centuries emphasized historical interpretations and rejected positivism in favor of phenomenological and hermeneutical descriptions and interpretations of cultural experience. For example, the philosophical writings of Johann Herder (1744–1803), Johann Fichte (1762–1814), Friedrich Schelling (1775–1854), Georg Hegel (1770–1831), Arthur Schopenhauer (1788–1860), Friedrich Nietzsche (1844–1900), and Wilhelm Dilthey (1833–1911) raised questions about self-identity, spiritual identity, group identity, and human identity with reference to the reality of cultural distinctiveness and development. Frequently referred to as the German idealist tradition, the study of worldviews and values (*Weltanschauungen*) combined with scientific and romantic currents. Freud and Weber combined these currents in their work, with the former often manifesting hostility to religion (viewing it as analogous to childish fantasy, or irrational, neurotic behavior) and the latter manifesting neutrality to religion (viewing it as having irrational or rational components).

THE PSYCHOLOGY OF PROJECTION AND RELIGIOUS SYMBOLISM

[The] conviction I acquired a quarter of a century ago, when I wrote my book on *Totem and Taboo* (in 1912), and it has only become stronger since. From then on I have never doubted that religious phenomena are to be understood only on the model of the neurotic symptoms of the individual, which are so familiar to us, as a return of long-forgotten important happenings in the primeval history of the human family, that they owe their obsessive character to that very origin and therefore derive their effect on mankind from the historical truth they contain. (Sigmund Freud 1947 [1938]: 89)

In *Totem und Tabu* it was not my purpose to explain the origin of religions, but only of totemism. Can you from any standpoint known to you explain the fact that the first form in which the protecting deity revealed itself to men was that of an animal, that a prohibition existed against killing or eating this animal, and that yet it was the solemn custom to kill it and eat it communally once a year? It is just this that takes place in totemism. And it is hardly to the purpose to argue whether totemism should be called a religion. It has intimate connections with the later god-religions; the totem animals become the sacred animals of the gods; and the earliest, and the most profound, moral restrictions—the murder prohibition and the incest prohibition—originate in totemism. (Sigmund Freud in *The Future of an Illusion* n.d. [1927]: 37)

In his writings, Freud searched for the true meaning of certain events and for the meaning of the representations of the events. He analyzed the symbolisms of various domains of human life such as the human family, sexuality, and religion and interpreted the interconnectedness of the symbols. Specifically, Freud's anthropological theory of religion has three components: (1) his assumption that primitive humans were like irrational infants—a view common in the late nineteenth and early twentieth centuries; (2) his borrowing of Smith's ideas to construct a theory of totemism and taboo; and (3) his contribution to the development of the theory of religion as a projective system.

Freud's theory that religion is "an infantile obsessional neurosis" raises questions about the nature of human biology, psychology, sexuality, and culture. He was one of several scholars in the late nineteenth and early twentieth centuries who explained primitive humans as having remained developmentally at an infantile mental stage, and who subscribed to the Haeckelian notion that "ontogeny recapitulates phylogeny" (i.e., that the individual organism in its development replicates the developmental stages of the species). The distinctive feature of Freud's theory is that he sees a correspondence (and a parallel) between neurotic and religious behavior.

Like Smith (from whom Freud borrowed the idea that totemism is a primordial sacrificial ritual), Freud notes that the totem represents the father or founder of the group or clan, but he goes beyond Smith to offer a psychoanalytic theory that explains the origin of taboo and civilization (viewed as constraints on the innate pleasure-seeking orientation of humans). The investigation of totemism as a form of religion (and as a form of social organization) was an important aspect of anthropological discourse during the late nineteenth and early twentieth centuries. Scholars were seeking to identify the most primitive or elemental forms of culture, particularly those of religion and kinship. Totemism, as a symbol of primitive kinship and religiosity, loomed large in their consciousness.

Freud's scenario of why primitive humans established the institutions of totemic worship and clan exogamy (taboo against sex within the lineage group) is well known. Freud assumed, as many did in his time, that primitive humans lived in a horde. He also assumed that a patriarchal founder-male probably had exclusive sexual privileges with the women of the horde. The other males (sons) of the group, in frustration and resentment, killed the patriarch to gain sexual access to the women (mothers and sisters). But this act of parricide must have created guilt feelings and remorse, and to overcome such feelings, the sons compensated by propitiating the dead father as a sacred entity and by excluding sexual relationships with mothers and sisters. The acts of propitiation and sexual exclusion constituted the beginning of the ritual affirmation of the lineage bond between the sacrificed father and the sons, and this lineage affinity was commemorated periodically through the performance of a sacrificial ritual. Animal (symbolic) substitutes came to represent the sacrificed father, and these substitutes were slaughtered and ritually consumed in order to reaffirm the lineage unity that prohibited sex within the group. Freud's theory of the origin of totem and taboo implies that such customs are genetically determined, although he does not provide an adequate model to illustrate the interaction between genes, psychology, and culture.

In many ways, Freud's theory of incest taboo is like the sociobiological theory of altruism. Most anthropologists tend to dismiss sociobiological theories of cultural phenomena because we do not have any scientific evidence to suggest that there is a correspondence between particular genetic structures and particular cultural orientations. The nature and practice of altruism differs from culture to culture, although altruism can be seen in all cultures, just as the incest taboo exists in every culture. Well-known anthropologists such as Claude Levi-Strauss and Leslie White, despite their very different theoretical assumptions about the nature of culture, agree that the incest taboo needs to be understood as a cultural device for exchanging women between different groups (for economic and political reasons), a device that brings about cooperation between groups and thereby contributes to their survival. Scholars point out that if the incest taboo had innate genetic and/or psychological foundations, there would be no need to have cultural prohibitions against incest.

Freud's psychoanalytic theory of psychosexual development explains that children pass through stages of love and hate toward the parents; boys manifest the desire to possess the mother and are hostile toward the father (Oedipus complex), but these feelings of ambivalence are generally resolved once one reaches maturity, and the father is idealized or glorified. Those who fail to resolve these conflicts manifest neurotic symptoms, and religion is a part of the same manifestation of unresolved tensions and conflicts. For Freud, totemism, as a religious expression, is a phenomenon borne out of the Oepidal conflict.

Freud makes use of Smith's interpretation of totemism extensively, but as Beidelman (1974: 60–61) points out, he "turned Smith's argument about, and what for Smith was a cathartic feast cementing society by reaffirming affectual bonds became a guilt-ridden and covertly hostile rite of expiation by which aggression against authority is both denied through taboo and yet reconfirmed through periodic symbolic ingestion of the father in the form of the prohibited father object." Various scholars have noted that Freud's writings on taboo and other religious beliefs have provided the foundation for the study and explanation of religion as "a projective system, that is to say, a system for structuring the outer world and one's relation to it in accordance with a pattern laid down in an earlier experience during ontogenesis" (Kardiner and Preble 1961: 206).

> Religion, according to Freud, is a social illusion to overcome the individual's feeling of helplessness against the forces of nature. By personifying the forces of nature into specific entities like deities, man acquired a technique for dealing with them thus putting them to some degree under human control.
>
> Freud showed that the techniques advocated by religion to placate or move the deity are the very ones that the child learns in order to placate his parents and to guarantee for himself their continued solicitude and protection.
>
> Freud recognized that they were based on a prototype of real experience—that of a child with his parents. Religion thus can be seen as having a remarkable governing function: it tended to regulate relations between individuals in society, and served as a protection against dangers of the outer world. (Kardiner and Preble 1961: 206)

The idea of a "projective system" is by no means Freud's original idea. It has been around for more than 2,000 years, and as I pointed out earlier, the ancient Greeks and many recent scholars used the idea of projection to explain religion. Freud's contribution was in the development of a coherent theory that explained the psychological mechanisms of projection, and in this regard he was like Darwin, who explained the mechanism of biological evolution for the first time (the idea of evolution had been discussed in Western and other cultures for several millennia).

The idea of a projective system enables us to understand the psychological principles or mechanisms involved in the creation of the supernatural world. The symbols that represent the supernatural world are modeled after human experiences, particularly as such experiences occur in the human family. The child's experiences with the father and mother are crucial in the development of "human nature." Parents (and other authority figures) serve as significant symbols of the sacred other because the child "accepts" the definitions and explanations offered by authority figures without questioning their validity, and the child represents his or her identity with the use of these symbols. From a child's helpless position, the authority figures (symbols of significant others) fuse the known and the unknown and synthesize various kinds of conceptions and experiences. The child does not or cannot verify whether the authority figures represent empirical reality as such or whether they represent a supernatural reality.

The child does not and cannot verify what the self is, but a representation of self is crucial to the child's cognitive and emotional development, and the representation is modeled after that of the significant other.

The foregoing interpretation of a projective system supports the perspective of this book. The Freud-inspired "culture and personality" orientation of American anthropology can be used to understand the relationship between symbols of the sacred other and the sacred self. The Chinese-born American anthropologist Francis L.K. Hsu in his book *Under the Ancestors' Shadow* (1967) shows how the sacred symbols are created and how they are used in the representation of the sacred self in traditional China. The dead ancestors (sacred other) and their descendents are linked together through the cultural themes of "father–son identification" and "ancestral authority." Both the living father and sons are under the protection and authority of dead ancestors, and both have responsibility and obligations to glorify the dead ancestors. Thus in traditional Chinese society, the dead ancestors are the preeminent or significant symbols of sacred others that enable the Chinese to represent the sacredness of the self. There is little hostility between the living father and the sons because, according to Hsu, the living are engaged in enhancing the authority and sacredness of the dead ancestors, who, in turn, are committed to aid and protect the living.

Morris Carstairs in his book *The Twice-Born* (1967) provides a psychoanalytic explanation of Hindu beliefs and practices associated with the god Siva and goddess Kali. He suggests that Freud's psychoanalytic theory is the key to the relationship between the emotional life of the Hindus and religious phenomena. Melford Spiro in his book *Burmese Supernaturalism* (1967) has combined psychoanalytic theory and functionalism to explain beliefs in shamanism. Gananath Obeyesekere applies Freudian concepts to religion in his book *Medusa's Hair: An Essay on Personal Symbols and Religious Experience* (1981). Edmund Leach's influential paper "Pulleyar and the Lord Buddha" (1962) uses Freudian psychoanalytic concepts and structuralist premises to explain Hindu beliefs.

Weston LaBarre in his book *The Ghost Dance: The Origins of Religion* (1970) has used Freudian ideas to explore how different kinds of religious specialists emerge in society and how different kinds of deities are created. He contends that, for the most part, we can see how the human family serves as a model of the divine world: The manifestation of power relationships, awe, and helplessness in the family is the basis for creating the images of the supernatural world.

LaBarre concludes that religion originates in psychic trauma caused by a culture's failure to provide solutions to life's problems and that the shaman plays a crucial role in curing this trauma and in formulating an external spiritual reality.

THE INTERPRETIVE SOCIOLOGY OF MEANINGFUL ACTION

Max Weber (1864–1920), the German sociologist, wrote extensively on the dynamic role of religion in Europe (*The Protestant Ethic and the Spirit of Capitalism*, 1958 [1930]), China (*The Religion of China*, 1964 [1951]), and India (*The Religion of India*, 1958). His ideas on religion were expressed in other monographs and papers as well.

Various scholars (for example, Talcott Parsons, who translated from German into English most of Weber's works, and C.K. Yang, who wrote an introduction to Weber's *Religion in China*) have noted that Weber differed significantly from Durkheim in focusing on the relationship between religion and social/economic change. Durkheim, in contrast, focused on the relationship between religion and social values. The differences between these two seminal thinkers encouraged different approaches to the sociological understanding of society. Weber was much more open to the contributions of individual motivations, intentionality, and meaning, as well as of historical factors, to social action.

As Martindale (1960: 385) notes:

> Weber assumes that the subjectively intended meaning present in an action is a causal component of it. Sociology is concerned with action only so far as it possesses meanings.
>
> Meaning [according to Weber] does not necessarily refer to an objectively correct meaning or one true in a metaphysical sense. The meaning is the one held by actors in situations and not the meaning the situation may have to a scientist or metaphysician.

The interpretation of meaning from the actors' perspective is important because it sheds light on how individuals in a society define and conceptualize the relationship between the self and the other in different contexts.

Other Weberian concepts are also important for the study of the symbol-self. Weber, in his study of the relationship between the protestant worldview and capitalist enterprise, showed that the Calvinist concepts such as "calling" and "grace" were congruent with and fostered capitalist activity, raising the question of the consequences of representing the self in relation to certain types of symbols of the sacred other. Puritan Christians constructed the self in relation to the Calvinist theological interpretations of the "will of God" and the "signs of being chosen or saved."

According to Weber, the study of the nature of the relationship between the representations of self and sacred other is a crucial one in the discussion of economic, social, and authority systems. Weber shows in his studies of the religions of India, China, and medieval Europe that there were major differences in how the self was represented and defined as sacred, and how these differences in self-representation were related to different kinds of economic and social developments. The Calvinist–protestant ethic or worldview was conducive to the development of "rational" economic and social institutions. (I do not agree with Weber's analysis of rationality in all respects. He seemed to believe that the West was qualitatively different from the non-West in the development of rationality in all human enterprises, a commitment that, according to him, was the foundation of pursuits to discover the principles of nature. Weber was a product of the period, and he possibly shared in many of the German cultural biases.)

In his writings, Weber devotes considerable attention to the concept of *charisma*. He offers different interpretations and meanings of charisma, but as I noted earlier (cf. Martindale's discussion of meaning), the differences come from his effort to understand how charisma is used in different situations.

Charisma is a way of conceptualizing supernatural power. Weber (1963: 2) notes that the recognition of extraordinary powers is the basis for charisma: In this respect charisma is an attribute of certain objects and people, and charisma is the same as *mana, orenda,* or the Iranian *maga* ("the term from which the word magic is derived") and Weber employs the word *charisma* "for such extraordinary powers." He identifies two types: Primary charisma "is a gift that inheres in an object or person simply by virtue of natural endowment"; the other type of charisma "may be produced artificially in an object or person through some extraordinary means."

With reference to authority structures, the role of the shaman or prophet and the meaning of the "gift of grace," Weber (1947: 358) offers the following definition of charisma: "The term 'charisma' will be applied to a certain quality of an individual personality by virtue of which he is set apart from ordinary men and treated as endowed with supernatural, superhuman, or at least specifically exceptional powers or qualities."

Weber's discussion of the concept of theodicy (religious explanation of human suffering) and the problem of meaning is generally viewed as an important aspect of his analysis of religion. Weber (1963: 138–149) investigated messianic, millenarian eschatologies and the karma–reincarnation eschatologies to show the consequences of different theodicies/eschatologies for human action. I discuss this in a later chapter.

Weber's approach to the study of religion in anthropology acquired significance through the writings of Talcott Parsons (who, incidentally, defined cultures as systems of symbols and meaning, a definition that has become popular in contemporary anthropology). Parsons has influenced a number of contemporary anthropologists, particularly Clifford Geertz, whose views I will discuss in a later chapter.

THE MAGIC CIRCLE OF THE SELF

Carl Gustav Jung (1875–1961), like Freud, dealt with unconscious motivations and shared in the German idealist tradition. Unlike Freud, he interpreted religion as a therapeutic device for synthesizing or harmonizing the unconscious orientations of the self with the archetypes of the "collective unconscious" of humanity and of specific "races." Jung believed that the archetypes were primordial images of humanity and that they manifested in religious phenomena; he saw himself as providing a phenomenological description of these religious or spiritual realities. Jung said that scientists cannot verify whether the claims concerning the existence of gods are factual: The student of religion must investigate why religious experiences occur and analyze the structure and meaning of such experiences.

> That religious experiences exist no longer needs proof. But it will always remain doubtful whether what metaphysics and theology call Gods and gods is the real ground of these experiences. The question is idle, actually, and answers itself by reason of the subjectively overwhelming numinosity of the experience. (Jung 1957: 102)

In his books *Psychology and Religion* (1938) and *The Undiscovered Self* (1957), Jung discusses the relationships between the collective unconscious, archetypes or primordial images, and religion. Jung believes that all significant archetypes are component parts of the racial or collective unconscious (psychic residue formed as a result of primordial experiences of humankind). All human beings are born with similar structural components (archetypes) of the unconscious and have the potential to reenact the conceptualizations (or images) of the ancestors as well as revive the memories of ancestral experiences. However, an individual's present life may or may not be conducive for reenacting the images or reviving the memories. Cultures differ in the extent to which they foster continuity with ancestral memory, and religious traditions differ in the extent to which they stimulate individuals to participate in the collective unconscious.

Jung contends that although the archetypes are deeply buried in the unconscious, they become manifest in the symbols of dreams, visions, myths, and art; and that the archetypes also shape human action. Representations of birth, death and rebirth, mother-cow, father-bull, supreme god, demon, unity, self, and so on are recurring themes of the archetype because these themes have become engraved on the collective memory of the human species.

Jung, as I noted earlier, focused on the role of self in unifying personal experiences and linking them with the collective unconscious. According to Jung (1957), symbols such as the mandala ("the magic circle") express the human search for the wholeness of the self, for integration and equilibrium.

CHAPTER SEVEN
Functional Analysis of Religion

THE NATURAL SCIENCE
OF HUMAN SOCIETY

Social scientists have often conceptualized human relationships by using the biological analogue of the organism and have described or explained the structure and function of "social organisms." Many ancient treatises on society contain an implicit functional analysis, and Scottish and French studies on human institutions in the seventeenth and eighteenth centuries state explicitly that certain customs contribute to the welfare of society; but only during the past hundred years have scholars theorized on the nature of the relationship between social structure and social function in the maintenance of society. Scholars such as Herbert Spencer (1820–1903), William Robertson Smith (1846–1894), and Emile Durkheim (1858–1917) have been identified as the early leading proponents of functional analysis. Within British social anthropology, the two leading functionalists, A.R. Radcliffe-Brown (1881–1955) and Bronislaw Malinowski (1884–1942), criticized each other's version of functionalism and thereby refined the concept of function and made it an operationally valid, "scientific" concept. Within American sociology, Talcott Parsons and Robert K. Merton contributed to the theoretical development of a "functionalist" school.

By the middle of the twentieth century, however, functionalist studies no longer monopolized anthropology and sociology. Functional analysis was accused of being philosophically linked with a conservative or imperialist political ideology, and other analytic models were proposed to study social conflict and social change. In a paper called "The Myth of Functional Analysis as a Special Method in Sociology and Anthropology," Kingsley Davis (1959) argued that because all sociological/anthropological inquiries dealt with the analysis of the functional interrelationships of sociocultural phenomena, it was unnecessary to identify functional analysis as a special type of analysis. He suggested that functional analysis and sociological analysis were one and the same.

In general, scholars who use the analogy of organism conceptualize society or culture as a system with interdependent subsystems or institutions that contribute to the maintenance of the system. Radcliffe-Brown's model is identified as "structural functionalism": The social organism is a system of relations that constitute the structure; the structure is maintained by the activities of institutions that function to meet the needs of the social system. Malinowski's model is identified as "biopsychological functionalism": In this perspective, institutions arise and exist to meet the biopsychological needs of the individual. The biological concept of "adaptation" is frequently used by functionalists to suggest that a social or cultural system must be internally and externally adapted: Ecological and psychological functionalists of American cultural anthropology describe how the various parts of a culture are congruent with one another and integrated; a culture must also have a viable relationship with or be adapted to its environment, including the physical and social realities.

Religion has been viewed, from the foregoing perspectives of functionalism, as contributing to social cohesion, as allaying anxieties, or as regulating equilibrium. In the following sections I present brief discussions of these views. Anthropologists have often used Merton's distinction between "manifest" and "latent" function to suggest that the function of a belief, custom, or activity may be one that is different from what is visible to or defined by the participants. For example, the people who perform rituals may believe that they communicate with supernatural beings and powers; the manifest function of the ritual is to secure supernatural power or the help of supernatural beings. The underlying, latent function of the ritual is to bring the members of the group together and to maintain the social relationships.

ANXIETY AND IMMORTALITY

Bronislaw Malinowski, the Polish intellectual who was attracted to anthropology by James Frazer's *Golden Bough* and who subsequently made a lasting contribution to the development of British social anthropology, discusses the nature of magic and religion in several of his books, but his systematic formulations on religion and magic are contained in his posthumously published *Magic, Science and Religion* (1954).

The significance of Malinowski's theory of magic is that although he agreed with Frazer that magic is pseudo-science, he emphasized that magic serves an important cultural function by allaying or assuaging anxiety arising out of unpredictable aspects of human life. In this respect, Malinowski's theory supports my suggestion that during times of stress and anxiety the shamanistic or magical orientation acquires relevance in the life of human beings. Malinowski notes:

> The integral function of magic . . . consists in the bridging-over of gaps and inadequacies in highly important activities not yet completely mastered by man. In order to achieve this end, magic supplies primitive man with a firm belief in his power of succeeding; it provides him also with a definite mental or pragmatic technique wherever his ordinary means fail him. It thus enables man to carry out with confidence his most vital tasks, and to maintain his poise and his mental integrity under circumstances which, without the help of magic, would demoralize him by despair and anxiety, by fear and hatred, by unrequited love and impotent hate. (Malinowski 1954: 140)

The function of religion, according to Malinowski, is to provide the group with integration. There are many events in the life and history of a group when the harmony and unity of the group are threatened, and of such events the most threatening is death. Thus, elaborate rituals surround the event of death: "Of all sources of religion, the supreme and final crisis of life—death—is of the greatest importance." Malinowski goes on to state that human beings emotionally and intellectually deny death and assure for themselves immortality through various cultural means:

> Man's conviction of continued life is one of the supreme gifts of religion, which judges and selects the better of the two alternatives suggested by self-preservation—the hope of continued life and the fear of annihilation. The belief in spirits is the result of the belief in immortality . . . Religion saves man from a surrender to death and destruction, and in doing this it merely makes use of the observations of dreams, shadows, and visions. The real nucleus of animism lies in the deepest emotional fact of human nature, the desire for life. (Malinowski 1954: 51)

A.R. Radcliffe-Brown, an influential thinker in the tradition of British social anthropology, was critical of Malinowski's theoretical contributions despite the fact that both were "functionalists" who analyzed the interdependence of beliefs and institutions in the maintenance of systemic wholes. Their differences stemmed in part from Malinowski's use of the concept of culture and his theorizing about how institutions evolved to serve various human needs, as opposed to Radcliffe-Brown's use of the concepts of social structure or society and his theorizing about how institutions such as religion served to maintain the social structure (relationship of individuals and groups) and ensure the ongoing survival of society.

Radcliffe-Brown disagreed with Malinowski's assumption that anxiety was an innate human orientation and that magic or religion could be explained as cultural adaptations that alleviate anxiety; he said that anxiety and other feelings were generated by society. The beliefs given to individuals by society created the need to perform magical or religious rituals, which in turn helped unify the people. In his essay *Taboo*, Radcliffe-Brown notes:

> . . . while one anthropological theory is that magic and religion give man confidence, comfort, and a sense of security, it could equally well be argued that they give men fears and anxieties from which they would otherwise be free—the fear of black magic or of spirits, fear of God, of the Devil, of Hell.
>
> Actually in our fears or anxieties as well as in our hopes we are conditioned (as the phrase goes) by the community in which we live. And it is largely by the sharing of hopes and fears, by what I have called common concern in events or eventualities, that human beings are linked together in temporary or permanent associations. (Radcliffe-Brown 1972 [1939]: 81)

Dozens of monographs on religion, using the British social anthropological framework, describe and explain the congruence or correspondence between social structure and religious beliefs; religious beliefs are generally assumed to be derivatives of the social structure. Famous monographs include E.E. Evans-Pritchard's *Witchcraft, Oracles and Magic Among the Azande* (1937) and *Nuer Religion* (1956), Reo Fortune's *Sorcerers of Dobu* (1932), Godfrey Lienhardt's *Divinity and Experience: The Religion of the Dinka* (1961), and John Middleton's *Lugbara Religion* (1965). Hundreds of papers on religion were published by British social anthropologists and American cultural anthropologists during the period from 1930 to 1960, most of them following the functionalist perspective. Since 1960, new theoretical and methodological developments have led to different ways of interpreting religious phenomena. I will discuss the more recent anthropological studies of religion in later chapters.

American cultural anthropologists have used a more eclectic theoretical approach than the British social anthropologists in their study of the function of religion. Many have combined psychological and sociological theories to analyze the adaptive or adjustive function of religion in the maintenance and continuity of culture (conceptualized as a historically evolved configuration of beliefs and practices). I have already referred to the contributions of Ruth Benedict (Chapter 3). Some of the more recent studies by the American cultural anthropologists will be discussed in the section on ecology of religion. In the following paragraphs of this section, I give a sample of pre-1970 studies that have theorized on how religion functions to reduce anxiety.

Paul Radin (1883–1959), the American cultural anthropologist, in his book *Primitive Religion: Its Nature and Origin* (1937) takes the position that magic preceded religion and that religion did not specifically grow out of magic. Magic, according to him, is infantile and subjective as well as a creation dedicated to the compulsive power of thought; magic provides humans with techniques for what is believed to be the ability to control and coerce nature. Radin says that economic insecurity is the biggest source of fear that confronts human beings; religion alleviates anxiety and helps to preserve society through the affirmation of values necessary to maintain society.

The American cultural anthropologist Clyde Kluckhohn (1905–1960) analyzes the adjustive and integrative function of myth and ritual. In his book *Navaho Witchcraft* (1944), he theorizes about the implicit function of witchcraft practices and describes the relationship of witchcraft beliefs and practices to other aspects of Navaho society. His book explains the decrease or increase in witchcraft accusations and how witchcraft beliefs are part of a general worldview.

Melford Spiro, the American cultural anthropologist, explains religion within a framework that combines psychoanalytic and functionalist interpretations. In his explanation of Ifaluk religion (1952), he suggests that beliefs in supernatural beings were adaptive on the island of Ifaluk because the people could project their hostilities onto the outer world and thus reduce the possibility of conflict among themselves. In his book *Burmese Supernaturalism* (1967), Spiro explains how different types of religious beliefs coexist and function to serve the emotional and social needs of a group. Because this study is representative of functional analysis in American cultural anthropology, I discuss it briefly here.

Spiro attempts to explain why two distinct systems of religion—Buddhism and "supernaturalism"—exist in Burma. He notes that an important function of religion is to furnish a theodicy that explains suffering. Buddhism, the Great Tradition of Burma, does not provide answers to alleviate the suffering in the present (current) existence. Buddhism affirms world renunciation, gives formulae for attaining nirvana, and advocates annihilation of human desires. Accumulation of merit or demerit in one's karma does not alter one's present condition; karma decides the future condition or type of rebirth, and thus suffering in the present is due to a person's actions in a previous birth.

Because of this rationalistic and self-denying explanation, Buddhism leaves a void in resolving humans' day-to-day suffering. This void is filled by "supernaturalism." Supernaturalism provides alternate explanations for suffering (in the present existence) and thereby meets the existential needs of the people. It provides channels through which people can seek the help of good spirits and blame the evil spirits for their suffering. Thus, supernaturalism and Buddhism are compatible. Not only are they compatible, but according to Spiro, had there been no system of supernaturalistic beliefs, Buddhism could not have survived and prospered in Burma. Whereas Buddhism stresses restraint and asceticism, supernaturalism provides avenues for the expression of sensuousness. The former appeals to the rational and the "sacred," the latter to the "irrational" and the profane. The Buddhist monk is serene and composed in contrast to the shaman, who is turbulent. Belief in both systems (Buddhism and supernaturalism) is almost universal in Burma. Buddhist powers are propitiated as equally as are the *nats*, or spirits of supernaturalism. Often the Buddhist formulae safeguard the people against the evil *nats*.

> For the Burmese there is no question about what is Buddhism and what is animism. Still, though they are committed Buddhists, the Burmese are yet drawn to both goals and the means of animism. Using Buddhist means, they pursue natlike, non-Buddhist ends; cathecting Buddhist goals, they attempt to achieve them by natlike, non-Buddhist means. In short, between the polar extremes of animism and Buddhism, we see a continuum of beliefs and practices which show attributes of both systems. (Spiro 1967: 271)

In 1966 the cultural anthropologist Anthony Wallace published a provocative study of religion. It provided (1) a typology of religious systems, (2) a theory of religious movements that he had earlier formulated in 1956 as a processual model of "revitalization," (3) an analysis of the function of religion in achieving self or identity integration as well as cultural integration, and (4) a theory of the relationship between ritual and religion.

To Wallace, explanations of sociocultural phenomena as "social facts" or "cultural facts" are incomplete. It is necessary to analyze how such facts are generated and maintained in relation to the self, identity, or personality, taking into account biological and psychological factors. Thus it is important to discuss personality configurations, disorders, stress, disorientation, and crisis when explaining phenomena such as shamanism and religious movements. Wallace (1966: 139–158) argues that religious orientations are intimately connected with curing identity disorders:

> When identity is seriously impaired, therefore, we can expect that the experience will call for strenuous efforts to understand and repair the damage to self-esteem; the deeper the impairment, the more desperate the efforts to find a solution. Sometimes, of course, the efforts at resynthesis of identity are inadequate to maintain or restore a tolerable level of self-esteem; but frequently, if the effort is supported and guided by others and if some sort of model of the transformation process is provided by the culture, the effort is successful. And, although there are many avenues to identity renewal, they all involve some kind of identification with an admired model of the human personality, and differentiation from a despised model. Perhaps the most ancient, most widespread, and most successful of these procedures is provided by religious ritual. In religious identity renewal—salvation, to use the familiar term—the identification is with, or the differentiation is from, a supernatural being.

. . . when the person's identity (or image of self) is unsatisfactory, religion is a source of ritual to which he may turn in order to achieve salvation. Most, if not all, cultures recognize at least some such identity problems in individual instances and provide culturally standardized ways for the unfortunate victim of identity conflict to achieve relief, by way of possession, becoming a shaman, mystical withdrawal, or good works.

RELIGIOUS REGULATION OF ECOLOGY

In this section, I offer an interpretation of theories that explain religious beliefs and practices as cultural-ecological adaptations that are systemically involved in the maintenance of human ecosystems.

During the mid–twentieth century, cultural-ecological theories (which explain how cultures historically develop patterns of internal and external adjustment and adaptations to food environments) acquired significance through the writings of Leslie White (1900–1975) and Julian Steward (1902–1972). White's approach to the study of culture has two components: One is to investigate the development of culture (in a general sense) as an energy-harnessing system determined by technological advancements, and the other is to investigate human behavior as cultural behavior determined by the unique symboling activity of the human species. Unfortunately, most scholars do not recognize the two features of White's theory of culture, and, as a result, he is often dismissed as a "mechanistic materialist." White's commitment to intellectual honesty and free inquiry often led to major conflicts with anthropological colleagues and others. In particular, his analysis and interpretation of religion was viewed by some as anti-American. The following two excerpts from an essay by White's former student convey White's views on religion, as well as the public reaction to his views.

The biggest uproar of all resulted from a paper entitled "Anthropological Approaches to Religion," which White read at the annual meeting of the American Anthropological Association in Chicago in December of 1957. Ruth Benedict (1948: 589) had once written: "Man is a creature of such freedom of action that he can . . . at any stage of technological development create his gods in the most diverse forms." White disagreed with this assertion, and his paper was designed to show that a society's religious system was not idiosyncratic at all but reflected its socioeconomic system. He pointed out that the notion "the Lord is my Shepherd" reflected a pastoral economy. He argued that a society subsisting on wild food, with no knowledge of monarchy, could hardly have a conception of "Great God, our King," or speak of "Christ, our Royal Master." "Contrariwise," he continued, "a monarchical cultural system is not likely to have a bear . . . for a god." A few months earlier the Russians had placed the first Sputnik into orbit, and White concluded his paper saying, "A cultural system that can launch earth satellites can dispense with gods entirely."

The next day, the New York Times carried a full-column story of the meetings, mentioning a number of the papers presented. In the middle of the article was a paragraph about White's paper which quoted the above line without comment. The Detroit papers, with a ready eye for an issue they could sensationalize, picked up the story from the Times. They called various clergymen in the state, asking them to comment on the fateful line. The clergy were only too happy to oblige, and denounced White for his irreligion. The Episcopal Bishop of Michigan accused White of "playing into the hands of people who would undermine the spiritual heritage of the Western world" (The Detroit News, December 28, 1957). The Michigan Catholic of January 2, 1958 headlined a front-page editorial, "How Long Will UM Let White Deride God?" Once again, pressure was mounted to dismiss White, but discomfited though the university administration was, it again held firm.

In a reply to his critics, which White prepared for private circulation, he commented wryly: "One wonders . . . at the vehemence of the clergy. If a puny anthropologist should in fact 'deride God,' does He need a protective clergyman to defend Him? Did the reaction of the clergy, their unwillingness to countenance a free competition of ideas, express a sense of insecurity on their part? Or, was it, perhaps . . . the prospect . . . of technological unemployment?" (Carneiro 1981: 222–223)

In the cultural-ecological perspective, religion is viewed as a part of the ideological subsystem; the ideological subsystem is explained as deriving from the social-political subsystem, which is explained as deriving from the technological-economic subsystem. In this view, although religious structures are caused by other basic structures of a society, religious structures are congruent with (or correspond to) the other structures and often function to maintain the other structures. Steward made a substantial contribution to the analysis of how sequential changes occur in these structures and to the study of whether there are worldwide regularities or recurrences in the sequential development of systemic structures.

Marvin Harris and Roy Rappaport are among those American anthropologists who have attempted to apply cultural-ecological theory to explain religious beliefs and behavior.

Harris has developed a theory of religion based on "cultural materialism." He examines the systemic (functional) adaptations of certain beliefs that appear to be irrational or nonfunctional, such as the Hindu taboo against eating cow and the Jewish/Islamic taboo against eating pig. The following discussion is based on views stated in his books *Cows, Pigs, Wars and Witches* (1974) and *Cannibals and Kings* (1977). He notes:

An established principle of ecological analysis states that communities of organisms are adapted not to average but to extreme conditions. The relevant situation in India is the recurrent failure of the monsoon rains. To evaluate the economic significance of the anti-slaughter and anti-beef-eating taboos, we have to consider what those taboos mean in the context of periodic droughts and famine. (1974: 20–21)

Contrary to expectations, studies of energy costs and energy yields show that India makes more efficient use of its cattle than the United States. (1974: 31)

In his essay on "the origin of the sacred cow," Harris shows that beef was an important part of the diet in India until about 600 B.C. After that period, cattle became scarce, and eating beef became the monopoly of the Brahmin priests and upper-caste, wealthy Hindus, demonstrating their high status; but during the next thousand years or so the killing of cattle became a religious taboo, and only the poor untouchables ate carrion cow meat, demonstrating their inferior status. Harris explains this development by pointing out that keeping the cow alive was adaptive for the farmer's ecosystem where water was scarce; the cow contributed to the long-range viability of the system. Thus, gradually, the protection of cows against slaughter became common in drought-ridden places. The Brahmins, as priests, provided legitimacy for such a practice, and when the Muslims began to invade and settle in India, the meat-eating elites used the preexisting cultural-ecological adaptation as a political symbol of resistance against Islam. A dichotomy between the meat-eating Muslims and the vegetarian Hindus established a political, social boundary for Hinduism: The cow was defined and explained as sacred, and an elaborate theology of "cow as mother" developed in India. Harris argues that:

> The tabooing of beef was the cumulative result of the individual decisions of millions of individual farmers, some of whom were better able than others to resist the temptation of slaughtering their livestock because they strongly believed that the life of a cow or an ox was a holy thing. Those who held such beliefs were much more likely to hold onto their farms, and to pass them on to their children, than those who believed differently. (1977: 147)

The religious taboo against eating pig exists, according to Harris, because it is maladaptive to raise pigs in the desert environment of Judaism and Islam: Pigs compete for the same food that humans eat, and they cannot survive the extreme heat of the Middle East unless they are provided with shade as well as water to moisten themselves. Harris (1974: 40) notes: ". . . the Bible and Koran condemned the pig because pig farming was a threat to the integrity of the basic cultural and natural ecosystems of the Middle East."

Harris refers approvingly to Rappaport's study of pig-raising communities in New Guinea that shows how various beliefs and practices contribute to the maintenance of pigs as an ecologically viable practice. Rappaport, in his book *Pigs for the Ancestors* (1968), examines the systemic role of ancestor worship and ritual in order to show how ritual links the various subsystems to maintain or regulate the total ecosystem's equilibrium. He notes (1968: 164–165):

> Information from the Tsembaga and other Maring groups [of New Guinea] support the suggestion made by Vayda, Leeds, and Smith (1961: 72) that pig festivals "help to maintain a long-term balance between Melanesian man and the crops and fauna from which he draws his sustenance."

As a ritual of ancestor worship, the massive slaughter of pigs among the Maring groups of New Guinea occurs every twelve years. Rappaport's study makes it clear that this ritual is linked to factors such as welfare, protein requirements, land use, and the increase in the number of pigs.

The study shows that the ritual is a regulatory mechanism or thermostat. About every twelve years, the number of pigs increases to the point that the viability of the cultural system is threatened because pigs compete with humans for food resources. The year-long festival of pig slaughter (conceptualized as offerings for the ancestors) and warfare start; the ritual stops when it is necessary to clear forests to produce food crops and raise more pigs, a period when warfare is not promoted.

The ecological perspective provides models that can be used to illustrate the functional relationships of institutions about which people may or may not be aware. Religious beliefs and practices correspond to the requirements of the cultural systems, and such beliefs and practices provide legitimacy for maintaining the relationships of the system. It is important to realize, however, that one can recognize the importance of the ecological perspective without being a "cultural materialist." If economics were the only determinants of human life, cultural models would probably be much more efficient than they are. The limitations and possibilities of the environments are themselves created by cultures that exist in a dialectical relationship with the environment.

CHAPTER EIGHT
Structural-Symbolic Analysis of Religion

THE LINGUISTIC SCIENCE OF CULTURAL COMMUNICATION

The philosophical-mythological-scientific traditions of all societies include some form of inquiry into how and why different kinds of cultural or symbolic systems originate, and how and why these systems are maintained. Within Western civilization many philosophers/scientists have tried to answer these questions by attempting to reveal the underlying principles of nature and the human mind; they speculated that there may be a correspondence between the laws of mind and the laws of nature. For example, Plato suggested that the laws of nature were none other than the eternal, universal ideas or forms and that these forms manifested in human consciousness, although imperfectly. The Stoics promoted the view that human problems and misery arose in societies that did not correspond to the natural law. The French philosopher Rene Descartes believed that through rigorous logical and mathematical calculations, the human mind could comprehend the laws of nature. The German philosophers Immanuel Kant and W.F.G. Hegel extended the foregoing ideas: Kant made a distinction between *a priori* and *a posteriori* systems and suggested that human beings were born with innate *(a priori)* mental structures (categories of understanding) to comprehend phenomena; Hegel argued that the Universal Spirit or Idea manifested itself and evolved through the dialectical resolution of opposing kinds of consciousness, becoming more and more perfect in this process.

Claude Levi-Strauss, the French philosopher-anthropologist, has inherited the above-stated Western intellectual legacy and, based on it, has built an intellectual movement called structuralism. Before I discuss this brand of structuralism, embodied in the works of Levi-Strauss, I will identify some of the other anthropological writings that have also dealt with the study of "organization" and "structure" in human behavior.

Several types of structural studies developed in the early twentieth century in British social anthropology and American cultural anthropology. The empiricist tradition of British social anthropology focused on discovering the social laws that governed or determined the emergence of similar types of social arrangements. In this view, the organizing principles or the laws of social structure could be discovered through the investigation of the institutions that functioned to maintain the structure; individuals acquired these institutions and, in turn, were linked with one another, making human behavior "structured" and predictable.

American cultural anthropologists sought to discover the patterns or structures of cultural traditions—for example, how certain types of values, worldviews, and themes fit together to become a coherent cultural whole, and how linguistic categories determine and are directly involved in the maintenance of the cultural configurations. Many American cultural anthropologists acquired skills in ethnohistorical and linguistic studies, and by the middle of the twentieth century a highly specialized way of recording cultural traditions had developed. This specialized approach has different labels, such as American structuralism, ethnosemantics, descriptive structuralism, ethnoscience, structural semantics, formal ethnography, new ethnography, cognitive anthropology, and semantic anthropology. In recent theoretical studies, cognitive anthropology, semantic anthropology, and symbolic anthropology have become broad subdisciplinary theoretical orientations within anthropology.

American structuralism and the French structuralism of Levi-Strauss have one thing in common, namely, the methodology of structural linguistics; cultures are conceptualized as communication systems. By using the linguistic analogue as opposed to the organic analogue, the anthropologist discovers or reveals the "grammar" or grammatical structures of cultures.

Beyond the foregoing similarity, American structuralism and Levi-Straussian structuralism differ in their objectives. The American structuralist uses the methodology of linguistics to identify the semantic domains and conceptual models that are significant in a particular culture. Just as a linguist describes the rules that govern the language of a community, the anthropologist constructs a model of a group's conceptual and meaning systems that enables an individual to behave or function appropriately as a member of the group. Just as the speaker of a language may not be aware of the grammatical rules that lie behind effective functioning in a speech community, the people in a culture may not be aware of the models that lie behind the organization of their experiences.

Levi-Strauss, on the other hand, seeks to reveal the structure of the human mind. This structure operates at an unconscious level to produce the surface structures of culture and their various transformations in different cultural settings (these surface structures, like the grammar of the language, are also not conscious; thus the anthropologist is engaging in a double sleight of hand by inferring models of surface structure that reveal universal deep structure). In other words, Levi-Strauss attempts to show, through his studies of kinship and myth, how the logic of the mind (which he identifies as the binary structure or logic) is involved in producing various types of cultural models of communication. The goal of this kind of structuralism, as Hawkes (1977) points out, is to describe the coherence, transformations, and self-regulatory principles of structure. A structure, by the very nature of its logical relationships, has coherence, is capable of transforming or reconstituting the relationship, and creates a boundary. The importance of structuralism is in showing that "the world does not consist of independently existing objects, whose concrete features can be perceived clearly and individually, and whose nature can be classified accordingly. . . . *In consequence, the true nature of things may be said to lie not in things themselves, but in relationships which we construct, and then perceive between them*" (Hawkes 1977: 17 [emphasis mine]).

In the following section I discuss the contributions of Levi-Strauss to structural-symbolic analysis, and in the third section of this chapter I discuss briefly a type of structural analysis that is linked theoretically with "cognitive" or "semantic" anthropology.

BINARISM OF THE MIND
AND RELIGIOUS MEDIATION

According to Levi-Strauss, both culture and language have unconscious, universal structural attributes that result from the innate nature of the human mind. Just as it is possible to unravel linguistic transformations of the unconscious structure, it is possible to decipher or decode cultural transformations of the unconscious structure as they are manifested in phenomena such as totemism, myth, and kinship. Because the mind structures reality through the operation of binary logic, this logic underlies all cultural forms. Structural analysis enables us to understand how the deep binary logic is used to create diverse cultural models, and ultimately we gain an understanding of how the mind works. The role of the anthropologist is to record the synchronic transformations of the basic or deep structure as they are manifested in different cultures. Thus, on one level, the ethnographer investigates the surface structures of a given culture but at another level investigates the universal mental structure of humankind.

We will encounter Levi-Strauss again in the chapter on myth, but I wish to comment here on the relevance or significance of structural analysis for the study of religion in general.

A central premise of structuralism is that the meaning of an object or element does not reside in the element or object but in the perceived relations between elements. Structural anthropologists are not concerned with analyzing how religion, as an institution, develops and functions in relation to other institutions, but with decoding the categories of thought and the oppositional relationships of the categories. Religious categories are identified as mediating categories or models that help resolve contradictions generated by other categories. Thus, rather than explaining how a particular religious myth or ritual helps to promote social or psychological integration, the structuralist deciphers the existence of contradictions or oppositions that pose a threat to the logical order of culture and interprets how these contradictions are mediated through categories that incorporate the oppositions and represent plausible solutions to these oppositions. Religious models or categories most commonly resolve the opposition between life and death.

As I mentioned earlier, the structuralist premise of Levi-Strauss is that our perceptions and conceptions are determined by the nature of the mind, which structures oppositions to generate models of reality. An implicit assumption in the structuralist position is that the mind and the universe share a common logic that makes approximations of reality possible. The mind creates models of reality based upon the perceived oppositions and correspondences of oppositions. In totemism, for example, humans do not necessarily have affinity with totemic animals because of their perceived sameness or identity but because of the perceived correspondences or homology between the differences among groups (cultures) and the differences among animals (nature). Totemism is a model that illustrates that just as group A is different from group B, the animal species C is different from the animal species D. What is perceived in nature may be used to construct cultural forms, and as a result the natural and cultural forms will exhibit the corresponding oppositions.

Levi-Strauss's view of binarism applies also to how the self is perceived. Pettit (1975: 75) notes that Levi-Strauss "argues—though without giving detail—that consciousness of the self presupposes, not so much consciousness of the opposition between the self and the other, as consciousness of the other as being already contained within different oppositions." In this sense, according to Pettit, Levi-Strauss "means presumably that I can be conscious of the self which I oppose to it—only if I can give the other 'oppositional' identity of its own. He assumes that oppositions which operate in such a case take a simplest binary form." Despite these ambiguities, the structuralism of Levi-Strauss offers a useful perspective to formulate a semiotic concept of the self.

Levi-Strauss, however, is not concerned with human intentionality, motivations, and self-conscious orientations but with the unconscious, invariant principles of binary logic. He has been accused by his critics of being a metaphysical anthropologist attempting to build an edifice of a dehumanized physics of culture. His theory of knowledge, which may be called biogenetic epistemology, suggests that the study of anthropology must reveal how the structure of the human mind operates mechanically in producing the wide range of logically coherent cultural systems. As Leach (1970: 26) notes, Levi-Strauss believes that "in investigating the elementary structures of cultural phenomena, we are also making discoveries about the nature of Man—facts which are true of you and me as of the naked savages of Central Brazil."

Although many scholars disagree with Levi-Strauss's theory of knowledge, they have been influenced by his views and have modified and incorporated them in their own studies. Few contemporary students of the anthropology of religion have escaped Levi-Strauss's shadow. He suggests that mythic systems bring together and establish correspondences of different representations of events and thereby deal with certain basic contradictions that arise in how humans explain the origin of human life, death, sexuality, and so on. I discuss in a later chapter his theory of and method for the analysis of myth.

Binary opposition may be an important principle by which order is imposed on human experience, but it is not the only principle. The following discussion of the contributions of Mary Douglas sheds light on this issue.

ORDER AND RELIGIOUS BOUNDARIES

Mary Douglas, the British social anthropologist, in books such as *Purity and Danger* (1966) and *Implicit Meanings* (1975) points out that human beings create sacred boundaries through the use or application of certain concepts of propriety. The creation of sacred boundaries can be seen in how order is maintained by excluding those items that would contravene order. We identify certain things as "dirt" not because they are inherently dirty, but because they are dirt in relation to how we order the domains of existence. For example, "Shoes are not dirty in themselves, but it is dirty to place them on the dining table; food is not dirty in itself, but it is dirty to leave cooking utensils in the bedroom, or food bespattered on clothing. . . . In short, our pollution behavior is the reaction which condemns any object or idea likely to confuse or contradict cherished classifications" (1966: 35–36).

Douglas develops the foregoing idea to explain Jewish dietary customs. She notes that in order to understand any taboo, or ideas about pollution, purity, and defilement, we must examine the "total structure of thought" because these ideas are not isolates but are related to "a systematic ordering of ideas." Certain principles are used to classify and create order, and those items that do not fit in the classificatory schema are excluded from order, and order becomes sacred or holy to maintain its boundary. "To be holy is to be whole, to be one; holiness is unity, integrity, perfection of the individual and of the kind. The dietary rules merely develop the metaphor of holiness on the same lines" (1966: 54). The animals that do not fit into the classificatory order (of holiness) are anomalous and hence are outside order and unclean. She suggests "that originally the sole reason for its [the pig] being counted as unclean is its failure as a wild boar to get into the antelope class, and that in this it is on the same footing as the camel . . . [which is cloven-hoofed but not ruminant]."

Wuthnow et al. (1984: 84) summarize the views of Douglas on pollution and order as follows:

> If dirt is the by-product of ordering and classifying, and society is the source of rules and categories, then dirt is very much a normal part of social life, like crime and deviance. The presence of order—society—makes disorder possible. Rules, boundaries, categories and all sorts of cognitive and moral classification systems create lines that are crossed and categories of things for which there are exceptions. Not everything fits, and what doesn't becomes deviant, odd, strange, or criminal. From this point of view crime and dirt are the same phenomena. Both represent something out of place. For crime, it is behavior which violates the normative and legal order; for dirt, it is matter which is not in its correct place. When things get out of place the normative and legal order is challenged and society re-establishes that order by taking ritual action. For individuals and crime there is punishment. For dirt there is cleanup (we often speak of "cleaning up" crime too).

CHAPTER NINE

Phenomenological-Symbolic Analysis of Religion

THE CULTURAL SCIENCE OF HUMAN EXPERIENCE AND MEANING

In the nineteenth and early twentieth centuries, when positivist sociology and anthropology were popular in other European intellectual traditions, Germany emphasized the study of meaning and history (see Hughes 1958). Phenomenology, rather than natural science, was considered more appropriate for understanding culture. For German scholars, the concept of *kultur* (culture) represented "spiritual" or "moral" features of a group; conceptions of "cultural pluralism," "cultural relativism," "national character," and "genius of a people" became popular. The writings of Wilhelm Dilthey, the German historian, and Johann Herder, the German theologian-anthropologist, became central to the discourse on all cultural sciences, and their contributions had an impact on early-twentieth-century American cultural anthropology. American cultural anthropology shares with German scholarship an emphasis on the study of history and meaning of cultural configurations.

In a general sense, the ethnographies written by cultural/social anthropologists constitute a descriptive or phenomenological activity rather than a "natural science" activity of formulating and testing hypotheses.

Philosophers of science have distinguished between "naturalistic" and "phenomenological" approaches in the social sciences for a long time: Goldstein (1961: 225) notes that "naturalistic social science seeks to explain how sociocultural phenomena come to be as they are, how they develop and change." The phenomenological approach is identified by him as "one that is primarily oriented toward description, not theory formation, and in which the vantage point of subjectivity, in a way to be made clear, is of first importance."

Phenomenological subjectivity is not the same as psychological subjectivity. Phenomenological description attempts to bracket the phenomenon that is described to exclude possible biases and to reveal the essential structure and meaning of the phenomenon. However, as Davis (1986) argues, descriptive knowledge cannot be the same as the experienced reality, and the science of phenomena (phenomenology) must also investigate the conceptualization of the study of experience. In his article "'That's Classic!' The Phenomenology and Rhetoric of Successful Social Theories," Davis has this to say about phenomenological description of experience.

> Phenomenology has usually studied the 'perception' of natural and social objects from the point of view of the observing subject, but it can also study the 'conception' of intellectual objects from this same point of view. A study that draws on this aspect of phenomenology would be especially appropriate for groups, like intellectuals and academics, whose mental life is largely constituted by cognitive phenomena. (Davis 1986: 285–301)

The comparative approach of anthropology enables the anthropologist to understand phenomenologically the universal structures in the cultural formulations of experience. The British social anthropologist Evans-Pritchard (1965: 17) observes that the method used in the anthropological study of religion is phenomenological—"a comparative study of beliefs and rites, such as god, sacrament, and sacrifice, to determine their meaning and social significance." The Italian cultural anthropologist Lanternari (1963: v) views phenomenological study as describing and analyzing the nature and development of particular cultural phenomena without linking them to other phenomena. For Lanternari, phenomenological studies are historical studies. The following quote is from his book on religious movements, *The Religions of the Oppressed: A Study of Modern Messianic Cults:*

> Some prefer to present the facts pertaining to the religious life of a given civilization as viewed from within the closed circle of the subject itself. . . . This type of historian is a phenomenologist, who is concerned mainly with discovering and identifying the universal and unchanging religious "structures" (Lanternari 1963: v)

Phenomenological-symbolic analysis has affinities with structuralist, functionalist, and semiotic approaches in anthropology. In American cultural anthropology, phenomenological-symbolic analysis is linked with Ruth Benedict's configurationalist analysis in particular, and with the study of themes, values, worldviews, and meaning in general.

In the previous chapter, I identified the characteristics of structural-symbolic analysis. Structural-symbolic analysis attempts to reveal the unconscious or hidden meanings and to analyze the interconnectedness of symbols (syntactics), whereas phenomenological-symbolic analysis focuses on the conscious referents or meanings of symbols (semantics) and the use of symbols by the individuals to engage in meaningful, goal-oriented activities. In this respect, phenomenological-symbolic analysis is similar to hermeneutic or interpretive methodology in the cultural sciences. As Rossi (1974) has pointed out, phenomenological-symbolic analysis is a self-reflective activity that offers "hermeneutic understanding" of phenomena:

> Structuralism intends to separate the structure of an institution or myth from the personal experience of the investigator to conduct an objective investigation. On the contrary, hermeneutics wants to reach the meaning of an institution through the conscious effort of the interpreter, who enters into the semantic field he studies. . . . (Rossi 1974: 65)

THE SYMBOLIC COHERENCE OF RELIGION AND SOCIETY

E. E. Evans-Pritchard (1902–1973) was an early proponent of symbolic analysis in British social anthropology and as such went against the dominant intellectual trend in British social anthropology, which was positivistic. Most scholars viewed their discipline as a natural science, were functionalists of one sort or another, and frequently used the biological analogue of the organism to conceptualize society. In contrast, Evans-Pritchard formulated the concept of society as a moral or symbolic system and conceived of social anthropology as a historical discipline.

Evans-Pritchard's studies of religion and society focused on description and interpretation of the symbolic coherence of the various beliefs, and he repeatedly pointed out that only through an understanding of the total system could a researcher discover the internal logic and coherence of religious beliefs and behavior. He argues that ". . . we have to account for religious facts in terms of the totality of the culture and society in which they are found, to try to understand them in terms of what the Gestalt psychologists called the kulturganze, or what Mauss called *fait total*" (Evans-Pritchard 1965: 112).

In his monographs on the Azande and the Nuer of the Sudan (in northern Africa), Evans-Pritchard explores the logic and symbolic associations of various religious representations. The Azande have very elaborate oracles to reveal future events and the guilt or innocence of people who are accused of witchcraft, adultery, and so on. Oracles, as a kind of divination, have widespread distribution in Africa; the Azande use the rubbing-board oracle, the termite oracle, and the poison oracle. The Azande do not consider the natural and supernatural world to be contradictory; for example, it is natural for an individual to get sick or die because of witchcraft. But the Azande do not mistake ordinary objects for spiritual entities; they attribute supernatural qualities to the objects when the objects are used to derive oracular, that is, supernatural information, and such a use does not contradict their cultural assumptions of reality.

> Azande observe the action of the poison oracle as we observe it, but their observations are always subordinated to their beliefs and are incorporated into their beliefs and made to explain them and justify them. Let the reader consider any argument that would utterly demolish all Zande claims for the power of the oracle. If it were translated into Zande modes of thought it would serve to support their entire structure of belief. For their mystical notions are eminently coherent, being interrelated by a network of logical ties, and are so ordered that they never too crudely contradict sensory experience but, instead, experience seems to justify them. The Zande is immersed in a sea of mystical notions, and if he speaks about his poison oracle he must speak in a mystical idiom. (Evans-Pritchard 1937: 319–320)

In a discussion of Nuer beliefs about their totems and twins, Evans-Pritchard takes pains to show that the Nuer distinguish clearly between the natural and the supernatural. For example, a particular individual or group may symbolically refer to a crocodile or some other animal as Spirit in order to conceptualize the individual's or group's association with the Spirit, but this does not mean that the Nuer believe that animals are Spirits. Likewise, when the Nuer say that twins are birds, it does not mean that they are birds in a literal sense, but that they are above nature and therefore associated with Spirit. "Birds are children of God on account of their being in the air, and twins belong to the air on account of their being children of God by the manner of their conception and birth." (Evans-Pritchard 1956: 131)

EXPERIENCE OF CHAOS
AND THE SYMBOLS OF SACRED COSMOS

Peter Berger, the American phenomenological sociologist, has written extensively on the subject of religion (Berger and Luckman 1966, Berger 1969). He investigates how subjective experiences are externalized into objectively meaningful realities that become distinctive cultural products, which in turn are intelligible to and used by other human beings. The human propensity for reification (the tendency to view human creations as objective realities) enables the human species to construct models of reality in dealing with experience. The maintenance of these models is a dialectical process. As Wuthnow et al. (1984: 38) point out, the concepts of identity and self are central to Berger's theorizing about the construction and maintenance of the sociocultural world:

> Berger maintains that all reality is in a constant dialectic with itself. None the less, two dialectical processes are particularly important to human experience in the world and play a part in Berger's writing: a dialectical between the self and the body (or organism and identity), and the dialectic between the self and the sociocultural world. The last is at the heart of Berger's theory of culture.

According to Berger, the sacred order of the universe, or the sacred cosmos that humans create, is to protect the cultural order that is in constant danger of disintegrating. Experiences such as suffering, meaninglessness, and death must be explained if cultural order is to be maintained. Religious symbols and systems offer explanations and justifications for the maintenance of the cultural order that include explanations of suffering with different kinds of theodicy such as karma and millenarianism. The cultural order is affirmed and reaffirmed again and again through the creation and dramatization of a sacred cosmic order in belief and ritual. Religion is, in other words, a protective cover for the cultural construction and maintenance of reality. The following excerpts from Berger's book *The Sacred Canopy* (1969) illustrate his interpretation of religion.

> Religion is the human enterprise by which a sacred cosmos is established. Put differently, religion is cosmization in a sacred mode. By sacred is meant here a quality of mysterious and awesome power, other than man and yet related to him, which is believed to reside in certain objects of experience. This quality may be attributed to natural or artificial objects, to animals, or to men, or to the objectivations of human culture. There are sacred rocks, sacred tools, sacred cows. The chieftain may be sacred, as may be a particular custom or institution. Space and time may be assigned the same quality, as in sacred localities and sacred seasons. The quality may finally be embodied in sacred beings, from highly localized spirits to the great cosmic divinities. (1969: 25)

> On a deeper level, however, the sacred has another opposed category, that of chaos. The sacred cosmos emerges out of chaos and continues to confront the latter as its terrible contrary. This opposition of cosmos and chaos is frequently expressed in a variety of cosmogonic myths. The sacred cosmos, which transcends and includes man in its ordering of reality, thus provides man's ultimate shield against the terror of anomy. To be in a "right" relationship with the sacred cosmos is to be protected against the nightmare threats of chaos. To fall out of such a "right" relationship is to be abandoned on the edge of the abyss of meaninglessness. (1969: 26)

PRIMORDIAL CHAOS AND THE SYMBOLS OF SACRED COSMOS

Mircea Eliade (1957, 1969) argues that the conception of sacred cosmic order is the archetype or model for mythic conceptions and ritual enactments of order and notes that from a religious perspective, "all nature is capable of revealing itself as cosmic sacrality." Such a revelation or manifestation is identified as a "hierophany" or an "act of manifestation of the sacred," which is a "reality that does not belong to our world" (Eliade 1957: 11–12).

To Eliade, an archetype is a paradigmatic or exemplary model of culture. He believes that pristine or archaic culture was rooted in sacred archetypes:

> . . . for the man of traditional or archaic societies, the models for his institutions and the norms for his various categories of behavior are believed to have been "revealed" at the beginning of time, that consequently, they are regarded as having a superhuman and "transcendental" origin. (Eliade 1954: xiv)

> Through the experience of the sacred, the human mind grasped the difference between that which reveals itself as real, powerful, rich, and meaningful, and that which does not—i.e., the chaotic and dangerous flux of things, their fortuitous, meaningless appearances and disappearances. (Eliade 1969: i)

As a historian and a phenomenologist of religion, Eliade was concerned with (1) the study of invariant, universal structures that underlie the sacred archetypes, (2) the description of the historical developments in the uses of particular myths and rituals, and (3) the interpretation of the multiple meanings of religious symbols. In this regard, his approach to the study of religion was interdisciplinary: He combined anthropological, historical, linguistic, phenomenological, and heremeneutic orientations.

SYSTEMS OF SACRED SYMBOLS

According to Geertz (1969, 1973), religious symbols are "sacred symbols" that synthesize worldviews (orientations about the nature of reality) and ethos (orientations about a way of life); they provide the believers with a perspective on the world of human experience that protects the self against meaninglessness and creates moods and motivations that affirm the reality of the symbols. As Honigmann (1976: 318) points out:

> Much of the treatment of religion [according to Geertz] describes the capacity of religious concepts to provide, on the one hand, a general model of the

world, of the self, and of the relationship between the world and self and, on the other hand to establish long-lasting utterly convincing moods and motivations in individuals.

Geertz (1969) suggests that the study of public symbols in general, and of religious or sacred symbols in particular, has become an important theoretical concern in contemporary anthropology. In Geertz's view, it is important to interpret the meaning conveyed by the sacred symbols that have the function of fusing multiple referents, enabling the believers to tolerate, bear, or affirm their existence even when their experiences and the ideal conceptions of life contradict one another. In an exceptionally skillful interpretation of the lives and symbolic representations of two religious leaders (one from Morocco and another from Indonesia), Geertz (1969) shows that they, as symbols, synthesize diverse traditions and function as exemplary models or paradigms for their followers.

Anthropological enterprise, in his view, involves the interpretation of the symbol systems in terms of how they are used, and the identification of "the structures of signification." Culture is not an "occult entity" embedded in someone's head; culture is systems of meaning embedded in public symbols, and its continuity is dependent on its use and re-creation. According to Geertz (1973: 20), "there are three characteristics of ethnographic description: it is interpretive; what it is interpretive of is the flow of social discourse; and the interpreting involved consists in trying to rescue the 'said' of such discourse from its perishing occasions and fix it in persuable terms."

SYMBOLS OF LIMINAL EXPERIENCE

Victor Turner (1920–1983) made a lasting contribution to the study of ritual symbols. Like Geertz, he analyzed and interpreted "world religions." Based on his work in Africa among the Ndembu, Turner analyzed the symbolic structure of various healing rituals. I discuss in the chapter on ritual (Chapter 15) his analysis of a healing ritual.

Turner also drew our attention to the seminal writings of Arnold van Gennep, in particular his concept of "rites of passage," and made a significant theoretical study of the function of the ritual transitional phase and its similarity to other cultural dramas of change in individual and social life.

According to Turner, humans are distinctive in their capacity to alternate between socially structured behavior and situations of nonstructure, and to construct symbols of nonstructured experiences that affirm rather than destroy structure. As human beings are aware of the changes that happen to them and others and are confronted by the biological and social facts of disjunctions and discontinuities in their lives, the knowledge and experience of these changes and the discontinuities can be dysfunctional for cultural continuity. Situations of nonstructure enable individuals to experience the unity of life and timelessness. In these situations, paradigms of structure are affirmed or revised, and new paradigms are generated.

In his books *The Ritual Process* (1969) and *Dramas, Fields, and Metaphors* (1974), Turner develops the idea that human social life is characterized by the existence of an alternation between structured social roles and the blurring of the social roles ("anti-structure") that occurs in the ritual context. He finds anti-structure an essential feature of human existence because it is through the operation of anti-structure that human beings gain an understanding of their humanity. Structure and anti-structure are linked dialectically, the former providing continuity and the latter affirming the significance of both continuity and discontinuity. The operation of anti-structure is an essential component of rituals that dramatize changes in the stages of the life of individuals and groups. These rituals of passage have three phases, identified by van Gennep as separation, marge (limen or threshold), and aggregation. The middle marginal or liminal period does not operate with the social, hierarchical categories. The participants in liminality are liminal or threshold people whose structural position is ambiguous. "Liminal entities are neither here nor there; they are betwixt and between the positions assigned and arrayed by law, custom, convention, and ceremonial" (Turner 1969: 95). In the liminal period there emerges "an unstructured or rudimentarily structured and relatively undifferentiated comitatus, community, or even communion of equal individuals who submit together to the general authority of the ritual elders" (1969: 96). Turner develops his idea of liminality further as follows:

> Liminality is usually a sacred condition protected against secularity by taboos and in turn prevented by them from disrupting secular order, since liminality is a movement between fixed points and is essentially ambiguous, unsettled, and unsettling. (Turner 1974: 273–274)

Turner's concept of liminality is useful to understand why undifferentiated categories of human life are functional in the ritual context, and to understand religious movements as a kind of ritual process. Also, the concept of liminality can be applied to an understanding of the shamanistic sacred self. The merging of the symbols of the self and symbols of the sacred other is an aspect of liminality and communitas. Neophytes often go through a temporary period when they lack a separate identity but are soon provided with a new identity that is endowed with sacredness. This new identity is emotionally and cognitively ordained to protect the obligations associated with the new social role as sacred.

CHAPTER TEN
The Semiotics of the Sacred Self

THE SEMIOTIC THEORY
OF THE SYMBOL SELF

Human beings acquire representations of "who and what they are" through the internalization of shared significances or systems of significances of a cultural tradition. Thus, the study of the representations or symbols of the self is automatically the study of shared significances or systems of significances. At one level, we analyze the syntactic and semantic relationships of the symbols of the self and the symbols of the other; at another level, we analyze their pragmatics, or how these systems are used in "signifying acts."

Every cultural tradition has formulations about the locus and nature of the self. The West has had a long history of debates about the nature of the relationship between self and God and about the relationship between self and phenomenal reality. Western philosophical traditions have promoted a conceptual dichotomy or opposition between mind and body (which became a central issue in Cartesian discourse on the self), or between the "thing in itself" and "phenomena" (which became a central issue in Kantian discourse on the self). Anthropologists, until recently, seldom engaged in these debates about the nature of the self; the self-concept was not considered important in describing or theorizing about culture. But recent scholarship in semiotic cultural analysis (particularly semiotic theories of culture) has focused on the study of the relationship between self and culture to understand the creation and re-creation of cultural traditions.

Singer (1980) has formulated a semiotic theory of the self based on Pierce's general theory of signs. In such a formulation, "the locus, unity, and continuity of the self will be found in the systems of signs that constitute the dialogues between utterers and interpreters of signs" (1980: 485).

Geertz (1973: 3–30) explicitly promotes a semiotic approach to culture, defining culture as composed of "socially established structures of meaning" and identifying cultural analysis as "sorting out the structures of signification." Semiotic cultural analysis involves the interpretations of the cultural production of significances and meaning that occur in different contexts, and through this method we can reveal the constitution, maintenance, evaluation, and dramatization of the symbolic self. Central to Geertzian symbolic analysis is the identification of the role of public symbols that people use to conceptualize their experiences as well as to communicate their conceptualizations to others. Public symbols serve both semiotic and cybernetic functions as units of communication and organization.

> Thinking consists not of 'happenings in the head' (though happenings there and elsewhere are necessary for it to occur) but of a traffic in what have been called, by G.H. Mead and others, significant symbols—words for the most part but . . . anything, in fact, that is disengaged from its mere actuality and used to impose meaning upon experience. (Geertz 1973: 45)

SEMIOTIC-SYMBOLIC INTERACTIONIST THEORY

As Perinbanayagam (1985) notes, recent scholarship in semiotics (syntactics, semantics, and pragmatics) has influenced and reshaped the early formulations of the sociologically inspired symbolic interactionist theory. Symbolic interactionist theory posits that one's own self is a symbolic representation, an object in relation to the selves (objects) of others, and in this manner the self is created and re-created in the processes of human interaction. This approach to understanding human behavior is based on George Herbert Mead's initial formulation of the concept of the self and later elaborations of the relationship between culture and self by American sociologists such as Herbert Blumer, Ervin Goffman, and Peter Berger. Ritzer (1983: 165) identifies the major components of Mead's concept of the self as follows:

1. The ability to respond to one's self as others respond to it.
2. The ability to respond to one's self as the collectivity, the generalized other, responds to it.
3. The ability to take part in one's own conversation with others.
4. The ability to be aware of what one is saying and to use that awareness to determine what one is going to do next.

A semiotic view of symbolic interactionism, in which human interaction is not conceptualized as intersubjective communication, is clearly stated by Perinbanayagam in his book *Signifying Acts* (1985: 158):

> The relationship between self and other is then not described best as an intersubjective one, since there cannot be an interaction between two subjectivities; such a state of affairs is by the nature of the case an absurdity: what is subjective to a self will remain so and no interaction can hence be created on that basis. The relationship between selves is a relationship between a self and an other in which one is subject to himself and an object to the other and the other is subject to himself and an object to the initial self, simultaneously. To achieve this, each person objectifies—dramatizes—his motives, intentions, attitudes, moods, and values by engaging in signifying acts of one kind or another so that the other person can interact with him on a plausible basis. The relationship between self and other then, in the strict sense of the term, is a syntactical one rather than an intersubjective one; the self and other are predicated on each other, where they both are material, objectified, and vocal entities, which engage incessantly in signifying acts of one kind or another.

THE SEMIOTICS OF THE SACRED OTHER AND THE SACRED SELF

Abner Cohen (1977) draws our attention to the fact that symbolic formulations are related to the maintenance of the "totality of person" and notes that in the study of religious phenomena we are drawn to the analysis of how the self is protected.

> The precariousness of the self is created not only by the discrepant roles in which the person is involved but also by the perpetual threats of anomie and marginality posed by the unresolved problems of human existence like misfortune, evil, sickness, decay and, above all, death. . . . Almost everywhere they have been explained in mystical terms and dealt with by patterns of symbolic activities. (Cohen 1977: 124).

But Cohen does not clearly identify the fact that the religious or "mystical" explanations exist to provide coherence *for the culturally created self, or the symbolic self.* For an understanding of religious phenomena it is crucial that we identify the cultural locus of the self and show how the formulations of sacred beings or powers provide coherence for the symbolic self. Just as it is factually important and theoretically necessary to state that the symbolic self is made coherent by certain religious formulations about human suffering, death, and so on, it is also necessary to point out that human suffering and death are explained in different ways by different religious traditions and that a correspondence between these explanations and the explanations of the symbolic self must exist for the religious formulations to make the symbolic self coherent. In other words, the religious formulation of society A may not correspond to the symbolic self of society B. Religion does not eliminate suffering or death but eliminates the contradictions between cultural formulations of suffering, death, and so on by constituting and maintaining the symbolic self as sacred, rendering the symbolic self into a coherent, meaningful system of action despite the existence of inconsistencies between the biological and conceptual realities, or between nature and culture.

Symbols of the sacred self combine the characteristics of "key symbols" (Ortner) and "sacred symbols" (Geertz). Ortner (1973: 1339–1340) identifies two types of key symbols: "Summarizing symbols . . . are those symbols which are seen as summing up, expressing, representing for the participants in an emotionally powerful and relatively undifferentiated way, what the system means to them." Elaborating symbols, on the other hand, work in the opposite direction, providing vehicles for sorting out complex and undifferentiated feelings and ideas, making them comprehensible to oneself, communicable to others, and translatable into orderly action. The symbol of the sacred self can be interpreted as having the characteristics of both summarizing and elaborating symbols. Sacred symbols, according to Geertz (1966), function to synthesize conceptions of order and experiences of disorder as well as enable the users to fuse known and unknown realities, empirically verifiable and unverifiable facts, and engage in culturally appropriate action. Symbols of the sacred self embody the characteristics of key and sacred symbols and may be used in different ways in different contexts and used differently by different individuals.

I suggest that, in a cultural, semiotic perspective, the analysis involves the examination of how the various domains of religion (such as myth, ritual, shamanism, and witchcraft) operate to transform the "natural," biological human identity into supernatural (sacred), nonbiological human identity through establishing linkages or relationships between the symbolic self and symbols of the sacred other. The transformation of human identity is achieved through a number of different ways, but basically there are two polar types of transformation. One type of transformation produces the priestly sacred self, and the other type produces the shamanistic sacred self. These two transformations are aligned, respectively, with the human dimensions of social/political order and biological/psychological/health. Between these two types can exist symbols of sacred self that share in the characteristics of priestly or shamanistic sacred selves to a lesser or greater degree.

Ideally, the priestly self is constituted through the interaction with sacred others that signify social and political processes; and ideally, the shamanistic self is constituted through the interactions with sacred others that signify biological/psychological processes. The priestly self may be a representation of internalizing or rejecting the social/political characteristics or attributes of the sacred other; and the shamanistic self may be a representation of the merger or union with the biological/psychological characteristics or attributes of the sacred other. Symbols of the sacred other have multiple characteristics, and therefore the same symbol of the sacred other may be used in the constitution of the priestly or shamanistic sacred selves.

The priestly and shamanistic selves are ideal types, and combinations or variations of sacred selves occur in real action-orientations. For example, the same individual may represent shamanistic or priestly selves in different contexts, and individuals may represent a combination of priestly or shamanistic selves. The priestly self legitimizes the cultural order through making social and political conventions coherent. The shamanistic self is adaptive in situations of individual or group crisis; to be in contact with or merged with the sacred other is the ultimate source of integration or coherence for the symbolic self.

We can explain the priestly self with "reference group" theory and hypotheses: There can be positive emulation as well as negative emulation. Certain sacred others, or certain aspects of sacred others, from the believer's perspective, will be desirable or undesirable. For example, some gods, spirits, fetishes, ghosts, or powers can be good, and positive emulation of them is necessary to maintain social/political conventions and have a satisfying life; but some gods, spirits, fetishes, ghosts, or powers can be bad, and negative emulation is necessary to avoid them or prevent their intervention. There can be ancestor worship, inviting the spirits of the dead ancestors to participate in everyday life with the enactment of proper behavior among the living (positive emulation), or there can be cults of the dead, with rituals performed to exclude the spirits from any social involvement (negative emulation). Some religious perspectives have two opposite types of sacred other, with the god or the god's intermediaries serving as representations of perfection and goodness (symbols for positive emulation) as opposed to the devil or Satan and the devil's serving as representations of imperfection and evil (symbols for negative emulation).

We can explain the shamanistic self with the interpretation that rituals create transformations in individual psychobiological states to achieve certain results. Merger can be for negative or positive results. For example, the sorcerer's ritual may be directed toward negative results, and the sacred other may represent dangerous powers. An initiation ritual is directed toward achieving positive results, and the sacred other may represent benign powers. Hundreds of different combinations can occur in different rituals. Geertz (1966) correctly points out that in the ritual context there is fusion of the world as it is lived (experience) and the world as it is imagined (the sacred other). Turner (1967: 54) notes:

. . . ritual symbols are not merely signs representing known things; they are felt to possess ritual efficacy, to be charged with power from unknown sources, and to be capable of acting on persons and groups coming in contact with them in such a way as to change them for the better or in a desired direction.

And as Beck (1978: 88) observes:

[In ritual contexts] the participants do something (by the act of attending the proceedings) that opens them up to a diffuse set of sensory outputs by the ritual activities. These experiences are of processes that are defined as creative and energizing and viewed as communicating with a little-understood upper world of superhuman forms.

SHAMANISTIC AND PRIESTLY SACRED SELVES

In Part III of this book I present a detailed interpretation of the dynamics of shamanism, priesthood, and religious movements. In this section, I illustrate briefly the anthropological study of these phenomena. In the semiotic perspective on shamanistic and priestly sacred selves, such representations are not confined or restricted to the religious specialists who are identified as shamans or priests. Individuals may acquire shamanistic or priestly sacred selves in terms of how they use the symbols of the sacred other. Shamans and priests are those who professionalize the sacred selves in one way or another in order to perform certain socially recognized roles.

In anthropological discourse it is common to identify the shaman and the priest as contrasting types of religious practitioners and to identify the existence of other types of religious practitioners who share more or less in the characteristics attributed to the shaman and the priest. The shaman is considered to be a part-time religious practitioner whose religious authority derives from his or her ability to enter into an altered state of consciousness in order to participate in a non-ordinary reality or communicate directly with supernatural beings or powers. The priest, on the other hand, is generally defined as a full-time religious practitioner whose religious authority is legitimized by his knowledge and interpretation of the sacerdotal tradition and who engages in propitiating supernatural beings and in officiating over religious rituals. Such a typological distinction has been used by many scholars to differentiate certain religious beliefs according to whether they are associated with shamanism or priesthood. For example, belief in the existence of sacred power and practices such as divination and therapeutic rituals are often associated with shamanism; belief in the existence of sacred beings and practices such as communal worship and ritual validation of political power and hierarchy are often associated with priesthood.

The shaman represents empirically verifiable biological-psychological processes in relation to empirically unverifiable reality, and the priest represents empirically verifiable social-political processes in relation to empirically unverifiable reality. Believers who use the symbols of the sacred other to represent the self as sacred differ in the degree to which they represent either the shamanistic or priestly sacred self, and they may alternate between a shamanistic or a priestly orientation toward the symbols of the sacred other. The model that I have proposed has heuristic value for understanding the coexistence of shamanism and priesthood, and for understanding the diverse weighting of biological-psychological or social-political processes in the representation of the symbolic self as sacred.

The foregoing model is particularly useful to illustrate the structure and meaning of religious movements. Anthropological literature on religion and cultural change is replete with examples of "nativistic," "syncretic," "revivalistic," or "millenarian" movements. A common denominator of these movements appears to be their emergence during cultural disintegration and their attempt to create an integrated culture. The movements are led by prophets who promise a new way, and if the new way is socially organized, or is linked with political power, as in the case of Christianity, a new religious configuration or paradigm is established with an integrated culture.

By using the distinction that I have made between the representations of the self as sacred (in terms of the shamanistic self promoting the union of the symbols of the self and the sacred other, and the priestly self promoting a correspondence or approximation between the symbols of the self and the sacred other), I suggest that prophets of religious movements promote the shamanistic self in the construction of new symbols of the sacred self for themselves and their followers. Routinization or social organization of the movements may lead to the emergence of the priestly self as a representation of social-political processes with sacred attributes.

THE SACRED SELF IN MYTH AND RITUAL

Part IV of this book provides a comprehensive discussion of myth and ritual. The following brief statements on myth and ritual demonstrate that religious myths and rituals are the primary cultural domains in which the constitution, maintenance, evaluation, and dramatization of the sacred self occur.

Myth and ritual are human universals, but they are not necessarily religious. Myths reveal or communicate truths for their users not because they are constituted with scientifically testable facts but because they are coherent and communicate meaning and thus help individuals cope with contradictions, disharmony, injustice, suffering, and so on. Religious or sacred myths incorporate symbols of the sacred other in answering questions about the nature of life, death, cosmos, and so on and are often linked with racial, political, economic, and other social myths.

I suggest that religious myths are cultural discourses on the transformation of human identity, relating symbols of self and sacred other. Human life is made meaningful in religious myths that serve as mirrors to see and understand one's own sacredness in relation to the activities of the various sacred others who are depicted in the myths. Different kinds of myth exist, such as cosmogonic and eschatological myths, and each type conveys to the believer the meaning of a particular kind of sacred manifestation in relation to human identity.

Religious ritual is communication between the symbols of the self and the symbols of the sacred other and is a cultural domain to dramatize the sacred self. Biological and social transitions are often marked by performance of rituals. In general, events that are culturally recognized as crucial for the survival of the individual or the group are marked by enactments of religious rituals, and in such ritual contexts symbols of the sacred other are deployed, and the merging of the symbols of self and sacred other often occurs.

Different kinds of rituals exist, such as life-cycle rituals and social-renewal rituals. Most of these rituals acquire sacred or supernatural significance, and they function as cultural arenas in which the participants experience the transformation of human identity; the participants feel or see the presence of the sacred other and may merge their symbolic selves with that of the sacred others.

PART THREE
THE SEMIOTICS
OF SHAMANISM,
PRIESTHOOD,
AND RELIGIOUS MOVEMENTS

CHAPTER ELEVEN
Shamanism, Priesthood,
and the Symbols of the Sacred Self

THE SHAMAN AND SHAMANISM

Anthropologists generally distinguish the roles as well as the characteristics of religious specialists and consider shamans and priests to be two different types, identifying several others as sharing in more or less of the characteristics attributed to shamans or priests. The shaman's role is primarily to communicate *with* supernatural entities and to participate in the supernatural world to help individuals or groups achieve desired goals (divination, sorcery, and healing). Shamans experience ecstasy and transcendence and can achieve trance states with or without the aid of hallucinogenic drugs. The "classic" Siberian shaman is one who can undertake journeys or voyages to the spirit world and has spirit allies and familiars.

The role of the priest is primarily to communicate *to* supernatural entities through propitiation or supplication. The authority of priests stems from their religious training, and they officiate at group rituals and serve as the custodians of sacerdotal knowledge; they interpret and dramatize the mythological charters in public and uphold the social conventions and moral order. Other types of religious specialists such as prophets and theologians share aspects of the roles attributed to shamans and priests. Turner (1968: 439) offers the following distinction:

Priests may . . . be classified as institutional functionaries in the religious domain, while medium, shaman, and prophet may be regarded as subtypes of inspirational functionaries. This distinction is reflected in characteristically different modes of operation. The priest presides over a rite; the shaman or medium conducts a seance. Symbolic forms associated with these occasions differ correlatively: the symbols of a rite are sensorily perceptible to a congregation and have permanence in that they are culturally transmissible, while those of a seance are mostly in the mind of the entranced functionary as elements of his visions or fantasies and are often generated by and limited to the unique occasion. The inspirational functionary may describe what he has clairvoyantly perceived (or "been shown" as he might put it), but the institutional functionary manipulates symbolic objects with prescribed gestures in full view of his congregation.

Turner's characterization of the shaman as the "inspirational" or "entranced" functionary refers to the fact that shamanism deals with symbolization of psychological processes. The shaman may have a clear understanding of the cultural categories of perception and cognition and may function as an effective diviner and healer because of such an understanding, but his or her legitimacy derives from the capacity to merge with the symbols of the sacred other. The shaman is the prototype for total or partial union between the symbols of the self and the symbols of the sacred other. People differ in their capacity or inclination to attain such union, but in times of stress, sickness, and anxiety, and in the ritual context, direct contact and union with symbols of the sacred other is common.

Shaman is a Siberian Tungus word meaning an ecstatic religious specialist who communes with supernatural powers and beings. In the Siberian context the shaman is believed to journey to the outer world. The aspect of the shamanistic voyage to the outer world (the world above or below the Earth) is a distinguishable characteristic of functioning as a shaman in many cultural traditions. However, not all cultural traditions have elaborate symbology to represent shamanistic journeys. I believe that it is useful to have an all-inclusive category of shaman that includes a variety of religious specialists who have the capacity to commune with supernatural beings and powers rather than to restrict the concept of shaman to identify only those religious practitioners who experience journeys to the netherworld.

The shaman functions in non-urban (technologically primitive) societies as a preeminent healer and diviner. There are male and female shamans. They seldom function as full-time religious specialists.

The shaman and shamanistic orientation are universal, but in non-urban societies, particularly in certain non-urban cultural traditions, the shaman and shamanism have significance beyond the healing and divining functions. In some non-urban societies, shamanism operates with an elaborate system of symbolic classifications, and in these societies, the initiation of an individual into shamanism has great cultural significance. The shamanic worldview usually corresponds to the "magical" worldview, and beliefs in witchcraft and sorcery are components of this worldview. In complex, traditional societies, "mystical" orientations often coexist with orthodox scriptural traditions and have elaborate symbolic formulations about non-ordinary realities. These formulations may be linked with various systems of metaphysical healing and cults that promote altered states of consciousness.

The shaman is not constrained by social conventions and has, according to Harner (1980) and others, a worldview that does not correspond to what we perceive as real in everyday life. It is possible that these writers have painstakingly recorded the cultural assumptions, epistemologies, and techniques of the shamans; but it is also possible that they have become apologists for the shaman and shamanism, creating a worldview of shamanism that is derived from a number of different sources. In other words, are the anthropological creations of Don Juans (Casteneda 1970, 1971, 1972) fictions whose legitimacy is not from the recording of facts but from what the writings convey or communicate to the readers, as in the reading of novels? The apologists for the shaman as a culture hero who journeys into the depths of the inner self to bring back knowledge about eternal psychological truth frequently confuse psychological experiences of altered states of consciousness with the projected, external world of the shaman; this world is presented as a model of a reality that is different from what can be known through sensory perception and the observations of modern science. I will comment on this later in Part V.

Many complex, traditional societies have elaborate systems of shamanistic worldviews. The Tibetan Book of the Dead of Vajrayana Buddhism, Tao, Tantrism, Sufism, and Kabbala are examples of shamanistic, "mystical," or "magical" orientations that have focused on creating altered states of consciousness that enable the participants to transcend social categories and to merge their symbolic selves with the symbols of the sacred other. I will refer later to Mircea Eliade's study of shamanism in which he sees the parallels between the shamanism of non-urban societies and certain religious orientations such as Tibetan Lamaism, Hindu and Buddhist Tantrism, and Taoism.

THE SHAMAN IN NON-URBAN SOCIETIES

A person often becomes a shaman as a result of manifesting unusual characteristics. The ability to fall into a trance, self-induced or otherwise, has the greatest significance in this regard. In many societies, persons showing unusual characteristics are set apart. Some shamans may be albinos, epileptics, homosexuals, or transvestites, but there is no particular association between having certain biological or psychological attributes and being a shaman; in other words, not all albinos, epileptics, homosexuals, and transvestites are shamans. As Norbeck (1961) points out, although in some societies the shaman who is a homosexual or transvestite is viewed as the most powerful of all shamans, the transvestite *berdache* of North American societies is not always a shaman. (*Berdache* is a French word for North American Indian transvestites.)

Shamans attain altered states of consciousness by various means, such as rhythmic drumming and singing, breathing exercises that lead to super-oxygenation, fasting, body mutilations, and consumption of drugs. Shamans often speak in tongues (*glossolalia*) or communicate their wishes through interpreters (*ermeneglossia*). The language used in the state of trance may be a foreign language (*xenoglossia*). Shamans are frequently ventriloquists.

Shamans may "inherit" their attributes, or buy and learn the attributes. However, it is common for an individual to manifest behavior that is recognized as a calling for being a shaman. After a period of isolation that connotes "ritual death," during which he or she undergoes an "existential transformation," the individual is initiated as a confirmed shaman; the initiate may experience his or her journey to the world of spirits, where his or her body is dismembered and put together after a period of physical abuse and torture by the spirits; the initiate returns with a new body and with new knowledge acquired through such an experience.

Following are examples of how shamans are conceptualized in some of the non-urban societies that have been studied by anthropologists.

The Washo Indians (Downs 1966) believe that shamans have more power than others, and that they often derive this power from an animal. Disease is believed to be caused either by ghosts or by the sorcery of shamans, and shamans perform curing ceremonies to demonstrate their power.

Among the Mapuche Indians (Faron 1968), shamans are generally women. They cure sickness and divine the etiology of sickness. Shamans have their own guild that validates and supervises their activities. Shamans are considered to be on the side of "good," having "good" spirit familiars. Witches, on the other hand, are considered to be in league with evil spirits; witches are usually old women. The Mapuche do not make a distinction between witchcraft and sorcery.

Among the Huron (Trigger 1969) there are four kinds of shamans, and they all possess great supernatural power.

Among the Cibecue Apache (Basso 1970), shamans conduct curing, puberty, and other rituals. Shamans are believed to put power to good use. There are two types of witches, the sorcerer and the love witch. The latter practices witchcraft for sexual favors, and the former resorts to witchcraft to cause sickness, death, or loss of prosperity. The techniques of the sorcerer vary from using poison and shooting magical objects to casting spells.

Among the Eskimos of North America (Chance 1966), the most powerful leader is the shaman who has the power to cause and cure diseases. Disease is attributed to loss of soul or intrusion of foreign objects.

The Yanomamo (Chagnon 1968) believe that shamans control small-sized demons called *hekura;* the use of drugs is an integral aspect of shamanism. "Magic and curing are intimately bound up in shamanism, the practitioner devoting his efforts alternatively to causing and curing sickness" (Chagnon 1968: 52).

In Martinique, the group that Horowitz (1967) pseudonymously refers to as the people of Morne-Paysan, have shamans called *quiboiseurs* who cure diseases and harm people.

Mediums are the only religious practitioners among the Kalinga (Dozier 1967), and they are usually women who receive the calling to that profession through signs such as unusual fits and dreams. Although they are important functionaries whose services are in great demand to cope with malicious spirits, their status is low. Mediums function as diviners and curers, and they may use spirit familiars.

The clan chief of the Palauan (Barnett 1960) functions as the intermediary between the people and the spirits, but there is also an institution of spirit possession. When mentally unstable persons start proclaiming themselves to be gods and start acting like gods, such persons are called *korongs* or spirit mediums; *korongs* divine and cure and are wealthy. They are usually from the lower strata but are held high in social esteem. In the early twentieth century a nativistic movement (the Modekne cult) was founded by a person who at one stage of his life showed the characteristics of *korongs.*

Among the Ulithi (Lessa 1966b) there are four types of high magicians: the typhoon magician, the navigator magician, the fish magician, and the palm-leaf-knot diviner. Several lesser magicians are connected with the canoe, house, and other objects.

Among the Kapauku Papuans (Pospisil 1964), the shamans are very powerful and are second only to the headmen. They have the aid of several spirit familiars for counteracting evil spirits and for curing. Sorcerers have a low status and are ostracized. ". . . [U]nlike the shaman, the sorcerer possesses his own supernatural power that is believed to be independent of any spirit helper" (Pospisil 1964: 82).

THE SHAMAN IN COMPLEX, TRADITIONAL SOCIETIES

In many complex, traditional societies, differences in religious orientations are sustained by the literate and the folk traditions. The literate or "Great Tradition" is often associated with priesthood and discourse on the sacred texts, and the folk or "Little Tradition" is often associated with shamanism and related practices. These traditions overlap considerably and often coexist, influencing and complementing one another. A good example of their coexistence and function is found in Melford Spiro's *Burmese Supernaturalism* (1967). Buddhism in Burma coexists with the shamanist religious orientation, which Spiro identifies as "supernaturalism."

In Burma, the shamans are mostly female, and they function as diviners and mediums of *nats* (spirits). Shamans are held in very low esteem. They are considered immoral; only marriage to a *nat* makes a person a shaman. A few shamans are males, married to female *nats*. According to Spiro, most male shamans are latent homosexuals who, when they dance in the *nat* festivals, take on the characteristics of the female spirits. Spiro infers that the institution of shamanism provides an opportunity for members of the community to satisfy repressed sexual, dependency, prestige, and Dionysian needs. "By substituting a nat for a human being the shaman is allowed undistinguished satisfaction, albeit in fantasy, of prohibited sexual needs" (Spiro 1967: 219).

The exorcist in Burma is an occult practitioner who is also a devout Buddhist. He is a member of a semi-Buddhist sect called *gaings*. Membership in this sect confers occult powers. He seldom seeks the assistance of *nats* but interacts with the *nats* through the patient. His position is between that of the shaman and the Buddhist monk; he represents the intermediate stage between supernaturalism and Buddhism. "Like the shaman he recognizes the power of nats, but like the monk he does not invoke it. Like the monk, he utilizes this power to counter the nats" (Spiro 1967: 242). The motivational explanation that Spiro gives is that the person's desire for high esteem and power is met by his becoming an exorcist.

Spirit possession is treated by the exorcist. In most cases treatment is successful because an "exorcist seance is a form of psychotherapy" (Spiro 1967: 195). Feelings of guilt or shame and anxiety often induce persons to exhibit characteristics of spirit possession, which functions as an escape mechanism. Because exorcism ceremonies are conducted with community members present, patients get not only the support of the group but also a kind of approval that alleviates their guilt feelings and conflicts, thereby restoring them to normalcy.

In India, priestly Hinduism (sometimes referred to as the Great Tradition, which is transmitted by Brahmanical priesthood) coexists with the shamanistic Hinduism of villages (sometimes referred to as non-Brahmanical religion). The shamanistic or non-Brahmanical orientation is important, particularly in the villages where the priests of the temples often serve as shamans or mediums of particular deities and spirits. I discuss below the function of shamanism in a Tamil village of southern India. (Many sectarian orientations of Hinduism such as Tantrism have very elaborate shamanistic symbology and ritual, and these orientations are distinct from the village shamanism discussed below.)

In the Tamil society of southern India, a distinction is made between communal shamanism and family shamanism on the basis of their functions. The communal shaman who may or may not be the priest of village or *jati* temples is generally called upon by anyone in the *jati* group or the village community to divine causes of illness, exorcise evil spirits, and consult the supernatural in matters about which rational predictions are not possible. The communal shaman protects the villager through the aid of a familiar who could be a goddess, godling, or a spirit. The function of the family shaman is restricted in the sense that the primary duty is to protect the household with the aid of the family guardian deity who is normally the familiar of the shaman.

The family deity could be a member of the Hindu pantheon and could be an Amman (goddess) or her consort, or a spirit related to the communal cults. A deceased ancestor could come to be identified as an aspect of the goddess or a spirit, and with an appropriate suffix indicating the divinity the ancestor would be accepted by the members of the household as their guardian deity.

Any ritual associated with crisis in the household must have the approval and blessing of the family deity, and this approval and blessing are conveyed through the shaman of the family deity. When crisis rites are performed in households without a shaman, the family deity's approval and blessing are generally made explicit through the services of a village shaman or a priest.

Although a household may not have a shaman of the family deity at a given point in time, all members of the household are potential shamans, and this fact is crucial for the household to function as a religious unit and for the performance of household rituals. It is not necessary for family shamans to undergo special training: A person may experience possession by a godling, goddess, or spirit. When the supernatural being conveys to the other members of the household that it will protect the household, it is installed as the family deity. Or, a family deity may belong to a household for several generations and may select a favorite younger member through possession, indicating that it wishes to continue to protect the household after the death of its current shaman.

The most important feature of family shamanism is that members of the household are assured that the family deity can be activated or called upon to serve the needs of the household in moments of uncertainty. When a member of the household is installed as the family shaman, such an assurance is elicited from the deity, and the shaman's permanent relationship with the deity is confirmed with the seal of burning camphour placed on the tongue or palm.

The following is a description of a ritual that I recorded in 1970, in which a family deity and a family shaman were installed in the household of a successful merchant who had suffered several financial setbacks. Sickness and other family calamities occurred, and all these misfortunes were attributed to the nonperformance of appropriate mortuary rites for a daughter who had met an untimely death. It was believed that her spirit did not have a resting place and that proper rituals would make the spirit function as a family deity and thus prevent any more misfortunes in the family.

The services of two shamans were secured, and the two sons of the merchant were prepared to receive the daughter's spirit. Special preparations were made in the *nadu veedu* (center of the house) for the installation of her spirit as a family deity. A large photograph of the girl was placed on the wall, and below it an altar *(pathi)* was built where a pot *(kalasam)* was decorated with neem leaves and flower garlands. The lamp called *kamatchi-Amman vilakku* was placed on top of the pot. Cooked food and fruit were kept in front of the altar. The priests produced rhythmic music by drumming the tambourine *(Udukkai)* and tabla and by singing. They invoked the blessings of the community's goddesses, godlings, and spirits and sought to receive a message from them through the steady burning of the lamp, which served as the indicator of such a message.

The sons of the merchant were not possessed by the spirit of the deceased daughter (neither of them fell into a trance), but the merchant's sister-in-law began to sway. Although she showed every indication of possession, there was doubt as to its genuineness, and she came out of the trance. As this was occurring, a woman in the audience who was not related to the family was possessed by her familiar (not the spirit of the deceased girl), and the latter pointed out that a ritual item was missing on the altar. The priests sought forgiveness and gave the assurance that the ritual item would be procured; the woman's possession was over.

Following these two episodes of possession, the merchant's wife began to show signs that her daughter's spirit had entered her. The priests were convinced that this possession was genuine, and after a brief period of rapid singing and drumming they stopped and asked the merchant's wife who she was; she gave her daughter's name. The daughter, speaking through her mother, said that she had come to stay with them permanently and that she would protect everyone of the household. With further questioning, the daughter said that the merchant should go ahead with the arrangement of his son's marriage and the ear-piercing ceremonies of the other children. To make certain that the spirit had come to be a family deity who could be invoked and called upon to aid the family, burning camphour was handed to the merchant's wife and she swallowed it, thus confirming that the daughter's spirit had indeed become a family deity.

SHAMANIC SYMBOLOGY

Initiation of an individual into shamanism is often associated with symbolic death and rebirth. The initiate is introduced into the ways of the shaman and becomes a healer with the knowledge of supernatural reality.

In many non-urban societies and in many complex, traditional societies such as those of India, China, and Tibet, very elaborate ceremonies and knowledge systems are associated with shamanism. These types of shamanism have many distinguishable characteristics that are frequently interpreted as related to the religious and theological discourse on mysticism. They are markedly different from the types of shamanism that I have discussed in the foregoing paragraphs.

Mircea Eliade, in a number of books, presented detailed descriptions and discussions of the rituals and symbology of shamanism. In his book *Shamanism: Archaic Techniques of Ecstasy* (1964), he describes and analyzes the recruiting methods, initiation through symbolic death and rebirth, the shamanic cosmology and powers, and shamanic healing rituals. He also provides an excellent discussion of shamanic myths and symbology as they are used in India, China, Tibet, Mongolia, Korea, and Japan. As Eliade notes, certain forms of Hinduism and Buddhism are shamanistic in orientation: Tibetan Lamaism and the Hindu–Buddhist Tantrism are imbued with shamanic symbolism and mythology. Chinese Taoism has its foundation in shamanism as well. We may also include in shamanism various "mystery" cults and religious as well as mystical-religious traditions such as Kabbala and Sufism.

Eliade (1964: 508–509) notes that shamanism or shamans "have played an essential role in the defense of the psychic integrity of the community" and that shamanism "defends life, health, fertility, the world of 'light' against death, diseases, sterility, disaster, and the world of 'darkness.'" The following quotation illustrates the significance of shamanism as a system of knowledge about the supernatural reality and the shaman as one who is capable of undertaking "mystical journeys" to reveal the mysteries of humanity and the universe:

> It is as a further result of [the shaman's] ability to travel in the supernatural worlds and to see the superhuman beings (gods, demons, spirits of the dead, etc.) that the shaman has been able to contribute decisively to the knowledge of death. In all probability many features of "funerary geography," as well as some themes of the mythology of death, are the result of the ecstatic experiences of shamans. The lands that the shaman sees and the personages that he meets during his ecstatic journeys in the beyond are minutely described by the shaman himself, during or after his trance. The unknown and terrifying world of death assumes form, is organized in accordance with particular patterns; finally it displays a structure and, in course of time, becomes familiar and acceptable. In turn, the supernatural inhabitants of the world of death become visible; they show a form, display a personality, even a biography. Little by little the world of the dead becomes knowable, and death itself is evaluated primarily as a rite of passage to a spiritual mode of being. In the last analysis, the accounts of the shamans' ecstatic journeys contribute to 'spiritualizing' the world of the dead, at the same time that they enrich it with wondrous forms and figures. (Eliade 1964: 508–509)

Evidence suggests that not all shamans believe in shamanic world view. Claude Levi-Strauss (1963a) in his essay "The Sorcerer and His Magic" reviews the descriptions of a boy accused of sorcery among the Zuni of New Mexico (recorded by M.C. Stevenson in 1905), and of a shaman among the Kwakiutl who was skeptical of shamanistic healing (recorded by Franz Boas in 1930), to show how shamanistic or sorcery belief systems are socially created and maintained as valid models of misfortune and healing. Franz Boas (1930: 1–41) describes the life of a Kwakiutl shaman who conceived of himself as an actor but was considered by others to be a very powerful shaman. The following is a brief rendition of his autobiography.

A man named Giving-Potlatches-in-the-World wanted to find out whether shamanism was true or whether shamans only pretended to be shamans. Unexpectedly, he found himself chosen to become a shaman. Reasoning that this would provide him the opportunity to answer his question, he accepted the offer. He was initiated into shamanism and was taught the art of deception, which included self-induced "trembling," "fainting," and the vomiting of "blood and worm." He pretended to be a shaman and cured a sick person. After his success he was given the shaman name Qasalid. Qasalid visited several tribes, observed other shamans at work, and put them to shame by his successes in cases in which they had failed. He found out that in most cases the shamans were liars, posing as shamans only to make money. Qasalid was accepted by everyone as a great shaman, and other shamans tried to learn his techniques. He himself believed that he was a pretender whose main purpose was to investigate the ways of other shamans. He concluded that shamans were great pretenders. On the other hand, his life and activities were socially meaningful as valid models of being a shaman and healer.

Shamans are generally viewed as "culture heroes" in native South American cultures. Shamans have an intimate knowledge of hallucinogenic drugs, and they are also credited with the knowledge of how to "create" certain kinds of hallucinogenic experiences. An association is often made between shamanic personality and animals such as the jaguar, boa, or anaconda. The jaguar association is particularly prominent, and mysterious or supernatural powers are attributed to both the shaman and the jaguar; in some native South American culture, shamans are known as jaguars. In his study of shamanism among the Indians of the Vaupes in South America, Reichel-Dolmatoff (1975) notes that the shaman (who is known as *paye* in that region) is regarded as the most important specialist with knowledge of the cosmos, game animals, health, and cultural practices, combining the characteristics of the shaman and the priest. With reference to the beliefs that underlie the link between the shaman and the jaguar, he says:

. . . it is thought that a shaman can turn into a jaguar at will and that he can use the form of this animal as a disguise under which he can act as a helper, a protector, or an aggressor. After death, the shaman may turn permanently into a jaguar and can then manifest himself in that form to the living, both friend and foe, again in benevolent or malefic way, as the case may be. (Reichel-Dolmatoff 1975: 43)

PRIESTHOOD AND SOCIAL HIERARCHY

I have defined priests as religious practitioners whose symbols of the sacred self have referents in social processes, and I have suggested that the priestly sacred self represents a total or partial emulation (or rejection) of the symbols of the sacred other (gods, goddesses, spirits, etc.). Those who enter the priesthood become interpreters and exegists of the symbols of the sacred other and in turn become interpreters of social tradition and order. There is always a close association between priesthood and the political/economic order, even when political power is not vested in the priest, as in the case of "secular" societies. When a conflict exists between priesthood and the political/economic order, priesthood acquires a shamanistic orientation in the sense that some priests may function as prophets or "liberation theologians." This change in the nature and function of priesthood will be examined further in the discussion of religious movements in the text chapter.

As a result of the association between priesthood and the political/economic order, women are seldom admitted into priesthood, except in those societies in which they participate equally in the politico-economic system. The contrast between shamanism and priesthood is marked with regard to the participation of women. There are at least as many women as men who function as shamans; and in some societies, only women function as shamans. In both non-urban and urban societies, women function as mystics, seers, prophetesses, medicine women, and evangelicals and participate in large numbers in the so-called cultist (i.e., shamanistic) orientations.

The priest uses the sacred knowledge to communicate *to* (not with) the sacred others and functions as the guardian of that knowledge and those symbols of the sacred others. The priest usually embodies the morals and follows the taboos considered necessary to maintain the social order. The priest, by officiating over rituals and by propitiating sacred others, affirms or legitimizes social solidarity and social values. This fact impressed scholars such as Emile Durkheim, who by conceptualizing *a priori* existence to society, postulated the priority of religion over magic.

The priest is usually a full-time religious practitioner, but this statement needs to be qualified. Anthropologists have frequently suggested that priesthood is found more often in complex, traditional, and urban societies than in non-urban societies. This is a misleading interpretation because in non-urban societies, the male elders often function as priests. For example, among the Lugbara (Middleton 1965) the *ori* (ghosts of ancestors) have genealogical ties with the living and function to maintain traditional bonds, keeping harmony and so on. The elders, as the living custodians of tradition, can and do invoke the *ori* to sustain the social order and punish deviance.

A priestly "class" is often associated with rigid social stratification, usually serving to justify the system through the use of sacerdotal authority. The priestly class often (but not always) exists in urban societies and frequently uses a language—such as Arabic, Pali, Latin, or Sanskrit—that acquires religious significance. Certain religious systems are linked with political dominance and become powerful "world" religions, as in the case of Islam, Buddhism, Hinduism, and Christianity. I illustrate in the next section the role of priesthood in Hinduism as it occurs in India.

HINDUISM AND BRAHMANICAL PRIESTHOOD

Hinduism lacks an ecclesia, or a universally recognized, single church institution, but certain forms of Hinduism are organized around Brahmanical priesthood and sectarian orientations as well as regional goddess and other cults. Rooted in particular regional/cultural settings, Hinduism is characterized by the use of a multiplicity of regional-local deities and rituals. The symbolic content of Hindu beliefs and practices varies from one cultural region to another. From the believer's point of view, the deities function as symbols of the sacred other that embody regional values and are used as models of ideal behavior as well as to resolve various existential crises. At an abstract level it is possible to identify the deities as "Hindu," to relate them to "other Hindu" deities, and also to theorize about the nature and function of all-India Hinduism.

Brahmanical priesthood has great significance in representing the moral, social, and political order of the society. The priesthood is located at the apex of the social class–value hierarchy *(varna)* and is conceptualized as a link between the divine and the mundane. The social class–value hierarchy represents degrees of ritual/spiritual purity and social prestige and is legitimized in belief and ritual by the Brahmanical priesthood. Ritually defiling or polluting occupations have the least religious merit, and the groups undertaking them are ranked low in the social class–value hierarchy. Groups that undertake the most polluting occupations are placed within the "Untouchable" category, which is considered outside the Hindu social class hierarchical system. Those associated with the most pure occupations are classed as Brahmins. In between the Brahmins and the Untouchables are *jati* groups of Kshatriya, Vaisiya, and Shudra categories. *Jati* groups with the greatest economic and political power in a region or locality are conceptualized as belonging to the Kshatriya category; those that engage in trade and have little political power despite economic affluence are of the Vaisiya category; artisan and laborer *jati* groups, with neither economic nor political power, constitute the Shudra category.

Jati groups of Brahmin, Kshatriya, and Vaisiya categories have access to the scriptures in Sanskrit, and such education is considered an essential aspect of spiritual perfection. Members of *jati* groups belonging to these categories are initiated into the Sanskritic scriptures and are conceptually related to the role model of *varnashrama-dharma*, which identifies the social and spiritual functions of the different groups as well as of individuals in the different stages of life. The role model of *varnashrama-dharma* is in turn related to the *karma-samsara* doctrine (cosmic causation and retributive justice linked to the cycle of birth and rebirth), which provides a rationale for the hierarchical social/moral order.

Several "revolts" against Brahmanical priesthood and authority and the *varna* hierarchical system occurred during the past 3,000 years in different regions of India. Jainism and Buddhism, which became the sectarian orientations of large numbers of people within and outside India, may be used as examples of the reassertion and revitalization of non- or pre-Indo-Aryan cultural forms, possibly the extension of Dravidian philosophies and rituals (of the pre-Aryan period) that challenged the *varna* system and Brahmanic priesthood and authority. Also, the various Bakhti cults as well as the many philosophical treatises of the past 2,500 years had a pronounced anti-Brahmanical and anti-hierarchical approach to Hinduism and social order. A number of sectarian movements arose at different times in different regions, often in protest against Brahmanical authority and the *varna* system, using the symbols of particular regional, cultural traditions. The tenth-century Saiva Siddhantha movement of Tamil culture in southern India, the Lingayat movement of the twelfth-century in the Kannada culture of southern India, and the sixteenth-century Caitanya movement of the Bengali culture in northeastern India are examples of this phenomenon. The leaders and followers of these movements used the vernacular, or the language of the different regions, but Sanskrit was occasionally used to systematize their doctrines.

Despite the various revolts against priestly hierarchy, the Hindu social order with the Brahmanical priesthood and the caste hierarchy continues to exist.

THE ALTERNATION OF SHAMANISTIC
AND PRIESTLY SACRED SELVES

LaBarre, in his provocative book *The Ghost Dance: The Origins of Religion* (1970), notes that "the ancestor of god is the shaman himself, both historically and psychologically" and argues that "each religion is the ghost dance of a traumatized society." The shaman, in his view, is non-normal and is preeminently suited to deal with non-normal situations. Various other scholars such as Wallace (1966) and Bourguignon (1976) have theorized about the personality of the shaman and about contexts in which shamanic performances occur.

The perspective of this book, however, is to interpret shamanism as an affirmation and cultural formulation of the biological and psychological referents of the symbols of the self as sacred, using the symbols of the sacred other for this purpose. The shamanistic self is universal; all human beings participate in this orientation to a lesser or greater degree in different contexts and in different situations. Rituals are an important part of the shamanistic orientation.

Priesthood may be interpreted as an affirmation and cultural formulation of the social referents of the symbols of the self as sacred, using the sacred other for this purpose. The priestly self is universal, and myths are an important part of this orientation.

The theoretical model of the sacred self proposed in this book illustrates how the symbols of the self are constructed as sacred in two different ways, affirming either the biological/psychological or social realities as sacred. The shaman is the prototype for total or partial union between the symbols of the self and the symbols of the sacred other. People differ in their capacity, inclination, and motivation to attain such a union; but in the ritual context, direct contact with sacred symbols is common.

In the various religious phenomena that we identify as divination, witchcraft, sorcery, healing, and ecstasy, the symbols of the sacred other are experienced, and shamanistic religious practitioners often become identified with the symbols of the sacred other. These activities are directly or indirectly connected with the health and sickness of an individual or group. The shamanistic self orientation is made important in contexts of individual and social stress. In initiation rituals as well as in other transition rituals and religious movements, people dramatize their involvement with the symbols of the sacred other through contact or union with the sacred other.

We can see the operation of the shamanistic orientation clearly in the context of religious movements. Religious movements arise when the health of individuals of a group is at stake. The messiah or religious leader of the group adopts the shamanistic orientation in forging a paradigm to bring back the people to health. The similarity between religious move-ments and rituals of various kinds has been noted by scholars such as Victor Turner (1969). In the liminal (middle) phase of rituals and in re-ligious movements, the priestly self is temporarily suspended. Religious movements in their beginning stages are seldom socially connected. The movements either reject the existing social forms or strive to change the social forms through a new cultural formulation of human life.

We find a remarkable difference between the expected behavior of priests and shamans, and a marked difference in how they dramatize their sacred selves. In most societies it is inconceivable that a priest would get drunk or run around naked in public and still retain his status as a priest, but such behavior might, in fact, enhance the efficacy of the shaman. "De-viant" behavior on the part of the priest has social consequences that threaten the "order" of the society, whereas "deviance" on the part of the shaman may in fact be a path toward successful achievement of the co-herence of the symbolic self in certain contexts. As Spiro (1967) notes in his study of shamanism in Burma, and as various other scholars have noted, the shaman is often considered to be "immoral" or "non-normal."

Some societies generate conventions specifying that people who are in communion with the symbols of the sacred other should be excluded from the "normal," practical everyday concerns of the society and that these individuals should be given importance only in "abnormal" or crisis situations. It is not uncommon for religious systems to develop structural differences in priesthood itself, with some priests concerned with the maintenance of social order and tradition and others with mystical con-templation and communion with the sacred symbols. The latter are often separated from the priestly hierarchy, and they function in monasteries, ashrams, and so on. The "world" religions such as Christianity, Hinduism, Buddhism, and Islam manifest the structural dichotomy of "priest-admin-istrator" and "priest-mystic." Occasionally, these categories overlap, and frequently these categories complement one another.

The shamanistic orientation gets greater emphasis in situations of crisis. the crisis may be an individual's health problems or transition, or the group's cultural disintegration arising from famine, epidemic, or warfare. The priest has traditional authority because people accept the tradition as "normal," and the symbols of the sacred other validate tradition through the priestly sacred self. The priest epitomizes the priestly sacred self, but even those who do not officiate as priests maintain the priestly sacred self to a lesser or greater degree because they uphold the tradition and the symbols of the sacred other, which validate the tradition, to a lesser or greater degree.

When social disruptions occur, the traditional authority structure crumbles along with questions about efficacy of the symbols of the sacred other. The symbols of the sacred other no longer represent the tradition, and the priestly sacred self has less or no significance. It is in such situations that prophets emerge, promoting the shamanistic sacred self through intense rituals that establish direct contact with new or modified symbols of the sacred other. People become ecstatic, experience a non-ordinary reality, and may engage in ritual self-immolation or ritual killings. Generally, the prophetic stage is followed by socially recognized new patterns of relationships, but occasionally prophets and/or their lieutenants perpetuate the shamanistic self and keep the followers from achieving symbolic coherence through other means.

SHAMANISM AND THE NEW AGE/HUMAN POTENTIAL MOVEMENTS IN THE UNITED STATES

Anthropologists have, for a long time, theorized about the parallels between the shamanistic healing practices and psychiatric counseling practices. Both types operationalize metaphoric associations to produce physiological and/or psychological responses. Moerman (1979) and Dow (1986) have offered plausible interpretations of the symbolic structures and psychological mechanisms that are involved in healing. Anthropologists have also occasionally viewed shamans as "holistic healers" who function as an alternative model for healing to the mechanistic, allopathic physician or surgeon who is seen as constrained by Cartesian assumptions about the separation of mind and body. Other professionals in Western tradition have also idealized the role and significance of shamans and shamanism.

In recent times, a few anthropologists and other scholars have invented the shaman as having social-moral functions, an association that, as we have seen earlier, seldom exists in non-urban cultures. Members of the "counter-culture" movements often reject, explicitly or implicitly, what they perceive to be Western cosmological and social systems and strive to promote a shamanistic worldview. Ethnographic data on shamanism are occasionally used by those disenchanted with the "conventional morality" of the West, and in recent times the shaman and shamanism have become significant symbols of various counter-culture, human-potential, self-actualization, and psycho-therapeutic movements as well as among certain celebrities, psychics, mediums (who call themselves channellers), new-age proponents, and academics who wish to keep an "open mind" on beliefs in extraterrestrial life, astrology, UFOs, poltergeists, the occult, out-of-body experiences, auras, spiritual healing, and "para-normal phenomena" in general. The individuals who are committed to glorifying or idealizing the shaman and shamanism believe, in varying degrees, in the existence of forces and forms that are beyond or outside the laws of nature and assert with varying degrees of certainty that these forces and forms can be comprehended by the mind through hallucinogenic drugs or through rigorous meditative or ritual techniques with assistance from a "guru," "master," or "spiritual guide."

The intellectual justification for the acceptance of the shamanistic self-orientation is often provided by various publications which promote the view that modern science has shackled the human spirit and that we are at the verge of a new age in which consciousness raising and altered states of consciousness will be accepted as a part of human development. To the "new age" intellectual, the shaman is one who journeys into the inner depths of the self or the psyche and one who is not shackled or constrained by the social and political conventions that prevent the growth and realization of the inner self.

The shaman has been reinvented as the primordial, eternal, existential hero not only by persons such as Carlos Casteneda (1970, 1971, 1972) and Florinda Donner (1982), whose anthropological credentials and authenticity of data have been challenged by many professional anthropologists, but also by professional anthropologists such as Michael Harner (1973, 1980) and Holger Kalweit (1988). Popular books and papers on the use of hallucinogenic mushrooms in central Asia and on the use of various psychotropic plants among native South and North American cultures have created an impression among some students of anthropology that there is a "separate reality" more real than the reality of everyday life. Casteneda's "non-ordinary reality" looms large in the consciousness of these students, who claim that just as an anthropologist studies and discovers the realities (worldviews) of other cultures, we should study and discover the worldview of the shaman. Thus, there are studies that show that when we understand the cognitive map of the shamanic reality, it is possible to understand or "see" how shamanic transformations, healings, and divinations occur, just as when we understand the symbols and symbolic classifications of an alien cultural tradition we can "see" the rationality of the alien beliefs and behavior.

Many complex societies such as those of China, India, Korea, and Tibet have institutionalized shamanistic orientations, but such orientations usually are kept outside of social boundaries. The tantric and yogic traditions of India, in which anti-nomial beliefs and practices are promoted, and the Tao tradition of China, which is associated with alchemy and magic, are generally for people who function outside the traditional social order. In Korean society, shamanism is institutionalized in the organization called *sinkyo*, and there exists a class of women shamans known as *mutangs*, but their cultural significance is not great. In the traditional Tibetan tradition, the Lama is a reincarnated shaman who has the supernatural ability to defy space and time. Lamaistic shamanism combined with Buddhism and became the dominant religious orientation with different types of beliefs concerning the dead and the spirit world that were formalized in various sects and monasteries. Max Weber's books *The Religion of China* (1951) and *The Religion of India* (1958) provide some of the best interpretations of the coexistence of priestly and mystical/shamanic traditions of these two countries, elucidating how psychologically oriented nature-cults and the socially oriented religions have coexisted for centuries.

It is possible to interpret the Western intellectual involvement with mystical/shamanistic orientations, and the anthropological reinvention of the shaman, as vehicles of shamanistic symbolic self integration or coherence that frequently occurs in a social context of stress and anxiety. In the next chapter I present a detailed discussion of religious movements and suggest that a pattern of association links the shamanistic self orientation, cultural formulations of psychological/biological processes as sacred, and religious movements.

CHAPTER TWELVE
Disintegration and Reintegration of the Symbols of the Sacred Other and the Sacred Self

THE SYMBOLS
OF THE SACRED OTHER
AND THE SACRED SELF

Religious movements can be conceptualized as laboratories for the study of why and how symbols of the sacred other and the sacred self are constructed and maintained, and for the study of the alternation of shamanistic and priestly selves. In this section I discuss anthropological explanations of religious movements, in particular that of Wallace (1969), in order to illustrate how new or modified symbols of the sacred other and the sacred self are created and maintained.

In the last section of this chapter I offer brief descriptions and interpretations of two Afro-American polytheistic religious movements, namely, the Voodoo movement of Haiti and the Batuque movement of Brazil.

Anthropological descriptions and theories of religious movements are largely based on the study of non-urban (technologically primitive) societies that came into contact with the West through colonization after the fifteenth century. As these societies lost their political and economic autonomy, their social organization and culture changed, and prophets frequently emerged who promised to save the people from the accompanying disintegration of the symbols of the sacred other and the sacred self. As Norbeck (1961: 231) points out:

> The circumstances under which [religious movements] have emerged appear everywhere to be much alike, unrest and demoralization as a result of contact with Europeans and Americans, the loss of much of traditional culture without satisfactory adjustment to newly introduced ways, and often also great loss of life from warfare with the newcomers and the diseases introduced by them.

Anthropological study of religious movements is, therefore, intimately connected with the study of a particular kind of sociocultural change generated as a result of contact between West and non-West. In the early twentieth century, American anthropologists began using the concept of acculturation, which identified types of processes such as the incorporation of alien cultural traits (assimilation), the synthesis of native and alien cultural traits (syncretism), and the reaction against alien cultural traits (nativism or revivalism of old cultural traits). Assimilation, syncretism, and revivalism were often fostered by religious movements.

All social "movements" are characterized by collective efforts to bring about change. Ideally, they are self-conscious attempts to create a satisfying society or culture and an integrated or coherent symbolic self. We use the term *religious movements* when participants undertake such efforts in the name of religion, using existing sacred symbols in a new way or creating new sacred symbols to foster new or modified conceptions of the sacred self and to formulate a new way of life.

Cultural contact is not the only context that generates religious movements. Such movements can arise in societies in which internal factors such as famine conditions, epidemics, and other calamities cause a group to lose faith in its sacred symbols. Scholars have argued that certain kinds of millenarian religious orientations promote the development of religious movements as an ongoing process in some societies. I discuss these arguments in a later section. In the following paragraphs I discuss some of the anthropological views of religious movements.

Ralph Linton (1943), in discussing the factors that generate religious movements, notes that they arise as a result of reaction to an alien or dominant culture when the contact situation involves dominance and subordination. Linton (1943: 232) distinguishes between nativistic and non-nativistic religious movements by pointing out:

> In the nativistic movements the anticipated millennium is modeled directly on the past, usually with certain additions and modifications, and the symbols which are manipulated to bring it about are more or less familiar ele-

ments of the culture to which new meanings have been attached. In non-nativistic movements, the millennial conditions are represented as something new and unique and the symbols manipulated to bring it about tend to be new and unfamiliar.

He offers the following fourfold typology of nativistic movements with reference to whether the movements aim to revive or perpetuate cultural forms and whether this effort is performed through rational or magical means: (1) revivalistic-magical, (2) revivalistic-rational, (3) perpetuative-magical, and (4) perpetuative-rational.

Wallace (1956, 1966) proposes the term *revitalization movement* to include the variously labeled religious movements. He points out that nativistic movements, millenarian movements, reformative movements, and the like are not mutually exclusive phenomena. The dimensions of the movements vary, some aiming to restore the millennium, some to incorporate values of the alien or dominant culture, some to syncretize values for the in-group alone, and others to realize the utopia or the millennium in the distant future. But all of them manifest a similar processual structure that Wallace identifies as "revitalization." Religious movements undermine the existing institutions not with the aim of destroying the society but to bring about a new and meaningful integration through "manipulation of the real world." Wallace contends that "since revitalization becomes central to the analysis of the development of new religions, new denominations, new sects, new cults . . . it is attractive to speculate that all religions and religious productions, such as myths, and rituals, came into existence as parts of the program or code of revitalization movements" (1966: 30).

Wallace's (1956, 1966) significant contribution is his identification of the processual structure of revitalization in religious movements. When conditions of stress exist, a prophet emerges with a new cultural paradigm that if accepted becomes a new social reality or social order. Wallace delineates the sequential stages in the development of religious movements as follows: (1) steady state of culture, (2) period of individual stress, (3) period of cultural distortion, (4) revitalization, and (5) new steady state of culture.

Aberle (1966) rejects the feasibility of explaining religious movements as caused by boredom, utilitarian desires, or spiritual needs. He suggests that when there is a negative "discrepancy between legitimate expectation and actuality," the people may contemplate an ideal society in isolation or the violent overthrow of the existing social order (1966: 326). He points out that religious movements are activities of socially deprived groups aimed at "remedial action to overcome the discrepancy" (1962: 211). Deprivation is felt by members of a group only in relation to another group, which may happen to be the dominant one. Deprivation is relative in other terms also. The Ghost Dance Religion did not find adherents among the Navaho because although the political system was shattered, "relatively few were adversely affected by the loss of status in the process" (1966: 41). Also, Navahos have an abhorrence of death and ghosts that may have made them less receptive to the movement.

Aberle (1966) distinguished between transformative and redemptive movements, identifying the former as characterized by efforts to transform the natural and social order and the latter as characterized by efforts to achieve inner spiritual changes in the individual and "search for a new individual state." Jorgensen (1972) applies Aberle's model to interpret the Ghost Dance Movement as a transformative movement and the Sun Dance Movement as a redemption movement.

Anthropological descriptions include ethnohistorical accounts of the movements, as well as descriptions of the movements based on partici-pant-observation. These descriptions often provide detailed descriptions of the cultural patterns, themes, worldviews, and ethos as well as descrip-tions of political, economic, kinship, and religious organization. Through these studies we understand why certain types of movements become popular, why certain themes were emphasized by the leaders of the move-ments, and why the movements failed or succeeded.

Anthropologists have described movements that arose among indige-nous societies of the New World (in both South and North America), and most anthropological monographs written in the twentieth century contain information about the processes of change, including religious changes, generated from cultural contact. The Peyote Religious Movement (Native American Church) has been studied by several anthropologists (e.g., La-Barre 1969, Aberle 1966, and Slotkin 1956).

Anthropologists have also described and theorized about the signifi-cance of Oceanic religious movements, collectively known as Cargo Cult Movements, and we have detailed descriptions of movements such as the Hau Hau Movement among the Maori. (See, for example, Worsley 1957, Burridge 1960, and Lesson 1952.) The religious-political movements in Af-rica, Asia, and Europe have been investigated by sociologists, political scientists, historians, and anthropologists. (See, for example, Sundkler 1948, Fuchs 1965, and Farquhar 1929.) Anthropological papers and books that describe or theorize about religious movements include Aberle 1962, 1966; Allen 1974; Barber 1941; Beckford 1977; Barnett 1957; Cohn 1962; Collins 1950; Hill 1944; Lanternari 1963, 1974; Linton 1943; Mair 1959; Schwartz 1962; Slotkin 1956; Spindler 1952; Stanner 1958; and Thrupp 1962.

H.G. Barnett's *Indian Shakers* (1957), D. Aberle's *The Peyote Religion Among the Navaho* (1966), K.O.L. Burridge's *Mambu: A Melanesian Millen-nium* (1960) and A.F.C. Wallace's *The Death and Rebirth of the Seneca* (1969) are some of the best anthropological accounts of religious movements.

Wallace's book (1969) illustrates some of the distinctive features of the anthropological study of religious movements. The book is about the Seneca, their decline and cultural disintegration, and the emergence of a prophet named Handsome Lake who in the nineteenth century helped save the Seneca from extinction by founding a religious movement called The Old Way of Handsome Lake. This new Indian religion combined Iroquois and Christian religious elements. Of the approximately 20,000 Seneca living in New York, Quebec, and Ontario, about 5,000 are followers of the Old Way of Handsome Lake. The followers of the Old Way are sometimes called Longhouse People or the Pagans. Handsome Lakers sometimes attend Christian church services, and they invite Christians to attend theirs. They believe that there is good in both religions. The headquarters of the Old Way religion, a churchlike structure which was 150 years old when Wallace wrote the book, is on the Seneca reservation in New York.

The Seneca were one of the five or six Iroquois tribes united in a loose confederation. During the seventeenth and eighteenth centuries the Iroquois occupied extensive territory in northeastern North America and were involved as allies in the battles between the French and the English. The most prosperous of the different tribes of the northeastern region, they engaged in fur trade and were militarily the most powerful of all the tribes in North America. Their custom of blood-feud kept them constantly at war with tribes that did not come under the Iroquois confederation. The war council was composed of men and women, but war chiefs (men) often defied the rulings of peace-keeping councils, and frequent fighting depleted the number of men. Nomadic warriors often wandered off to distant places in search of their ideal manhood, searching out external enemies to demonstrate their valor and kin obligations. A matrilineal system and sexually tolerant orientation were important features of Iroquois society and culture; child-rearing practices included the swaddling of infants.

Iroquois religion traditionally had three types of rituals: (1) rituals of thanksgiving, (2) rituals of dreams, and (3) rituals of fear and mourning. The religion of the Iroquois enabled them to act out normally disallowed wishes. "In the opinion of the Iroquois themselves, these rituals prevented both mental illness and social disorder." Wallace notes that "Iroquois religion tended to be a means by which the disappointments and sacrifices entailed by living up to the ideal of autonomous responsibility could to some extent be compensated."

The rituals of thanksgiving were seasonal (calendrical) and were performed six times a year to express thanks to the spirit beings and hope that the spirits would continue to provide them with strawberries, green corn, and other staples. The ritual performed in midwinter was a testimonial to the creator, to give thanks for the blessings of the past year, and a supplication for future enjoyment.

The rituals of dreams were performed with the assumption that dreams provided guidance. The Iroquois had great respect for dreams and believed that secret desires of the soul were manifested in dreams. They distinguished between conscious and unconscious desires. They recognized the power of unconscious desires and were aware that frustration of desire could cause mental and physical illness. Wallace notes, "The Iroquois theory of dreams was basically psychoanalytic." He also observes, "Intuitively, the Iroquois had achieved a great degree of psychological sophistication." Iroquois medicine men were psychiatrists who penetrated the soul to discover the natural causes of desires and prescribe natural remedies. The Iroquois classified dreams into two categories, symptomatic and visitation dreams. The latter were visits from supernatural beings that could make people into prophets. Symptomatic dreams were revelations to act out, symbolically and literally, one's wishes.

Rituals of fear and mourning included practices to prevent witchcraft, to seek protection of a guarding spirit, and to seek cures. Rituals were also performed for protection against the dead, who were considered dangerous, and there were elaborate burial and mourning rituals.

The decline of the Iroquois began in the mid–eighteenth century. The policy of Iroquois neutrality came to an end when the Iroquois gave trading privileges to the English in 1740, and when the French retaliated, beginning in 1749. By the end of the eighteenth century, when the Americans won the war against the English (with whom the Iroquois had allied themselves), the Iroquois had lost everything. The establishment of the reservation system cost the Iroquois their economic and political autonomy, resulting in major changes in the traditional authority structures. Depopulation from war, disease, and starvation increased, as did psychological problems. Alcoholism became widespread, and accusation and fear of witchcraft increased—a collective paranoia had set in. It was in this context that Handsome Lake emerged as a prophet.

Handsome Lake grew up in an unvanquished Seneca tribal unit. He experienced visitation dreams, had visions of his journey to and meeting with Jesus, and proclaimed the Apocalyptic Gospel and a second Social Gospel. The first gospel included the teaching of the imminent destruction of the world, the definition of sin, and the prescription for salvation. Handsome Lake led a crusade against witchcraft. The second gospel proclaimed the good way of life. The heart of the Handsome Lake religion is the Gaiwiio, the good word, which is memorized and passed on.

Wallace, in a comprehensive analysis of the apocalyptic and social gospels of the prophet Handsome Lake, shows how Handsome Lake used the Seneca themes and symbols (interpretation of dreams, visions, rituals of thanksgiving and mourning) to introduce Christian themes such as sin, salvation, and punishment. Handsome Lake proposed major changes in Seneca beliefs and rituals; he rejected the role of medicine societies and mourning ceremonies and led a crusade against witchcraft.

In all of these proposed ritual innovations it is noteworthy that Handsome Lake was minimizing the traditional ceremonial opportunities for cathartic relief of the unsatisfied wishes of the soul. He disapproved of the False Faces and of other old and new medicine societies that had been formed in response to dreams; he deplored the indulgence of romantic fancies by the use of love magic; he grimly opposed any use of alcohol; he wished to do away with prolonged mourning. He demanded the repression of desire rather than its usual satisfaction and offered in place of human beings the more abstract images of the Creator and Punisher, of heaven and hell, and of the prophet as the objects of strivings for dependency. (Wallace 1969: 253)

Handsome Lake's social gospel was a combination of Seneca social ethics, Jeffersonian government policies, and the Quaker ethos. After 1800, Handsome Lake was more concerned with social matters: "The main values that the social gospel inculcated were temperance, peace and unity, land retention, acculturation, and a revised domestic morality" (Wallace 1969: 278).

Handsome Lake emphasized the social needs to foster (1) temperance, (2) peaceful coexistence and social solidarity, (3) protection of the tribe's territory, (4) economic transformation, or the shift from the traditional pattern of male–hunting and female–horticulture to male–agriculture and female–housekeeping, and (5) the stability of the nuclear family, focusing on domestic morality. This last, fifth aspect of the social gospel had a profound structural significance. It deemphasized father–son and husband–wife relationships. As Wallace (1969: 284) notes:

. . . in order to stabilize the nuclear family it was necessary to loosen the tie between mother and daughter. Furthermore, men were supposed to assume the role of heads of families, being economically responsible for their wives and children and not frittering away their energies on strong drink, gambling, dancing, and philandering, nor on mother-in-law trouble.

Handsome Lake died in 1815, the last decade of his life marked by political decline in his power among the Seneca. But he and his disciples were successful in carrying "the good word to other Iroquois reservations, and even to other tribes, and initiated a dramatic renaissance of Iroquois society" (Wallace 1969: 263). A generation after his death, his disciples "collated and revived his words and made them into the code of a new religion, a religion that survives today as Gaiwiio—The Old Way of Handsome Lake" (Wallace 1969: 303).

Handsome Lake succeeded in constructing new sacred symbols of the other and enabled his followers to interact with these symbols in constructing symbols of the sacred self. Initially, his orientation was shamanistic, but through formulations of ethical and moral conventions his movement acquired characteristics of the priestly orientation.

RELIGIOUS MOVEMENTS AND
THE MILLENARIAN THEODICY

In the foregoing discussion of the Handsome Lake movement, it is clear that prophets draw upon their distinctive historical, cultural heritage in formulating new symbols of the sacred other. The cultural specificity in the representation of new symbols of the sacred other is evident in how religious movements succeed in attracting followers. Also, certain cultural formulations about the problem and resolution of suffering as well as certain formulations about what happens to human life after death are conducive for the frequent, ongoing emergence of prophets who claim to have found a new way to deal with human suffering and death. The study of the rise and development of Christianity can contribute to an understanding of how the cultural formulations about suffering and death acquire distinctive features in different prophetic interpretations, how diverse interpretations emerge, and how a religious movement becomes linked with social-political orders.

Several scholars have pointed out that the millenarian theodicy (explanation of suffering with reference to the realization of happiness in the future) is conducive to "militant" religious movements. The absence of such a theodicy in places like China and India has had different consequences for the resolution of economic deprivation or social injustice. The following quotation describes the nature of the millenarian theodicy.

> The messianic-millenarian complex posits a theodicy by relativizing the suffering or injustice of the present in terms of their being overcome in a glorious future. In other words, the anomic phenomena are legitimated by reference to a future nomization, thus re-integrating them within an over all meaningful order. (Berger 1969: 69)

Cohn (1962) indicates that certain theodicies, such as the Hindu theodicy of karma, are capable of restricting millenarian aspirations, in contrast to the theodicies of Judaism, Christianity, and Islam, which encourage millenarian fantasies in times of stress and anxiety. Cohn (1962), in his significant study of medieval millenarism in Europe, attempts to show that there is little difference between the millenarian beliefs that prevailed during the Middle Ages and the nationalistic or socialistic ideologies of today. He advances the view that "for all their exploitation of the most modern technology, communism and nazism have been inspired by phantasies which are downright archaic" (1962: 309). Elucidating the many similarities between the millenarian movements and secular revolutionary movements, and drawing upon the parallels in ideology between these movements, Cohn arrives at the conclusion that "what Marx passed on to present day communism was not the fruit of long years of study in the fields of economics and sociology but a quasi-apocalyptic phantasy which as a young man, unquestioningly and almost unconsciously, he had assimilated from the crowd of obscure writers and journalists" (1961: 311).

According to Cohn (1962), millenarian movements are basically irrational means of expressing the psychological and social deprivations meted out by groups of people in the society. Millenarism, he holds, is a belief that gains credence under unbearable stress and anxiety in society. He contends that Nazism, Communism, or any other form of totalitarian movements could not have arisen where different groups of people were integrated and firmly rooted to traditional loyalties. Prophets could be effective only in "certain social situations." He notes that firmly integrated groups of the lower strata, although they may experience severe oppression, are less prone to accept millenarism as a way of solving their problems than are the surplus rural and urban populations that are not integrated to any particular group.

Worsley (1957, 1967) states that the emergence of millenarian movements reflects political consciousness among people living in "stateless" and "segmented" societies. He suggests that these movements should be studied as "rational" attempts by groups of people to solve irrational social conditions. The aspirations of the people are not to be regarded as fantasies stemming from an irrational and emotional milieu; they are "desperate searchings for more and more effective ways of understanding and modifying the environment" (1967: 345). Worsley defines millenarian movements as "movements in which the imminence of a radical and supernatural change in the social order is prophesied or expected, so as to lead to organization and activity, carried out in preparation for this event, on the part of the movement's adherents" (1967: 338). Millenarian movements arise among people who are not able to find satisfaction in the existing social order, and particularly among those barred from wielding authority in the existing social order. Referring to the Taiping Revolution in China, to the Ghost Dance Movement and other Prophetic Movements in North America, to the Cargo Cults in Oceania, to the Peasant Revolts in Europe, and to the Millenarian Movements of the European Middle Ages, Worsley points out that these movements arose either among the groups that were divided into discrete units, resembling "segmented" societies, or among the "stateless" societies lacking a unitary form of political organization.

Hobsbawm (1959) argues that millenarian movements arise notably among people who are socially deprived. He also observes that because there is a uniformity or regularity in the occurrence of these movements, they can be studied as phenomena of social change. While making a distinction between banditry and criminal organization on the one hand and anarchism, peasant communism, and labor sects on the other, Hobsbawm regards the former as a "cry of vengeance on the rich and the oppressors," aiming at justice and "not a new and perfect world." He considers the latter to be the articulation of "pre-political people who have not yet found, or only begun to find a specific language to express their aspirations about the world" (1959: 2–5). In his studies of Lazzarettism of nineteenth-century Italy, the Andalusian Anarchists Movement of Spain, and the Peasant Communism of Italy, Hobsbawm demonstrates that the Peasant Communism of Italy had a specific ideology of equalitarianism and a program for establishing a new social order, whereas the former two movements were considered heresies. On the basis of these studies Hobsbawm makes a distinction between movements that are either "reformist" or "revolutionary." Because the reformist movements do not strive to effect a transformation in the social order ad because they do not work to bring about an entirely new social order, they are not strictly millenarian movements. He suggests that in many instances, suppression of revolutionary movements leads to their becoming reformist movements. Conversely, the reformist movements in many instances laid the basis for the revolutionary movements, and according to this typology, reformist movements may be conceived as representing the first stage in the emergence of revolutionary movements.

Talmon (1962) attempts to demonstrate the relationship between millenarian movements and social change. Millenarism, she holds, is essentially "a connecting link between pre-political and political movements" (1962: 143). She contends that millenarism shares with secular revolutionism its emphasis on changing the existing social order, and secular revolutionism shares with millenarism its expectations of the fulfillment of the ideals. Both secular revolutionism and millenarism result from acute deprivation and disintegration of primary groups. Talmon holds that studies on millenarian movements can be carried out only through a combination of diachronic and synchronic analysis.

Mair (1959) notes that no distinction need be made between those movements that preach an immediate millennium and those that seek the millennium in the distant future. She observes that millenarian movements are usually opposed to the established religious institutions that validate the existing social order; they either modify the elements of the established beliefs or try to bring new elements into it.

Boardman (1962) points out that millenarian theodicy was introduced in the belief-system of the followings of the Taiping Rebellion at a late stage in its development. While the ideology of the Taiping Rebellion was greatly influenced by Buddhist, Confucian, Taoist, and, to a lesser extent, Christian eschatology, the "organizers of the Taiping movement realized the importance of an adequate eschatology and therefore set about constructing a system of reward and retribution in the hereafter" (1962: 73). The leaders made use of a modified form of the Christian concept of sin to mobilize the believers. "Taiping religion existed for two purposes, to provide other worldly solace and to inspire the realization of a Taiping heaven on earth" (1962: 77).

RELIGIOUS MOVEMENTS AND COMMUNITAS

The early phase of religious movements is characterized by the prophet promoting a shamanistic orientation through various rituals that foster contact and merger or union between the symbols of the sacred other (which could be the prophet) an the symbols of the self, separating the participants from preexisting social conventions. Unless this orientation is continued with the separation of the followers from socially organized activities, religious movements acquire organizational structures that promote priestly orientations. The ritual-shamanistic orientation of religious movements is analogous to rituals in general in the sense that participants are temporarily separated from the structured social conventions.

Victor Turner (1920–1983) has written extensively on the theme that religious movements are processes similar to rituals of transition. He elaborates upon the seminal contributions of Arnold van Gennep (1873–1957), who in his book *The Rites of Passage* (1960) points out that rituals dramatize the importance or significance of transition but are important vehicles for the maintenance of social continuity because they help to reintegrate into society individuals who experience changes in their life situations. According to van Gennep, rites of passage involve the passage or movement of individuals from an old social stage to a new stage. The middle period between the old and new is a liminal phase, and in Turner's analysis the liminal phase fosters the emergence of "communitas" among the participants. Turner notes that "liminality" and "communitas" constitute important aspects of religious movements as well as rituals.

In the liminal phase of rituals, the participants are "neither here nor there" and are between past and future social structural positions.

> The attributes of liminality or of liminal personae ("threshold people") are necessarily ambiguous, since this condition and these persons elude or slip through the network of classifications that normally locate stages and positions in cultural space. Liminal entities are neither here nor there; they are betwixt and between the positions assigned and arrayed by law, custom, and ceremonial. (Turner 1969: 95)

Turner (1969: 96–97) suggests that religious movements have the attributes of ritual transition (liminality) and that the liminal phase in both rituals and religious movements produces the communitas. Communitas is "unstructured or rudimentarily structured and relatively undifferentiated," and the participants experience "communion of equal individuals who submit together to the general authority of the ritual process." Society, as it is manifested in communitas, acquires the state of sanctity, where wrongs are righted, the mighty are humbled, the weak made powerful, and everyone is equal. Turner suggests that "social life is a type of dialectical process that involves successive experience of high and low, communitas and structure, homogeneity and differentiation, equality and inequality."

Millenarian movements exhibit the attributes of communitas that emerges in tribal rituals and in the lifestyle of American "hippies" who stress personal communion and low status over structured relationships. Structured societies like those of the Tallensi, the Nuer, and the Ashanti in South Africa, and groups in India, have the dimension of communitas expressed through rituals of various kinds. Liminality and, in turn, communitas emerge in times of rapid social change and in the rituals of tribal societies, as well as through the conceptual and ritual formulations of charismatic leaders.

Both communitas and structure are necessary: Whereas communitas purifies and rejuvenates the society, structure maintains continuity and order in society. In simple societies both communitas and structure are complementary to each other—that is, rituals reinforce structure, thereby reducing the chances of either existing independent of the other. In technologically elaborate societies, because of greater latitude in social relationships, existential communitas may emerge and have a separate, although temporary, existence.

Turner distinguishes three types of communitas: "existential," or "spontaneous" communitas; "normative" communitas; and "ideological" communitas. "Both normative and ideological communitas are already within the domain of structure, and it is the fate of all spontaneous communitas in history to undergo what most people see as a 'decline and fall' into structure and law" (Turner 1969: 132). The liminal phase of crisis rites falls in the realm of normative communitas. In history several men voluntarily became "outsiders" and tried to establish and perpetuate the communitas. For example, St. Francis of Assisi in the thirteenth century renounced property, a symbol of social position, and strove to keep the liminal phase a permanent state. Caitanya, a Hindu mystic of the fifteenth century, broke the sex laws of orthodox Hinduism, became casteless, and tried to do away with structured relationships. But in the course of time the movements begun by these men acquired structure. Men like Buddha, Mahavira, Gandhi, Tolstoy, and St. Francis held structurally high stations before their rejection of these estates. Turner holds that:

Those who feel the burdens of office, who have by birth or achievement come to occupy central positions in structure, may well feel that rituals and religious beliefs that stress the stripping or dissolution of structural ties and obligations offer what many historical religions call "release." (Turner 1969: 200)

In a later work, Turner (1974) points out that the concepts of liminality and communitas identify the existence of culturally sanctioned "anti-structure" in relation to structure and states that "gnosis, 'deep knowledge,' is highly characteristic of liminality. . . ." (Turner 1974: 250).

I pointed out earlier that shamanism affirms the cultural formulations of bio-psychological processes as sacred, using the symbols of the sacred other to represent such processes, and that the shamanistic sacred self represents a total or partial union with sacred symbols. Religious movements, in the perspective of this book, temporarily suspend the specific linkages with the existing social processes, and the priestly (social) sacred self is non-operationalized. New symbols of the sacred other are created and preexisting symbols of the sacred self are transformed in the processes generated by religious movements. The processes foster the creation of a community, often in opposition to the preexisting structure. The followers of the movement reject the preexisting structure, or perceive the structure as disintegrating or as not meaningful, and seek to promote the emergence of new knowledge of human life and identity. This occurs generally as the prophet becomes the symbol of the sacred other for representing the sacred human identity; initially the followers merge their sacred selves with the prophet, and gradually new structures become established with the symbols of the sacred other and the sacred self representing the new social conventions.

THE SIGNIFICANCE OF PROPHETS AS METAPHORS

Clifford Geertz, as we have seen, has contributed extensively to the anthropological study of religion. In his book *Islam Observed* (1969), he discusses the role of the prophet with examples from Morocco and Indonesia. The prophets are symbols or, more appropriately, metaphors, that represent multiple historical, social, and cultural images of the people. Their biographies are transformed to create systems of meaning with regard to what the people believe to be true spirituality. Geertz describes how this transformation occurs with reference to the sixteenth-century Javanese prince named Sunan Kalidjaga, and a seventeenth-century Berber mystic named Sidi Lahsen Lyusi.

In the history of any cultural tradition we can find many symbols or metaphors that people use to conceptualize their sacred selves. These metaphors are significant in their fusing several domains of experience in a manner that they serve as paradigms of human life, frameworks to understand the nature of the world and human existence as well as the meaning of historical changes, suffering, injustice, and so on.

CULTS AND RELIGIOUS MOVEMENTS

The term *cult* is often used by sociologists to characterize groups formed to promote particular religious beliefs and rituals that are subordinated to the will of the leader. The beliefs and rituals may be "anti-nomial" in the sense that they may be contrary to the normative aspects of a society. Cults may operate as separate, peripheral entities of a society, or as specific secret organizations within the society with elaborate rituals requiring initiation. Cults can have different functions. Thus we can speak of the "satanic cults" of the West that reverse the normative liturgy, the Sakti cults of India that blur social and sexual distinctions, the mystery cults of ancient Greece that dealt with oracular knowledge, the Katchina cult of the Hopi that imparted sacred values, and the various Hindu and Christian cults (such as the Hare Krishna or Holy Ghost People) that have dotted the American scene during the past five decades. (See Mary Daugherty's discussion of the Holy Ghost People in her article "Serpent Handling As Sacrament" 1976: 232–243).

Sociologists also use a typological model of religious organization, with cults at one end of the continuum and the ecclesia at the other end, with sects and denominations in the middle. The assumption behind such a typology is that the cult is a type of religious organization, with specific characteristics, that may transform into a sect and denomination as it acquires other characteristics.

The distinguishing feature of a cult is that it relies on cultural formulations of psychological aspects and is shamanistic (as I have defined the term). In fact, some of the various psychological movements of the past fifty years, such as est, have cultlike features, and similarly, religious movements in their early phases have cultlike features. We can theorize that religious movements are cultural formulations that make psychological processes sacred and that they become social movements and are established, in some instances, as social and/or political orders.

The following discussion sheds light on the cultlike features of religious movements.

Simpson (1962) in his study "The Ras Tafari Movement in Jamaica and

Its Millennial Aspects" suggests that cult activity is an escape mechanism for the disinherited, that followers of the movement find an outlet for their emotional tensions through violent or passive aggression in the form of self-induced trance and other mortifications. Kaminsky (1962) observes that because cults occur under conditions in which people experience psychological alienation, the cults should be analyzed in relation to particular psychological and social relationships. He points out that ". . . the principle of self-preservation requires the movement to maintain its total separation from the existing social order, by various forms of internal and external withdrawal, or by putting itself into a posture of violent nihilism vis-a-vis the establishment" (Kaminsky 1962: 215). The "Holy Ghost People," from the southern United States, whose church services include handling serpents and fire and drinking strychnine, are members of a Protestant Christian denomination that is "cultlike." They justify their rituals as part of the Christian teaching, found in the bible (St. Mark's gospel).

For other references to cults, see Adler and Hammett 1973; Bromley and Shupe 1981; Cambell 1978; Campbell 1977; Conway and Siegelman 1978; Cox 1977; Eister 1972; Glock and Bellah 1976; King 1972; Singer 1979; and Wallis 1974, 1975, 1976.

AFRO-AMERICAN POLYTHEISTIC RELIGIOUS MOVEMENTS

Caribbean and South American societies in which large numbers of Africans were used for slave labor produced Afro-American communities with distinctive cultural traditions. In these communities, African religious beliefs and practices coexist with Roman Catholic beliefs and practices; in some instances there has been synthesis or fusion of the diverse beliefs and practices, and in other instances a kind of religious pluralism or polytheism has developed. The Roman Catholic church, with its orientation of "saint worship," has been able to sustain, in different countries, a kind of tolerance of the incorporation of "indigenous" and "alien" deities into lower ranks of spirituality, but the church has frowned upon religious pluralism or polytheism that promotes "cultist rituals" dedicated to the worship of gods, godlings, and spirits and the practice of witchcraft and sorcery. Despite the official condemnation of such beliefs and practices, the believers in these polytheistic religious orientations consider themselves good Catholics. Often, the polytheistic orientation functions as a secret or private affair, and the public expression of spirituality corresponds to the Roman Catholic orientation.

Two polytheistic movements, the Voodoo cult of Haiti and the Batuque cult of Brazil, may be viewed as "syncretic religious" or as "shamanistic religious." These cults also resemble the religious beliefs and practices that occur in economically impoverished peasant villages in India, China, and Africa—thus raising the possibility that they are "religions of the oppressed peoples." Possession by spirits, divination, shamanistic symbology, and ritual healing are central aspects of these religions.

Voodoo gods and spirits are largely derived from the Yoruba Fon, Ibo, and Dahomean cultural traditions of West Africa. However, the gods and spirits have undergone major transformation. (See Karen Brown's essay "Voodoo" [1987].) Alfred Metraux (1972: 28, 362), in a detailed description and interpretation of Voodoo polytheism in Haiti, notes that in the Voodoo pantheon the "main divinities are still classified according to the tribe or region [in West Africa] from which they originate." The term *voodoo* is derived from the concept of *vodu* in Dahomey and Togo (West Africa): "[I]n Dahomey and Togo, among tribes belonging to the Fon language group, a 'Voodoo' is a 'god,' a 'spirit,' a 'sacred object,' in short all those things which the European understands by the word 'fetish.'"

Voodoo mythology and ritual derive from the Dahomean and other West African cultural archetypes of spirituality and power; the model of ritual specialists also is derived from the West African traditions. The priest (*hungan*) and priestess (*mambo*) have their followers "who voluntarily place themselves" under their authority. In the history of Haiti, revolutionary prophets and political leaders have frequently been associated with Voodoo religion, and this association was made explicitly when François Duvalier (Papa Doc) became the president in 1957. Papa Doc apparently practiced Voodooism, and he was known as having supernatural powers because of this association. (Papa Doc died in 1971.)

Some other distinguishable aspects of Voodooism are: elaborate initiation rituals, food offerings to the gods and spirits, spirit possession, worship of twins (believed to be supernatural—like the Nuer belief), cult of the dead, witchcraft, healing rituals, cult of sorceress. Metraux (1972: 323) notes: "Once when I asked a fervent Catholic whether he had finally finished with Voodoo, he replied that he would always be faithful to the Catholic Church but nothing could make him give up the worship of *loa* [spirits] who had always protected his family."

Another polytheistic Afro-American religion, called Batuque, is described in *Spirits of the Deep: A Study of an Afro-Brazilian Cult* (Leacock and Leacock 1975) as "a contemporary non-Christian religious sect found in Belem, Brazil." Batuque is one of several religious movements existing in urban Brazil that are labeled "Afro-Brazilian" to signify their linkage to both African and Roman Catholic cultural traditions. These sects can be identified as syncretic religious movements: They have adopted various diverse religious beliefs and rituals but have, in every region, formed a coherent system of beliefs and rituals. The Leacocks (1975: 2) note that "the development of these Afro-American religions has gone far beyond the mere borrowing stage, and in each local area a coherent, integrated system of belief has developed that is in some ways distinctive." The term *batuque* refers to the ritual of possession: Devotees get together and perform the ritual of possession with skeptics and believers witnessing the ritual.

> A visitor to a modern *batuque* should be prepared to witness a ceremony which has very little to do with the slaves or with Africa. The cult, of which the *batuque* is the central ceremony, has become a Brazilian religion, practiced by Brazilians, and dedicated to a group of supernatural beings most of whom have Brazilian names and speak only Portuguese. (Leacock and Leacock 1975: 3)

There is some confusion in how believers of Batuque religion and "outsiders" identify the religion.

> Today outsiders may occasionally call the cult "Batuque" but more frequently use the name "Macumba," adopting the term used in Rio de Janeiro for the Afro-Brazilian sects there. In Belem, the term "Macumba" has a somewhat derogatory connotation, perhaps the equivalent of "voodoo" in English, and cult members only employ the term when joking about themselves. When speaking more seriously, adherents call their religion either "Mina" or "Nago" or "Umbando." (Leacock and Leacock 1975: 50)

Batuque mythology-ritual complex is characterized by the existence of a set of ranked spirits called *encantado*. The *encantado* are different from the spirits of the saints (related to the Catholic tradition) who are worshipped along with the supreme god (who is identified with Jesus) and the Virgin Mary. The *encantado* are a class of spirits of the underworld, as opposed to the saints who are spirits of the heavens. There are several types of *encantado* who have specified or designated characteristics, and they can be harmful or can serve as guardians or spirit helpers in a variety of possession-states.

> The encantados are thought to live below the surface of the earth or seas in their own special dwelling places called *encantarias*. The nature and location of the *encantaria* varies with the type of encantado. American Indian encantados live in villages in the depths of virgin forests; water spirits have their *encantarias* under water in rivers, lakes, or the sea; while still other encantados live in elaborate cities that may be directly under human cities. While they remain "in" their *encantarias*, the encantados are thought to have bodies, but when they rise above the earth they rise as spirits, invisible to man, and it is thus they enter human bodies. (Leacock and Leacock 1975: 52–53)

The *encantados* have multiple origins: Some are of human origin (for example, King Louis XVI of France is now an *encantado*), and some have been eternally *encantados*; some *encantados* are etymologically linked with Brazilian Indian cultural traditions (for example, the animal spirits such as the Giant Snake, the turtle, the shark, and the jaguar), and some to the

European and Brazilian folklore tradition (for example, the folk healers such as Dom Carlos and Joao da Mata). Most importantly, many West African deities are associated with the encantados.

> Dahomean deities stand out most prominently among the vodus [understood as African spirit or deity] imported from Maranhao [an Afro-Brazilian region]: Aducu, Akossi-Sapata, Averekete, Bade, Ben Bocu, Legua Bagi, Noe. An indirect effect of borrowing from the Umbanda of Rio de Janeiro [another Afro-Brazilian region] has been the introduction or reemphasis of Yoruba-derived orixas such as Ogun, Oxossi, Oxun, Inhacan, Xango, Imanja, and Exu [the encantados]. (Leacock and Leacock 1975: 168)

While there are fundamental similarities between Voodoo and Batuque polytheistic religious movements, with both having a pantheon of African deities and spirits along with Roman Catholic Christian deities and spirits, and both emphasizing spirit possession, medium-channeling, divination, and healing, there are differences between Voodoo and Afro-Brazilian religions. Voodoo has, justly or unjustly, been viewed negatively by many Haitians and outsiders as a dangerous, mysterious system of ideas and practices that includes witchcraft, sorcery, and human sacrifice and has, as a result, been officially condemned by the state and the church and forced to function as a secret (underground) cult with priests, priestesses, and their followers subjected to social ostracism. Afro-Brazilian religions, on the other hand, focus on providing psychological and social support for the poor and "wretched of the earth." Because spirit possession and medium-channeling occur mostly in the public arena, often functioning as healing rituals, the involvement of the deities and spirits of non-Christian origin in the lives of the Roman Catholic Christians, or in the communities that are officially linked with the Roman Catholic Church, does not generate fear, hostility, and ridicule. Afro-Brazilian religions resemble, to some extent, the religious movements that search for redemption and psychological changes through performance of rituals that enable the participants to see themselves—their inner anxieties, conflicts, inadequacies, and strengths—in the personified spirits who possess them.

Film documentaries on Afro-Brazilian religions include one called *Bahia: Africa in the Americas* (produced by University of California Extension Media Center, 1988). The film demonstrates the importance of Candomble, an Afro-Brazilian religion, in the life of the people of Bahia, a province of Brazil located about 1,000 miles north of Rio de Janeiro. Candomble is derived from the traditional ancestral religion of the Yoruba of West Africa. When the Portuguese forced the Afro-Brazilians to abandon the worship of their divinized ancestors known as Orixas, they superimposed them on Catholic saints. The film examines the intermingling of Candomble and Catholicism and shows ceremonies in which rhythmic music and ritual dancing lead to trances and states of possession.

The Afro-Brazilian religions foster the shamanistic sacred self: Altered states of consciousness, possession, and ritual dancing are related to coping with poverty, sickness, and the stressful conditions of urban life. Religious movements flourish among "socially uprooted" peoples and in slums and other economically impoverished sections of society. Afro-Brazilian movements are unique in their use of African and other religious symbols.

RELIGIOUS MOVEMENTS AND THE ALTERNATION OF THE SHAMANISTIC AND PRIESTLY SACRED SELVES

Ideally, religious movements function to transform the disintegrated symbols of the sacred self into reintegrated symbols of the sacred self. Earlier sections have presented detailed discussions of how this transformation process occurs.

Religious movements arise in contexts in which existing symbols of the sacred other are perceived to have "failed" and are not used to represent the sacred self. In these contexts, the symbols of the sacred other do not represent social processes, or there is little correspondence between what exists and what is represented; an incongruence exists. Such an incongruence arises from the disorganization of social processes. A prophet or messiah emerges and may proclaim that he or she is the "new way" or has a new mandate from the symbols of the sacred other to bring about change. But the new way has to develop from the basic relationship that the prophet establishes with his or her followers; the representations of the symbols of the sacred other have the attributes of psychological processes rather than social processes. The symbols of the self of the followers contact and/or merge with the symbols of the sacred other through various rituals; it is not uncommon for the prophet to function as the "representative" on Earth of the sacred other, or as the sacred other (god or goddess). The representation of the sacred self in such a situation is essentially shamanistic. Gradually, if the movement becomes successful and is established, organizational structures develop, and the symbols of the sacred other begin to reflect social processes. At this stage the followers begin to affirm the social conventions as sacred, the prophet's role as the direct vehicle for communion with the symbols of the sacred other recedes, and the priestly sacred self acquires significance.

Afro-American religious movements constitute a type of religious movement that fosters a continuous shamanistic orientation and is linked with an established priestly orientation of the society. Rather than striving to alter or transform the society through the development of a new cultural configuration, the Afro-American movements such as Voodoo and Batuque have become "religions" that coexist with and supplement or complement the Roman Catholic religion.

PART FOUR
THE DIALECTICS OF THE SACRED OTHER AND SACRED SELF IN MYTH AND RITUAL

CHAPTER THIRTEEN
The Structure and Meaning of Myth

THE STUDY OF SACRED MYTHS

Lessa and Vogt (1972: 248) note: "In many respects the study of myth may be seen as a microcosm of the development of anthropology. Nearly all of the theoretical and methodological trends which have been current at one time or another in the past century in Europe and in America have had something to say about myth." In a review article on Joseph Campbell's book *Historical Atlas of World Mythology*, Wendy O'Flaherty (1983: 3) noted:

> Most attempts to synthesize world mythology rest on the assumption that there is an overarching pattern linking all myths. But the synthesizers disagree about what the pattern is. Structuralists like Claude Levi-Strauss say it is the universal need to impose logical order on our cognition of the world; Freudians say it is the universal experience of sexuality within the nuclear family; Jungians say it is inherited archetypes carried in the collective unconscious of the human race.

Sacred myths—or myths that incorporate the symbols of the sacred other and the sacred self—frequently explain the nature of the universe, human origins, creation of the universe, life after death, existence of gods and spirits, human suffering and injustice, and so on; these explanations cannot be empirically verified but are accepted by believers as true. Some of these explanations are categorized by scholars as fables, folklore, or simply as legends because the people who use them may not accept them as true. The important distinguishing characteristics of myths are that they are accepted as real or true by the believers, and they communicate to the believers messages that help the believers achieve coherence and meaning in their lives or in general achieve integration of the symbols of the self. Wallace suggests that there is no basic difference between myth and folklore and that theology, as a branch of knowledge about god, man, and the world, becomes distinguishable in certain cultures. He notes:

> Mythology and folklore . . . are stories which have a plot of some sort in which anthropomorphic beings strive toward and achieve with more or less difficulty, or fail to achieve, anthropomorphic goals. . . . Theology in advanced societies tends to become science; mythology tends to become literature. But in primitive societies the two are nearly indistinguishable. (Wallace 1966: 243)

Myths were often explained as primitive superstitions, or as irrational, anthropomorphic, or anthropopsychic representations of natural phenomena, and it was thought that through rational and scientific understanding these primitive forms would cease to exist. It may be pointed out that this view of myths itself often served as myth for many scholars because such a view was used to define humanity in a way that provided coherence and meaning for them as "rational scientists." As most scholars of the eighteenth, nineteenth, and early twentieth centuries subscribed to the view that there was a progressive development of the mind toward rationality, myths—the absurd, unverifiable stories—were thought to constitute primitive, infantile, or irrational expressions of the mind. Scholars such as Max Muller and Edward Tylor subscribed to this view, because they believed that primitive humans lived in a mythological, irrational world and that Western peoples lived in a scientific, rational world. The view that myths are irrational phenomena got a boost from the writings of Ernst Cassirer (1946), who witnessed the Nazi Holocaust and wondered whether this was an atavistic expression of the irrational impulses of humankind. He distinguished between "mythical thought" and "scientific thought" and suggested that the former was characterized by erroneous, symbolic connections between cause and effect.

Although Cassirer's analysis has validity, it must be pointed out that myths are "logical" when people share in the cultural conventions (Levi-Strauss has taken pains to show "the logic of myth"). When we identify a system as "irrational" we must examine the perspective that identifies a system of beliefs to be irrational. It is best to distinguish between "communicative" and "instrumental" rationalities (Ulin 1988) and show how myths are constructed with communicative rationality. The claims of myths cannot be supported empirically, but their claims acquire significance as "truths" for the users.

It is evident that myths are part of every culture, "primitive" or "civilized." Myths are "good" or "bad" in terms of their potential to uphold human dignity or cause human tragedy. In discussing the rationality or irrationality of cultural orientations, it is necessary to distinguish between the irrational, neurotic, or maladaptive behavior of particular individuals and the cultural logic of beliefs embodied in myths that may appear to be irrational from the perspective of those who do not use that logic. Myths are important cultural vehicles or domains in the construction of the symbolic self and the sacred self, and these constructions are accepted as valid not because they provide empirical proof for the existence of the self but because they provide a culturally significant and coherent model of the self. Myths may be viewed as models of meaning that relate human life in all its cultural ramifications to the world of experience and the conceptions of the world.

Myths have often been interpreted as allegories or parables that convey information about eternal truths and righteous action and function to regulate proper behavior; myths validate and prescribe right conduct. According to Malinowski (1925), myths "afford precedents and sanctions for social status and moral rules." Myths are, in this view, models of "what ought to be" for the believers; they are charters for social institutions and actions. To Malinowski, myth and ritual are interdependent, but myth serves as a moral foundation of culture.

> Myth fulfills in primitive culture an indispensable function: it expresses, enhances, and codifies belief; it safeguards and enforces morality; it vouches for the efficacy of ritual and contains practical rules for the guidance of man. Myth is thus a vital ingredient of human civilization; it is not an idle tale, but a hard-worked active force; it is not an intellectual explanation or an artistic imagery, but a pragmatic charter of primitive faith and moral wisdom. (Malinowski 1954: 101)

A similar but more sophisticated view is presented by Clyde Kluckhohn (1942), who suggests that Malinowski is right in certain respects but has erred in not examining the psychological, adjustive function of myth and ritual in reducing anxiety and resolving conflicts created by history, environment, and personality factors. It is common to suggest that myths are part of collective representations in the Durkheimian sense, or the derivatives of social structure in the Radcliffe-Brown genre. Between 1930 and 1955 British social anthropologists wrote a number of influential monographs that showed a correspondence between peoples' cosmogony, cosmology, and eschatology on the one hand and the social structure on the other. In this view myths are projections of social conventions and ensure the maintenance of the dominant values.

Myths are occasionally seen by scholars as rationalizations for rituals. The nineteenth-century Biblical scholar William Robertson Smith (whose seminal writings of "Semitic" religions gave rise to various theories on the function of totemic rituals) suggested that rituals had primary significance in the religiosity of primitive and archaic societies. The American anthropologist Anthony Wallace argues that ritual has "an instrumental priority" over myth: "[T]he goals of religion are to be achieved by performing rituals; myths are merely extremely valuable, and regularly employed, auxiliary equipment" (Wallace 1966: 104). As there are myths without corresponding rituals, and vice versa, it is problematic to argue that myths and rituals have an intrinsic or causal linkage. Questions of priority are of the chicken-or-egg variety.

Usually linked with but not confined to Freudian psychoanalytic assumptions, myths are often explained as expressions of unconscious/ subconscious wishes. This approach raises the issue of universals in mythic creations. Are there some innate, deep-seated, cognitively and emotionally unresolved aspects in human psychosocial and psychosexual development? Is myth rooted in this development as well as in the repressed memory of sexual or other conflicts? A classic example is the Oedipal myth of Greece, which Freud himself used to illustrate the psychosexual drama of humankind; but Claude Levi-Strauss has challenged Freudian interpretations and has offered an alternative explanation of the Oedipal myth that I will discuss shortly.

Alan Dundes (1962) in an intriguing paper called "Earth-Diver: Creation of the Mythopoeic Male" argues that many cultures have myths about men creating the earth with mud or dirt because males universally experience pregnancy envy and conceive of a cloacal theory of birth. According to him, this aspect of being male transcends cultural differences; and an examination of the earth-diver myth reveals a pan-human, universal psychological drama.

A discussion of the anthropological study of myth must include the contributions of the American cultural anthropologist Paul Radin, who collected and analyzed the trickster myths of the Native American cultural traditions. In his book *The Trickster: A Study in American Indian Mythology* (1956), Radin refers to the ambiguous physical, social, and moral characteristics of the trickster: ". . . . Trickster is at one and the same time creator and destroyer, giver and negator, he who dupes others and who is always duped himself. . . . He possesses no values, moral or social, is at the mercy of his passions and appetites, yet through his actions all values come into being" (Radin 1956: xxiii). Radin notes that trickster myths are created and re-created by each generation with characteristics that are neither solely human nor sacred, and that such creations help each generation to see some aspects of the human condition in relation to the cultural experience. Tricksters are mediators, he implies, in fusing the contradictory (and often opposite) characteristics. This theme of mediation has been elaborated by Claude Levi-Strauss in his structural analysis of myth.

STRUCTURAL-SYMBOLIC ANALYSIS OF SACRED MYTHS

In a general sense, structural-symbolic analysis decodes the hidden relationships of the components of myths. This analysis can be used to understand the meaning of culture-specific myths or the universal characteristics of myths.

The study of myth as logical, mediating model is closely associated with the seminal writings of Claude Levi-Strauss and his anthropological orientation called French Structuralism. Although Levi-Strauss ridicules the psychoanalytic approach, there is one similarity between the two approaches: Both claim to make visible the invisible through a model of the unconscious in order to reveal "what is universally true" of the human mind. But their approaches to the unconscious are poles apart, and their assumptions about the function of myth are diametrically opposed. To Freud, myths are "similar to dreams and neurotic behavior of the modern man." He proposes a tripartite conflict model of the human mind composed of id, ego, and superego.

Levi-Strauss suggests that it is the nature of the human mind to make binary discriminations and that all human creations (culture) are models based on this mechanical, unconscious structure of the mind. To him, the function of myth is to act as a mediating model to help humans cope with the discrepancies or contradictions generated by other models. To Levi-Strauss, myth is language, as are all other aspects of culture, because human reality is a symbolic reality of communications that obeys certain formal or logical laws of transformation and correspondences. Through the structural analysis of myth it is possible, he contends, to unravel the enduring, deep structure of myths.

The true meaning of myths is not in the narrative context (diachronic or historical) but in the arrangements of relationships in the narrative that integrate the diachronic and synchronic levels. Although the narrative may refer to an event that occurred in primordial times, the event's significance is everlasting and in the present. The meaning of myth is not in the isolated components or in the specific relationships of the components but is in arrangements of the relationships of the components that are not consciously known to the users of the myths. Once we discover the logic of the arrangements of the components, we can reconstitute the myth into a logical model, and we will immediately understand how the myth, as a logical model, helps the human mind cope with the discrepancies or contradictions generated by other models. Levi-Strauss argues that the analysis of myth is a key to understanding the nature of the human mind.

Levi-Strauss (1955), in his classic essay "The Structural Study of Myth," offers the following procedure for deriving the true meaning of the Oedipus myth. He points out that the myth conveys a story with events that occurred in primordial times; this is the diachronic, irreversible, statistical aspect of myth. We must also recognize that the myth conveys an everlasting or eternal message of how to cope with contradictory models of human origin and existence; this is the synchronic, reversible, mechanical aspect of myth. It is necessary to relate these two aspects (just as the user of the myth would integrate the two levels unconsciously), rearranging the relationships of the components of the myth.

First, isolate the particular or specific relationships into "shortest possible sentences." Second, identify the existence of similar features or characteristics and group them. If we follow two procedures correctly, we will be in a position to rearrange the relationships and fuse the diachronic and synchronic levels. The events can be grouped into four columns, signified as A, B, C, and D; then, A and B can cluster to contrast with the cluster of C and D to indicate that the relationship which exists between A and B is comparable or homologous to the relationship that exists between C and D.

In the Oedipus myth, there are the following significant events that occurred in primordial times.

Sequence	Narrative	Columns That Identify the Similar Relationships
1.	Kadmos seeks Europa	A
2.	Kadmos kills the dragon	C
3.	The Spartoi kill one another	B
4.	Oedipus kills his father	B
5.	Oedipus kills the sphinx	C
6.	Oedipus marries his mother	A
7.	Eteokles kills his brother	B
8.	Antigone buries her father	A
9.	The grandfather of Oedipus is lame	D
10.	The father of Oedipus is left-sided	D
11.	Oedipus is swollen-footed	D

There are four columns and eleven rows with each event boxed in one of the forty-four boxes.

A	B	C	D
1			
		2	
	3		
			9
	4		
			10
		5	
6			
	7		
			11
8			

In the above arrangement, columns A and B signify overrating and underrating, respectively, of blood relationships. The same contrasting type of relationship occurs in columns C and D, which signify denial of autochthonous origin of man and affirmation of autochthonous origin of man. Just as we perceive and tolerate the ambiguities of human relationships that can be loving or hostile, we can cope with the contradictory experiential model of human reproduction which signifies that humans reproduce sexually, and the conceptual-cosmogonic model of human origin that postulates that human beings primordially came from Earth (autochthony).

The above model can be represented as follows:

A : B::C : D or A is to B as C is to D

Levi-Strauss (1955) refers to the Zuni emergence myth to show that the basic opposition mediated in this myth is between life and death. He also points out that mediating models such as that of the trickster incorporate opposite characteristics and thereby acquire halfway, dual, or ambiguous features. "Not only can we account for the ambiguous character of the trickster, but we may also understand another property of mythical figures the world over, namely, that the same god may be endowed with contradictory attributes; for instance, he may be good and bad at the same time" (1955: 442).

According to Levi-Strauss, the Oedipal myth helps humans cope with the contradictory models that postulate autochthony (that humans are originally from Earth) and sexual conception (that humans are born as a result of copulation). The myth does not necessarily resolve the contradiction but makes life tolerable by affirming that comparable, contradictory situations are part of reality. Various criticisms have been offered of Levi-

Strauss's conclusions. Scholars may arrange the relationships of the myth differently and may reach different conclusions about the meaning of the myth. There is no way of knowing whether the receivers of the mythic message get it correctly (i.e., as the structuralist explains it) at the unconscious level. The same myth can convey a number of different meanings, and the anthropologist's version of meaning is only one of several versions. Also, the structuralist orientation often focuses on cognitive aspects and does not take into account the affective aspect of myths. (See Levi-Strauss 1955; Leach 1962, 1970; Willis 1967; Crick 1976.)

For Levi-Strauss, there is no fundamental difference between mythical and scientific thought processes. Both follow logical procedures in formulating the existence of relationships in the world of experience, and therefore it is wrong to delineate myth as an unscientific or primitive representation of reality. Although this is an important contribution to our understanding of myth and science, it must be noted that the models of science and the models of myth have different significations. The models of science approximate reality to show actual, phenomenal relationships, whereas the models of myth serve to formulate logical coherence and communicate meaning. It is logically coherent and meaningful to connect the symbols of the sacred other and the symbols of the sacred self, but the myths that incorporate these symbols cannot and ought not to be empirically verified, although the relationship is accepted by the believers to be true.

Levi-Strauss is not a positivistically oriented anthropologist who seeks to discover the cause-and-effect regularities in nature; he seeks to formulate a semilogical or communicative theory of mental and normative structures. He has excluded from his structural analysis the role of subjective consciousness and intentionality of human action, dismissing these notions as illusions. His brand of materialism excludes the possibility of promoting discourse on the role of symbols and myths as embodiments of cultural themes, emotions, values, and worldviews. For this kind of understanding we must turn to the symbolic analysis of myth.

PHENOMENOLOGICAL-SYMBOLIC ANALYSIS OF SACRED MYTHS

Several scholars have incorporated the views of Levi-Strauss into models that attempt to reveal the contextual meaning of myths. For example, in his paper "The Head and the Loins: Levi-Strauss and Beyond," Willis (1967) shows that the Fipa (an African Bantu-speaking group) sovereignty myth cannot be understood solely in structural terms.

The interpretation of the Fipa sovereignty myth . . . . does not preclude its analysis in terms of a system of binary discriminations in the standard Levi-Straussian manner. . . . But the central significance of the myth for the Fipa, it is argued, is its embodiment, at different cognitive levels, of what I have called "conceptual-affective" structures which directly reflect social organization. (Willis 1967: 533)

The historian of religion Wendy O'Flaherty has written extensively about myth, with particular reference to Hindu mythology. She correctly points out that it is necessary to understand how a particular myth defies meaninglessness in its cultural context. For example, the myths of Siva make sense only when you relate them to Hindu cultural orientations of pollution/purity, hierarchy, and spiritual power. Spiritual power can be gained in several ways, including the opening of the psychic centers through the flow of sexual energy; spiritual power can also be acquired through chastity or celibacy. Siva is an ascetic god but is also the god of virile sexuality and phallus; he has a permanently erect penis (ithyphallic), but he is eternally chaste. The myths of Siva have multiple meanings in terms of how and where they are used. The mythic image of the erect penis in Hindu cultural logic is also a representation of chastity; Siva, the ascetic god, conserves semen on the one hand and spills it on the other, but the spilling of semen is for creative regeneration of spiritual power.

O'Flaherty (1973) has adapted the ideas of Levi-Strauss to analyze how myths function in the Hindu cultural context. In her study of Siva, the erotic ascetic, she points out that mythic thought defies meaninglessness. People create different versions of the same myth using their cultural patterns or logic, ordering and reordering the myth; the same myth often has multiple meanings that vary according to context. The personae of myths acquire different attributes, depending on the context, to represent the various aspirations, desires, dilemmas, and experiences of the users. Myths accept human failures, the inconsistencies and contradictions that endanger society. Mythic resolution is not compromise but is attained through an exaggerated expression of the contradictions. This expression serves as a model of extreme possibilities. In this sense myths are divine dramas seen through a one-way mirror, wherein the personae act out anxieties, hopes, aspirations, desires, and fantasies. "Myths express unconscious wishes in the context of culturally stipulated paradoxes." Contradictions cannot be resolved by compromise. (What is the compromise between life and death, sexuality and asexuality?) The mythic figures absorb the contradictory aspects and serve as mediators. Mediation is achieved by introducing abnormality to the mediating figure, as in the case of the trickster or the Virgin Mother. Siva, the erotic ascetic, is abnormal.

It is the essential nature of the ambivalent mythological image to represent a reconciliation of oppositions which, in the factual and practical world, would seem impossible and immoral. This is the essence of the myth: the extreme positions are only imagined in order to show that they are untenable. (O'Flaherty 1973: 36)

O'Flaherty is quite right in her view that we cannot understand how the mediation is achieved by looking into one version of a myth. No single version deals with the paradox in its totality. Thus, we have to get several versions of a myth and discover the patterns of relationships and the themes that are represented. To the believer, the repetition of the myth in several versions renders the myth true in conveying the meaning.

UNIVERSALITY OF MYTHS OF ORIGIN AND MYTHS OF DEATH

Not all cultural traditions have myths of creation with sacred beings taking an active role in creation, and not all cultural traditions have conceptions of heaven, hell, or paradise, but it is likely that all cultural traditions have narratives that make some reference to human origins and human death in sacred or supernatural terms. Myths of origin and myths of death often proclaim that human life has an existence independent of what is visible and that the meaning and purpose of this existence can be comprehended through acceptance of the myths as valid. Malinowski (1954: 1126) notes:

> In certain versions of origin myths the existence of humanity underground is compared to the existence of human spirits after death in the present day world. Thus a mythological rapproachement is made between the primeval past and the immediate destiny of each man, another of those links with life which we find so important in the understanding of the psychology and the cultural value of myth.

For analytic purposes, we can identify creation (cosmogony) myths as a class or type of myths that can be subdivided into (1) those that deal with the creation of sacred beings, (2) those that explain the creation of the world; and (3) those that explain the creation of humankind. We can identify a separate class or type of myths that deals with death and explains what happens to human beings after death (eschatology).

The book of Genesis in the Bible is an excellent example for the study of how myths serve as mediating models to cope with the opposition between life and death, male and female, ignorance and knowledge, goodness and evil, and so on. As is well known, the Greeks and Romans had elaborate myths of creation and death, and mythological scholarship has a long history in the Western intellectual tradition. See Hamilton (1958) for brief descriptions and interpretations of Greek and Roman myths. See

Graves (1948) for an interpretation of how European goddess myths were gradually replaced by myths that focused on the activities of gods. Graves notes that the language of myths was "tampered with in late Minoan times when invaders from Central Asia began to substitute patrilinear for matrilinear institutions and remodel or falsify the myths to justify the social changes" (Graves 1948: vi).

Many ethnographies provide descriptions of how people use the myths of origin and death. For brief descriptions, see Kuper's (1986: 62) discussion of the creation and eschatological myth among the Swazi of South Africa; Chagnon's (1983: 93) discussion of the Yanomamo creation myth in South America; Hoebel's (1978: 89) discussion of the creation myth among the Cheyenne of the American Plains; Ohnuki-Tierney's (1974: 66) discussion of the mythical conception of death in the Ainu culture of Japan; Bascom's (1969: 80–81) description of Yoruba myths of creation in West Africa; and Furer-Haimendorf's (1969: 100) description of a myth of creation among the Konyak Nagas in India.

These myths "explain" why and how the world was created, why and how humanity was created, and why and how death was created. Conceptions of "heaven" and "hell" often coexist with conceptions of reincarnations: Such a coexistence of diverse conceptions is frequently found in Hindu/Buddhist cultural traditions and occasionally in those societies in which there are conceptions of multiple souls.

CHAPTER FOURTEEN

Cultural Archetypes of Spirituality

HISTORICAL AND CULTURAL CONTEXTS
OF MYTHICAL HEROES

Many myths assert the historicity of individuals and events that are described in the myths. Myths of this type have at least some historically valid referents: They are rooted in a particular cultural tradition, set in a particular historical period; they incorporate specific cultural themes and aspirations of a particular group, and the individual who is the object of the mythic narration serves as a cultural archetype, paradigm, or framework for the people to conceptualize and organize a variety of experiences in different domains of life. A good example of religious documents or myths incorporating historical facts is the Bible, which contains historical information on events and personalities of Egyptian, Babylonian, Persian, and Greco-Roman traditions.

As Leach and Aycock (1983) point out, the use of myths for historical documentation has little relevance for an anthropologist. In his essay "Anthropological Approaches to the Study of the Bible," Leach and Aycock (1983: 10) make the following pertinent remarks:

> Now if we consider the Bible as a totality, as I urge you to do, it is quite clearly a sacred tale and not a history book. But, if you take the totality to pieces after

the fashion of orthodox biblical scholarship, it is equally clear that substantial parts of it are written "as if" they were history, and the majority of biblical scholars seem to have persuaded themselves that these are, in fact, records of "true" history.

There is disagreement about just where legend ends and history begins but mostly it seems to be assumed that Moses (probably), and Saul and David (certainly), were real people who actually existed in the period 1250 to 1000 B.C., that is to say 500 years before the age of Herodotus and Thucydides.

Personally I find this most implausible. There is no archaeological evidence for the existence of these heroes or for the occurrence of any of the events with which they are associated. If it were not for the sacredness of these stories their historicity would certainly be rejected. Classical scholars do not now believe that the Trojan War was an historical event or that the kind of society depicted in the Iliad and the Odyssey ever actually existed; still less do they imagine that Achilles and Hector and Agamemnon and the rest were real people of flesh and blood. But Saul and David were reputedly their contemporaries.

In order for an individual (or, for that matter, an event) to become a sacred archetype of the cultural, myth makers (cultural handymen) associate numerous supernatural or sacred characteristics with the individual and events. In other words, a historical individual or event becomes a myth, with supernatural or sacred referents, and there is no way an anthropologist can verify the validity of such a myth as a historical document. From an analytic point of view, our concern is to investigate how a myth connects various themes, how it is coherent and meaningful, and how it is used. As I suggested earlier, a myth may contain historically and scientifically accurate information along with historically and scientifically inaccurate information. The significance of myths is not whether they are historically and scientifically accurate but whether they are accepted by the believers to be true, irrespective of whether they contain factual or nonfactual information. The myths cannot be subordinated to scientific or empirical verification.

I discuss in this chapter a Tamil (Hindu) cultural archetype, a Moroccan and an Indonesian (Islamic) cultural archetype, and a Spanish (Christian) cultural archetype. I also discuss the characteristics of Mohandas K. Gandhi of India and Martin Luther King Jr. of the United States and suggest that they are potential candidates to become cultural archetypes of spirituality. Some cultural archetypes, such as the goddess of chastity (the Tamil representation of female spirituality) and the Virgin of Guadalupe (the Mexican representation of the divine mother), are linked with certain "universal" themes of Hinduism and Christianity. The Tamil symbol is associated with Hindu mother goddess worship, and the Guadalupe symbol is associated with the "Madonna Complex" of Roman Catholic Christianity. Certain cultural archetypes have the potential to become universal archetypes of spirituality.

A TAMIL (HINDU) CULTURAL ARCHETYPE
OF FEMALE SPIRITUALITY

In the Tamil Hindu cultural tradition of India, a central religious theme that has persisted unchanged for more than 2,000 years is the conception of female chastity as connoting female spirituality. The principle of equating female chastity and female spirituality was elaborated upon in various myths by ancient Tamils as a category of sacred power. The attributes of this sacred power were discussed in great detail with reference to the spirituality of Tamil language, Tamil culture, Tamil family, and Tamil politics.

The following paragraphs provide a narration and interpretation of the myth of Kannagi, the cultural archetype of female chastity and female spirituality in the Tamil cultural tradition of India. The ancient Tamil "Epic of the Ankle Bracelet" (*Silapathikaram*), which was probably written between the first and third centuries A.D., narrates the life and times of a chaste wife named Kannagi. The author, Ilango Adigal, focused on Kannagi as a metaphor by means of which he could conceptualize the spirituality of political, cultural, and family experiences of the Tamil people. Tamil justice and culture are portrayed through Kannagi's experiences as a chaste woman. From the epic we understand that in spite of the occupational, religious, and political differentiation within Tamil society, notions of fate, love, chastity, morality, omens, justice, and divinity were the same for all Tamils; Ilango Adigal organized these themes around Kannagi's experiences in three Tamil kingdoms of southern India. Following is a summary of the Tamil epic.

Kannagi was the daughter of a prosperous merchant living in the Chola kingdom. She was trained in all the genteel arts and married a successful merchant named Kovalan. Their marriage was happy until Kovalan encountered a dancer of great charm and wit in the person of Madavi. The dancer's beauty and art attracted Kovalan to the extent that he took up residence with her, forgetting his chaste wife, Kannagi. This liaison between Kovalan and Madavi did not last long, however. At an annual Tamil ceremony, Kovalan sang a song which indicated to Madavi that he was thinking about another woman. In order to tease him, Madavi in turn composed a poem referring to another man. Kovalan, suspecting that Madavi was unfaithful to him, severed his ties with her.

Kovalan returned to his wife a broken man. He had lost all his wealth in his relationship with Madavi and was depressed at his bleak prospects. But Kannagi consoled him and gave him her diamond-embedded ankle bracelets. Deciding to sell the ankle bracelets to start a new business, he went to Madurai, the capital city of the Pandiya kingdom.

On reaching Madurai, Kovalan concluded that it would be better for Kannagi, who had come with him, to find temporary residence somewhere in the city.

Kavunthi Adigal, a Jain woman ascetic who had accompanied them, suggested that Kannagi could stay with a woman named Mathari. When the couple arrived at Mathari's house in the city, Kannagi cooked an elaborate meal that was fated to be Kovalan's last. After resting briefly, Kovalan proceeded to the bazaar along with one of Kannagi's ankle bracelets.

In the bazaar, Kovalan saw the chief goldsmith of the Pandiya king and, hoping that he could sell the ankle bracelet to the queen, asked the goldsmith to estimate its price. The goldsmith, however, had recently stolen an ankle bracelet belonging to the queen; as Kovalan asked him to evaluate Kannagi's ankle bracelet, the thief contemplated a scheme to implicate Kovalan. Because the ankle bracelet produced by Kovalan resembled the queen's, the goldsmith believed that he could convince the king that Kovalan was the thief and ask for his execution, thus covering up his own guilt. While Kovalan waited trustingly, the goldsmith proceeded to the king. The king, eager to please the queen by giving her the ankle bracelet, accepted the word of the goldsmith without verification and bade his soldiers recover the ankle bracelet and execute Kovalan. The goldsmith took the soldiers to his house, where Kovalan was waiting. Although the soldiers doubted whether a person of Kovalan's countenance could have committed such a crime, the goldsmith succeeded in goading one of them to accomplish the king's command to behead him.

Kannagi, anxiously waiting for Kovalan's return at Mathari's house, soon heard that he had been executed. In uncontrollable grief and anger she ran to Kovalan, whose corpse appeared to come alive and proclaim the injustice done. Kannagi proceeded to the king's palace to declare her husband's innocence and challenge the king's authority. The king, courteous during his audience with her, reasoned that it was his duty to render justice by killing a thief. Kannagi protested that her husband was innocent, claiming that the ankle bracelet which Kovalan had in his possession was one of the two belonging to her, and she mentioned that they contained diamonds. As the queen's ankle bracelet contained pearls, the king commanded his soldier to bring the ankle bracelet recovered from Kovalan. Kannagi dashed the ankle bracelet to the floor, dislodging a diamond, which struck the king's mouth. The king, who could not bear the idea that he had rendered injustice and had himself become a thief and murderer in the process, fell from his throne in despair and died. The queen, seeing the death of her husband, also died of despair.

Outside the palace, Kannagi tore her right breast with her hand and to avenge the wrongful execution of her husband cursed the city of Madurai where the calamity had occurred. Fire broke out wherever the drops of her blood fell, and the city was engulfed in flames. For fourteen days Kannagi wandered toward the Chera kingdom and was seen being transported to the skies in a chariot.

The deification of Kannagi as the Goddess of Chastity was ordered by the Chera king, who was told of Kannagi's transcendence and of her experiences in the Pandiya kingdom. Deciding to dedicate a temple in her honor, the king took a long journey across the north of India to the Himalayan mountains to secure the proper stone to build her idol. After the successful completion and dedication of the temple, Kannagi was proclaimed the Tamil Goddess of Chastity.

The myth of Kannagi incorporates several themes associated with different domains of cultural experience, such as politics and ethnicity; Kannagi embodies spirituality and chastity and evokes deep emotions in the believers. The Tamil male considered it his spiritual obligation to protect the "chastity" of Tamil language, culture, and womanhood.

Kannagi is not worshipped as a goddess by all Tamils, although her image is often associated with mother goddess worship, which is very popular among the Tamils. However, every child growing up in Tamil society acquires an understanding of the significance of the myth of Kannagi for the Tamils. A full understanding of the structure, meaning, and referents of the Kannagi myth can be gained only by examining the myth's historical evolution, along with its use in different social contexts. The component elements of the myth may draw on one another's referential empirical reality (such as politics, family, and ethnicity), and the believers may selectively use the components relevant to their social or personal needs. However, the totality of the myth's meaning is evident to the Tamils even when the entire myth is not used.

INDONESIAN AND MOROCCAN ARCHETYPES OF ISLAMIC SPIRITUALITY

In Chapter 9, I referred to the book *Islam Observed* in which Geertz (1969) interprets the role of two Muslim leaders, one in Indonesia and another in Morocco. Despite the fact that these leaders propagated the same religious faith, they were accepted in their respective countries not because of Islam but because they manifested the cultural archetypes of their respective cultural traditions. They symbolized the conflicts, contradictions, and themes of their cultural traditions and became cultural vehicles for the people of the two different traditions to conceptualize Islamic faith.

Sunan Kalidjaga, the sixteenth-century Javanese prince, who is regarded as the propagator of Islam in Java, became a mythic hero in linking or mediating the Hindu god-kings and Islamic shrines-sultans as well as the Hindu ritual-priests and Islamic Koranic scholars-mosques. The myth of Kalidjaga's conversion from Hinduism to Islam is a narration of how an inner, redemptive change occurred, transforming him from a thief, drunkard, gambler, womanizer, and robber into a saint. Kalidjaga met a saint named Bonang one day; after Bonang performed a miracle, Kalidjaga meditated for several years. Bonang returned to meet Kalidjaga several years later and asked him to spread Islam. Kalidjaga had not studied the Koran but had become a Muslim through an inner transformation, a "self-produced inner state."

The myth of Kalidjaga's conversion was a formulation compatible to the Indonesian cultural tradition. He was a yogi who sought inner harmony and manifested stoical quietism, comparable to that of a Hindu ascetic. The cultural archetype of Indonesia is settled life, hierarchical and metaphysical, with an adaptive and pragmatic orientation. In this cultural context, the myth of Kalidjaga made sense, and Kalidjaga could function as a symbol of the sacred other for the formulation of the sacred self for Indonesians.

In contrast to the foregoing mythic hero, the Moroccan cultural tradition produced an Islamic symbol of the sacred other with very different characteristics. Lyusi was a seventeenth-century Koranic scholar in Morocco who became a focal cultural expression of *Maraboutism,* the Islamic holy order. During Lyusi's time, *Marabouts* or holy men who had great supernatural power (*baraka*), founded various holy orders. In his youth, Lyusi met a teacher named Nasir who was ill with an incurable disease. Lyusi washed Nasir's clothing and upon drinking the washing water was possessed of *baraka*. This event rendered Lyusi a saint, a *marabout*. After years of learning and wandering from one *maraboutic* center to another, Lyusi challenged the evil king, Sultan Ismail, and performed a miracle before returning to preach and propagate Islam.

The myth of Lyusi depicts him as a puritan zealot with extraordinary physical courage and ecstatic moral intensity. This corresponds to the Moroccan cultural archetypes such as aggressive fundamentalism and piety, moral perfectionism, magical power, and visionary reform. Thus Lyusi could function as a symbol of the sacred other in Moroccan cultural tradition in the constitution, maintenance, evaluation, and dramatization of the sacred self.

CATHOLIC ARCHETYPES
OF PATRON SAINTS

Eric Wolf (1958: 34) in his analysis "The Virgin of Guadalupe: A Mexican National Symbol" notes that "Occasionally, we encounter a symbol which seems to enshrine the major hopes and aspirations of an entire society. Such a master symbol is represented by the Virgin of Guadalupe, Mexico's patron saint." The Guadalupe symbol belongs to the same genre as the Virgin Mary (as she is represented in different cultures), and the symbol is also similar to the widely accepted cultural orientation of "Saint worship" in Roman Catholic countries. However, the Guadalupe symbol's characteristics and meaning are uniquely Mexican in orientation. In one sense, the symbol is the microcosm of Mexican social and political realities. The complexity of the hierarchical relationships between and among the various ethnic groups and between the sexes (and the family) is embodied in the symbol.

> The Guadalupe symbol thus links together family, politics and religion; colonial past and independent present, Indian and Mexican. It reflects the salient social relationships of Mexican life, and embodies the emotions which they generate. It provides a cultural idiom through which the tenor and emotions of these relationships can be expressed. It is, ultimately, a way of talking about Mexico: a "collective representation of Mexican society." (Wolf 1958: 38)

Saint worship is an important feature of Catholic Christianity: For example, Christian (1972) in his ethnography of a village community in Spain provides a detailed description of saint worship and its significance to the villagers in terms of how the saints serve as sacred metaphors or intermediaries in the life and communal affairs of people.

> The saints of importance to collectives are statues holding fixed positions in the landscape, whether in chapels or in parish churches. There are many such devotions, spatially based, geographically located. In time each has to have a territory of grace, an area over which its benevolent power seems especially manifest. Such images, even if in terms of name and design they are not unique in the vicinity, are considered particularly powerful. . . . [W]e will call them *shrine images*. Their location, whether it be a chapel or a parish church, we call a *shrine*. (Christian 1972: 44)

EXEMPLARY RELIGIOUS MODELS
AND CULTURAL CONTEXT

Perhaps every reader can identify or recognize someone who served (or serves) as an exemplary model (with religious connotations). Mohandas K. Gandhi (1869–1948) of India and Martin Luther King Jr. (1929–1968) of the United States appear at first glance to be similar in their characteristics as exemplary religious models. Both had strong religious commitments, and both preached nonviolence as a spiritual force; both resisted political and social oppression, sought to reconcile the conflicts between different ethnic groups, and promoted the ideas of human dignity, egalitarianism, and peaceful coexistence. Both were assassinated. Yet they were so profoundly rooted in their cultural traditions that it is inconceivable that they could have communicated their messages in any other cultural tradition; no matter how similar their characteristics, they could not have been socially or politically effective in each other's cultural traditions.

Gandhi was a devotee of the god Rama, but he was like Siva, a yogi and an erotic ascetic. He saw his life as an experiment in operationalizing truth and believed that truth was the essence of God and the natural order.

Thus he was not afraid to reveal his personal fears and strengths, desires and frustrations, spiritual detatchment, and unity with God at the same time.

King, a minister of the Christian Baptist Church, had great spiritual, moral, and physical courage but was also troubled by self-doubt, carnal desires, and setbacks. He preached a gospel of hope, and a social gospel of the unity and equality of humankind. To him, Jesus was both an exemplary model and god, and thus King may have anticipated early death and perhaps even sought salvation in death.

To a large extent, King and Gandhi have become exemplary religious models. In the years to come, they will be reinvented again and again with characteristics and attributes that will correspond to the experiences of the succeeding generations. It may also be noted that although their gospels had special significant meanings to the people of their generations and cultural traditions, they stood for and embodied certain universal human aspirations. Thus, they have the potential to be used as pan-human religious models.

CHAPTER FIFTEEN
The Structure and Meaning of Ritual

THE NATURE OF RITUAL COMMUNICATION

Ethological studies of animal rituals suggest that humans are genetically constituted for repetitive, stereotypic behavior in personal and social communication. Among humans, such behavior occurs in a culturally defined manner, with different cultures establishing boundaries for its expression. Just as each language selects certain sounds as significant in the construction of meaning systems, each culture selects certain body movements in association with the performance of ritual communication (verbal or nonverbal).

Ritual communication occurs with reference to specific, culturally defined, personal or social goals. Anthropologists often point out that rituals have both "expressive" and "instrumental" functions. Rituals may be expressive of values and/or part of the ideational culture, and rituals may accomplish or achieve results other than what they explicitly indicate. For example, rain rituals may or may not produce rain, but they bring people together and allay their anxiety over drought; the same explanation can be offered for curing and other such rituals.

The anthropological study of ritual differs from the ethological and psychological study of ritual, although biological and psychological anthropologists may use the findings of ethologists and psychologists. Anthony Wallace, the American anthropologist, has theorized on the nature of ritual, using ethological and psychological studies. According to him,

> Ritual may be defined as stereotyped communication, solitary or interpersonal, which reduces anxiety, prepares the organism to act, and (in social rituals) coordinates the preparation for action among several organisms, and which does all this more quickly and reliably than can be accomplished (given the characteristics of the organisms and the circumstances) by non-stereotyped, informational communication. (Wallace 1966: 236)

> An organism overwhelmed by information overload is incapable of discriminating response; ritual, by reducing the information content of experience below the often bewildering level of complexity and disorder with which reality confronts him, permits adaptive response. In this sense, the goal of science and the goal of ritual and myth are the same: to create the image of a simple orderly world. (Wallace 1966: 239)

Several other anthropologists have also theorized about the "adaptive functions" of human ritual. For example, the following quotes suggest that rituals function to provide human beings with conceptions of moral and social certitudes, and that individuals contact the sacred other and experience the sacred or supernatural reality in the ritual context.

> An unbroken set of steps leads from ritual's invariance to certainty, acceptance, and conviction, from them to the unquestionable and from the unquestionable to its special cases—legitimacy, propriety, correctness and truth. Sanctity, then, is a product of the invariant recurrence in ritual of that which is taken to be never-changing. Sanctity and eternity, although not quite one and the same, are both generated by the performance of invariance and, as such, are, as it were, brother and sister. That which is sacred is not only true but eternally true. Conversely, the eternal verities represented in ritual are sacred. (Rappaport 1986)

> We assume man is a rule-making and order-seeking creature to whom transition and change represent a challenge, if not actual threat. The cataclysms that menace the fabric of social coherence range from epidemics and assassinations to the transition from youth to manhood, birth to death, and spring into winter. Societies tend to meet these situations of crisis with ritual, which presents the enduring validity of certain principles of order. (Crocker 1973)

A ritual is a stereotyped sequence of activities involving gestures, words, and objects, performed in a sequestered place, and designated to influence preternatural entities or forces on behalf of the actor's goals and interests (Turner 1973).

Rituals, for the most part, incorporate techniques of reversal, or the performance of activities or behaviors that are not condoned in nonritual contexts. Cultures differ in the acts that are reversed: Some acts of reversal are related to social hierarchy and therefore occur only in stratified societies; and certain acts of reversal occur in cultures with elaborate shaman-istic symbologies or witchcraft-divination-healing beliefs.

In the following section I present examples of the techniques of rever-sal and offer a brief discussion of reversals that occur in the ritual contexts.

THE TECHNIQUES OF REVERSAL
IN RITUAL CONTEXT

Reversal of biological and social roles, and reversal of what is considered to be ordinary biological or social states of existence and behavior, occur uni-versally in the ritual context. Ethnographies are full of data on reversals such as nudity, impersonation, sexual license, inverted speech, inverted walking, regurgitation, devouring filth, fire-walking, mortification of the flesh, and scatological acts that occur during religious and nonreligious rituals.

A perusal of recent ethnographies indicates that reversals occur in all societies in one form or another as part of most rituals. It is reasonable to conclude that ritual reversals are universal, or that they are not confined to any one region or type of society. For example, among the Magars of Nepal, scatological acts occur in the context of naming and funeral rituals (Hitchcock 1966: 59, 54); Diamond (1969: 48–49, 91) reports on the occur-rence of various forms of reversals during funeral and cyclical rituals; nudity is part of funeral rituals among the Konyak Nagas of South Asia (Furer-Haimendorf 1969: 12); reversal of sexual roles occurs in peasant villages of Ireland (Messenger 1969: 99); impersonation is reported among the peasants of Central Asia (Dunn and Dunn 1967: 29); impersonation and clowning occur among the peasants of modern Greece (Friedl 1962: 100); reversal of sexual roles is noted in the Lugbara society (Middleton 1965: 70); among the Gururumba of New Guinea, practices such as the devouring of filth, impersonation, and regurgitation occur during crisis and cyclical ritu-als (Newman 1965: 69–80); acts such as inverted walking and inverted dancing occur among the Kapauku Papuans of West New Guinea in the context of crisis and cyclical rituals (Pospisil 1964: 68–81).

There is abundant information on ritual reversals among the North American Indians. Nudity is a common form of reversal: In some instances males and females strip naked in order to ridicule the dead of different clans; sometimes women strip naked and engage in sexual license in order to increase crop production. Inverted speech and inverted walking as well as self-torture are common forms of reversal that occur in association with war rituals. In the context of healing rituals, medicine men handle fire and boiling liquid. Devouring of filth and urine as well as other scatological acts have been observed among North American Indians (Pandian 1970).

To these examples may be added acts such as circumcision, subincision, and clitoridectomy as well as the widespread acts of self-mortification, the sexual excesses associated with various cultist ceremonies, the Black Mass, and the Mardi Gras.

The foregoing statements are not meant to be an exhaustive summary of the acts of reversal but are meant to show that reversals are universal and that acts of reversal constitute an important aspect of almost all rituals. Many scholars have identified this kind of behavior and have asked numerous questions. Why is the technique or method of reversal employed universally in ritual contexts? Do common motivational factors underlie these reversals? Does the structure of the mind impose an opposition between ordinary and non-ordinary forms of social interaction, thus necessitating the performance of reversal in non-ordinary forms of interaction? Do reversals in ritual communicate messages that oppose the biological and/or the social order? Do these reversals occur more or less often in certain types of societies? If so, is the occurrence of reversals in ritual associated with certain types of social/political structure and religious beliefs? Are acts of reversal a product of "magical thinking" to gain control and power? Or are these acts symbolic forms that convey specific meanings and messages to bring about personal and group harmony or equilibrium?

Durkheim (1915) noted that such actions were magical or anti-social. In his book *Religion in Primitive Society*, Norbeck (1961: 55, 74, 151, 204–212) uses the term *ritual reversal* to categorize behaviors such as role inversion, burlesquing, clowning, inverted speech, scatology, and sexual license that occur in various ritual contexts. He suggests that it is legitimate to view some of these acts as expressions of magical thinking and notes that some reversals serve as a source of individual or social catharsis and entertainment. Norbeck (1974: 35–39, 50–54) notes that a functional congruence or relationship may exist between certain forms of ritual reversals and human play. He suggests that activities of this kind have the common attribute of transcendence: Certain forms of ritual reversal can be categorized as forms of play; and it is also legitimate to explore the adaptive significance of reversals and play in the maintenance of the social order and in their contribution to the psychological well-being. However, he holds that "ritual reversals of behavior cover a much broader range than play as a substitution for work" (1974: 50) and observes that "the prevalence of ritualized acts that reverse the ordinary is puzzling. Perhaps they represent a universal and innate way of thinking of the human species, a 'principle' or 'structure' of human thought" (1974: 54).

According to the perspective taken in this book, the phenomenon of reversal in the ritual context may be seen as part of the shamanistic orientation of the self. The shamanistic self is created through the merger of the self and sacred symbols, and contrariness or reversals often serve to test the validity of the merger as well as the power of the sacred self, and in turn the power of the sacred other. Turner (1969) has used the concept of liminality to point out that the ritual context promotes anti-structure, in which the participants do not operate within the social categories. On the one hand the participants gain an understanding of mystical oneness with their fellow humans and sacred others, and on the other hand the participants have the opportunity to engage in extreme forms of behavior that are not permitted in the structured or social realm of human existence.

The phenomenon of ritual reversal is not confined to non-urban (technologically primitive) societies. In traditional-urban societies, as in India (Marriott 1966), ritual reversals constitute an important aspect of all religious ceremonies. Ritual reversal is also an important aspect of cultist religious movements which oppose the existing standards of a society. Many religious traditions tolerate or incorporate ritual reversals; examples of this can be found in medieval Europe, China, India, and Tibet. As Barbara Tuchman (1979: 32–33) has pointed out, ritual reversal was a common phenomenon in medieval Europe:

> As an integral part of life, religion was both subjected to burlesque and unharmed by it. In that annual Feast of Fools at Christmas time, every rite and article of the church no matter how sacred was celebrated in mockery. A dominus festi, or lord of the revels, was elected from the inferior clergy—the cures, subdeacons, vicars, and choir clerks, mostly ill-educated, ill-paid, and ill-disciplined—whose day it was to turn everything topsy-turvy.

I suggest that ritual reversals introduce affirmation to and of the sacred self through "testing" the validity of the symbols of the sacred other. In my discussion of myth I pointed out that myth is a theoretical dimension that is not tested, and that a myth's validity is in its nontestability and acceptance. Ritual, on the other hand, is enactment of certain techniques, and certain results are expected—such as solidarity, cures, and so on. Religious rituals use sacred others to attain these results and therefore test the validity of sacred others. The identification or contact with sacred others, by itself, is experiential, and this results in affirmation of the symbols of the sacred other even when the required results are not experienced.

Ritual reversals "prove" that the symbols of the sacred other are valid because the sacred self is capable of experiencing and demonstrating various kinds of biological and social transformations, which by themselves are proof of the existence of the sacred other. The participants may undergo bodily mutilation, defy fire, perform as clowns, go naked, and desecrate the sacred arena by performing contrary acts in ritual contexts. These behaviors, in different ways, become experimental tests for the validity of the symbols of the sacred other because the sacred self is able to engage in such practices. Certain ritual reversals enact the affirmation of the sacredness of particular status positions or the community as a whole, and cultural traditions vary in the importance and elaborateness associated with them—and the "reversals" that have significance. The Arunta of Australia have elaborate initiation rituals, particularly for the boys who undergo rites that include circumcisions, being tossed in the air, subincision, fire ordeals, and bloodletting before being accepted as adults with sacred knowledge of the *churinga* (the totemic representation of the sacred values). Ritual reversals are more common when the shamanistic aspect of religion is emphasized, as in the founding of religious movements and in various crisis-contexts.

In Chapter 16, I discuss two healing rituals that manifest techniques of reversal. One of these rituals explicitly dramatizes the reversal of gender roles. The existence of such rituals—that is, some rituals dramatizing reversal of roles or some other specific characteristic—has raised the question of whether there is a class of rituals that can be identified as "rituals of reversal." As I indicate in Chapter 16, the delineation of some rituals in that manner is misleading: The "acts" of reversal occur in different ritual contexts, and the reversal of behaviors may be in relation to particular types of behavior in a certain society; and, in a general sense, "ritual" itself may be viewed as a reversal of what is enacted as "normal" in the everyday social context.

Max Gluckman (1954), the British social anthropologist, was one of the first scholars to show that certain rituals in southern African cultures focused on the expression of "rebellion" and resolution of rebellion, and since then various scholars such as Edward Norbeck (1961, 1974), Victor Turner (1969), and Peter Rigby (1968) have made theoretical contributions to the understanding of rituals that incorporate aspects of rebellion, conflict, or reversal. I will discuss the significance of their views in Chapter 16.

In a recent paper entitled "Annual Rituals of Conflict," Robert Dirks (1988: 856) argues that "annual rituals of conflict occur disproportionately among societies situated in environments prone to seasonal hunger and possessing political systems strongly inclined to favor communal over individual decision making." According to Dirks, "such rites originate in a spontaneous reaction to sudden, drastic uptakes of food energy."

I am not certain whether a combination of ecological, social, and psychological variables is the most appropriate framework to understand the phenomenon of reversal in the ritual context. There is little doubt that "stress" is an important factor in the occurrence and the "function" of ritual, but the physiological/psychological state of stress itself is culturally formulated in a number of different ways. As Dirks himself suggests, we must undertake in-depth historical and cultural-contextual studies of specific rituals to analyze their "origins" and "functions." As Kuper (1986) points out, the annual ritual of kingship among the Swazi of southern Africa has been interpreted as a "ritual of rebellion," but the ritual affirms the political and cultural orientations of the Swazi so that this reversal may be viewed more appropriately as a ritual of "social renewal," a category of ritual that I discuss in Chapter 18.

CHAPTER SIXTEEN
Divination, Witchcraft, and Healing

THE WORLDVIEW OF DIVINATION, WITCHCRAFT, AND HEALING

Divination, witchcraft, and healing can be lumped together as a ritual-set. This ritual-set is predicated on and rooted in the existence of cultural formulations that identify or explain supernatural or sacred beings and powers as being involved in the processes of knowing and causing harm or cures. Certain ritual actions are believed to initiate and/or interpret the involvement of sacred beings and powers. Divinatory, witchcraft, and healing rituals reinforce one another in affirming the role of sacred beings and sacred powers in human affairs; together they constitute a coherent worldview for the believers.

Beliefs and rituals associated with divination, witchcraft, and healing occur all over the world, but their existence has different consequences in urban (technologically advanced) and non-urban (technologically "primitive") societies. In most non-urban societies, the worldviews and values incorporate theories of pathogenesis that include the sacred other in various characteristics as causal factors. Often, divinatory-healing and witchcraft-sorcery beliefs and rituals indirectly support or affirm the social structure and dramatize the importance of equal distribution of wealth (riches arouse suspicion), homogeneity of culture (nonconformists are suspect), channel anxiety (scapegoat phenomenon), and promote social control (fear of deviance). In many societies, a distinction is made between the activities of a witch and the activities of a sorcerer. A witch, in such a formulation, is an evil person who inherits evil powers; a sorcerer is a person who learns witchcraft that may be good or bad.

The diviner, healer, witch, and sorcerer may have distinguishable roles in many societies, but it is not uncommon to have these roles combined in the person of the shaman (who is anthropologically defined as someone who has the ability to commune directly with supernatural beings and powers). Divining and healing rituals frequently combine (or go together) because healing involves divination. The perspective of this book suggests that all these activities belong to the shamanistic orientation with a particular kind of relationship between the symbols of the sacred other and the symbolic self. The diviner, healer, witch, and sorcerer establish contact with the symbols of the sacred other and may merge the symbols of the self with those of the sacred other; among the participants, their rituals foster contact or union with the symbols of the sacred other.

RITUALS OF DIVINATION

Divinatory information may be attained through cultural assumptions about intervention of deities or spirits or through visions; people may also believe that such information may be attained by interpreting natural phenomena or by using special techniques that are not scientifically verifiable or predictable but are accepted as valid. Diviners are usually shamans who secure information through communion with the symbols of the sacred other and thus have important positions in non-urban societies. In urban societies, diviners such as astrologers, palmists, and psychics may claim to be "scientists" even when their methods cannot be subjected to scientific verification. They may exist on the fringes of society, often attacking the scientific method, frequently functioning as entertainers.

Malefijt (1968: 216–225) offers the following classification of divination. Under "divination without human experiment," she includes (1) *augury* (reading omens), (2) *ornithomancy* (prophecy through bird watching), (3) *geomancy* (interpreting mud cracks), (4) *pyromancy* (interpreting the shape of flames), (5) *lithomancy* (interpreting the shape of rocks), (6) *hydromancy* (interpreting the flow of water), (7) *astrology* (interpreting stars and planets), (8) *somatomancy* (interpreting the shape of the body), (9) *neomancy* (interpreting moles), (10) *phrenology* (interpreting cranial shape), (11) *ophthalmoscopy* (interpreting eyes), (12) *palmistry* (interpreting lines on the palm), (13) *metascopy* (interpreting forehead and planets), and (14) *physiognomy* (interpreting the body and the zodiac).

Under "divination involving human experiment" she includes (1) *ordeal* (oracle to determine guilt or innocence), (2) *haruspicy* (inspection of entrails), (3) *hepatoscopy* (inspection of liver), and (4) *scapulimancy* (interpretation of shoulder blades).

Under divination through dreams and trances, she includes (1) *oneiromancy* (interpretation of dreams) and (2) *chrematismos* (revelation).

Witch hunts often occur at times of strife and stress in both urban and non-urban societies. In urban societies witch hunts have occasionally resulted from the conflict between religious orthodoxy and those who are labeled heretics, and people of science have been condemned as witches because their theories conflicted with existing cosmologies. H.R. Trevor-Roper (1967) in his book *The European Witch-Craze of the Sixteenth and Seventeenth Centuries* argues that the Roman Catholic Church, in its effort to conserve a crumbling social order, helped develop a trend of demonology that was used to destroy nonconformists, including the Jews. However, Margaret Murray (1921) in her book *The Witch-Cult in Western Europe* suggests that "the witch-cult was a survival of a pre-Christian religion in Western Europe, a fertility cult which was called Dianic and which first may have developed in Egypt."

WITCHCRAFT AND SORCERY

Witchcraft and sorcery are generally identified as "magical," and James Frazer's theory of "sympathetic magic" is often used to explain how the sorcerer makes a false connection between objects that look alike (and objects that were together at one time) to create certain effects on people. As I suggested in Chapters 2 and 4, it is more valid to interpret witchcraft-sorcery rituals as using the technique of conditioning (like Pavlov's dog): In societies in which people believe in and are culturally conditioned to respond to witchcraft-sorcery accusations (and cures) in a certain manner, the sorcerer's techniques are effective. As early as 1942, Walter B. Cannon brilliantly showed how people die of fear and other emotional reactions: Physiological changes occur that cause a breakdown in bodily functions. In a paper entitled "'Voodoo' Death," Cannon (1942) interpreted how or why people die when they break cultural/religious taboos and when they believe that they have been bewitched. Levi-Strauss (1962: 162) refers to the efficacy of magic as a function of the belief in magic by the sorcerer, his or her victim, and the group: "[F]irst, the sorcerer's belief in the effectiveness of his techniques; second, the patient's or victim's belief in the sorcerer's power; and, finally, the faith and expectations of the group. . . ."

Terms such as *voodoo* and *voodoo doll* are commonly used to identify certain types of witchcraft-sorcery rituals, but it is important to note that the term *voodoo* technically refers to the polytheistic religious movement of Haiti and that many scholars refer to the African syncretic religious movements of the New World as "voodoo cults." See Chapter 12 for a discussion of voodoo-witchcraft rituals in African religious movements of the New World.

In the following paragraphs I discuss J.R. Crawford's (1967) book, *Witchcraft and Sorcery in Rhodesia.* Crawford provides a detailed account of the society and culture of the Shona tribe of Rhodesia (modern Zimbabwe) and discusses the nature and function of beliefs and practices that are identified as witchcraft, sorcery, and divination. Crawford's study is an example of the positivistic functionalist studies promoted by British social anthropologists such as Radcliffe-Brown; information on the meaning of various symbols among the Shona is limited.

Crawford's book is based on Rhodesian court records of "wizardry" (which includes witchcraft, sorcery, and divination) for the years 1956 to 1962. Crawford describes Rhodesian society, its ruling white minority, and the ambiguous position of chieftains and headmen who, although they are appointed by the government, represent their people because they are members of the dominant patrilineage. A detailed account of the confessions and other statements of wizardry are given along with a discussion of belief in wizardry and its connection to beliefs in spirits and ritual practices. Because certain members of the society and "certain categories of people" are generally accused of wizardry, Crawford examines its relation to kinship structure and analyzes the consequences of wizardry accusations in terms of how the people accused of witchcraft react and how the community solves the problems of the existence of a witch in its midst.

Crawford notes that beliefs in wizardry provide answers to problems that arise out of social tension due to structural anachronisms, rapid social change, and misfortunes that cannot be interpreted or explained in rational terms. Pentecostal churches help persons adapt themselves to new social conditions and provide emotional solutions, as in the case of the traditional beliefs in spirits. Belief in wizardry is rampant in areas that have been least affected (but still disturbed) by modernization. People living in towns are emotionally less involved in wizardry. Economic regression and political instability encourage the belief in and practice of wizardry. Accusation of wizardry is very often an effective means of manipulating public opinion. Suppression of traditional and institutionalized methods of placing the guilt on socially repugnant individuals (ordeal once being nearly universal in Africa) has resulted in the emergence of secret societies such as anti-sorcery cults. Proximity in space and status is a main factor in a person's suspecting another of wizardry.

In many instances accusations of wizardry create more social tension and conflict than they reduce. Witches are usually believe to be women, and sorcerers men. The only way a helpless woman accused of witchcraft can survive is to boast of cannibalism and spirit possession; these admissions, which create fear in others, place her in a superior position. Many witches flee the village while others commit suicide because of ostracism and guilt feelings; a few who have the support of a father, husband, or brother are reintegrated into the community after clearing themselves through ordeals and/or purificatory rites. Charges against agnatic kin are rarely made since this would endanger the unity of the patrilineage. "In a patrilineal society with virilocal marriage . . . witchcraft allegations are, in the main made against the wives and mothers of lineage members and . . . sorcery allegations are made against lineage members" (Crawford 1967: 287).

Witchcraft is distinct from sorcery among the Shona even though in some communities there may be only one term to characterize both. Witchcraft does not entail the performance of magical rites because the witch is believed to have inherited or acquired the evil spirit, and this is sufficient to cause misfortune to others. Sorcery is less serious, as it can be practiced by any person with the use of objects that are believed to have attributes that can cause harm. Whereas the presence of a witch is considered a social threat, the sorcerer and diviner may not be looked upon as such. There is some evidence to support the view that witchcraft is more common in unilineal social organizations that have definite rules concerning ownership and maintenance of property. The Shona, who do not have definite rules about who can live in the village community, believe in both witchcraft and sorcery.

Crawford says that belief in wizardry in one form or another is universal in Africa because an African's hypotheses about causal relationships in relation to tangible and intangible phenomena "are, objectively speaking, erroneous" (Crawford 1967: 67). The belief explains why a particular person meets with the misfortune. But only when the misfortune is socially relevant does it call for punitive actions from the community. Injury or death of an elderly person is less relevant to the community, but the death of a child or barrenness of a woman affects it because these misfortunes signal the possible extinction of the community. Crawford notes that "wizardry beliefs have relevance because they combine a theory of causation with a personification of those forces which the community detests" (Crawford 1967: 72).

Crawford discusses the religious beliefs of the Shona primarily to explain how belief in witchcraft is interwoven with beliefs in spirits. For example, the *shave* cults, which focus upon spirit possession, function to set right the wrongs committed in the community. The cults "have been particularly prevalent during the years following the occupation of the country by Europeans, being presumably associated with social changes of the time. At present they are losing ground to the prophets of the Pentecostal churches" (Crawford 1967: 83). These prophets usually also engage in divination and curing of witches. The traditional diviners are sometimes called upon to identify the witch or the sorcerer.

Crawford classifies divination into three types: "psychic," in which the diviner is supposedly possessed (temporarily) by spirits; "psychological," in which the diviner may use the technique of hypnotism; and "causal," which rests on chance finding. For the most part, diviners have a good knowledge of their clients. Crawford notes that divination through ordeal—the poison ordeal, the boiling water ordeal, and the Muchapi ordeal (administering muchapi medicine, which "proves" the innocence of the victim if he or she survives)—is common throughout Rhodesia.

For more information on the anthropological study of witchcraft, sorcery, and divination, see *Magic, Witchcraft and Curing*, edited by J. Middleton (1967); *Witchcraft and Sorcery*, edited by M. Marwick (1970); *Witchcraft* by L. Mair (1969); and *Magic, Witchcraft, and Religion*, edited by A.C. Lehman and J. E. Myers (1985).

HEALING AND THE RITUAL INTEGRATION
OF THE SACRED SELF

There has been some confusion in the description and interpretation of rituals variously labeled "rituals of rebellion" (Gluckman 1954), "rituals of status reversal" (Turner 1969), or "rituals of conflict" (Norbeck 1961).

Gluckman (1954) identified a particular type of ritual performance in southern African cultures as "rituals of rebellion." Such rituals, according to him, help to resolve conflict and antagonism between those who hold political authority and those who have no political power. He theorized that ritual enactments that include verbal assaults and ridicule occur in stable societies with clearly defined social roles of political dominance and subordination. Marriott's (1966) description of the Holi Festival in India, in which the low-ranking castes "reverse" their roles vis-à-vis the high-ranking castes and ridicule their political/economic superiors, lends support to Gluckman's theory, but as Norbeck (1961, 1974) points out, "reversals" occur in many different kinds of rituals. Reversal of sex roles and scatological acts may occur in all types of rituals.

It is perhaps misleading to identify any one type of ritual as "ritual of reversal" or "ritual of conflict." If there is social antagonism between the sexes, such an antagonism or stress may be resolved through men and women wearing each other's clothes and reversing each other's roles in the ritual context; likewise, if there is social conflict or stress arising from hierarchical roles, the social hierarchy may be reversed in the ritual context. If there is stress or anxiety in the changing of social roles, from one generation to another, the ritual context provides an arena where the reversals, that is, changes from childhood to adulthood, can be enacted. The specific acts of reversal such as nudity, sexual license, singing lewd songs, clowning, and contrary walking or speaking vary: Different cultural traditions historically acquire particular forms of reversal as ritually appropriate.

Victor Turner (1978: 287) in his commentary on the anthology entitled *The Reversible World* notes:

> One aspect of symbolic inversion may be to break people out of their culturally defined, even biologically ascribed roles, by making them play precisely the opposite roles. Psychologists who employ the socio-drama method as a therapeutic technique claim that by assigning to patients the roles of those with whom they are in conflict, a whole conflict-ridden group can reach a deep level of mutual understanding.

Thus, it may be that all rituals are to some extent enactments of resolution of social contradictions and conflict, and that ritual contexts may be viewed as arenas for the blurring of social classifications, hierarchies, or separations in order to foster or achieve a unity of human oneness (cf. Turner 1969, 1974). In an illuminating interpretation of a healing ritual, Rigby (1968) describes the social roles of males and females in the Gogo society (in eastern Africa), wherein the tending of cattle is a male occupation but the curing of cattle through social/ritual reversal of sex roles is a female occupation. This healing ritual is identified by Rigby as a "ritual of purification" to show that the healing of the cattle is symbolically achieved through the purification of the ritual state of the society.

The Gogo are divided into several patrilineal clans that are neither corporate nor exogamous. The residential unit is the homestead, composed of the agnatic head of the family and members of the extended family, as well as other dependents. The ritual leader (head of the homestead) is entrusted with the responsibility of keeping the region occupied by the group in a state of ritual purity, thus assuring prosperity. Rituals of purification take place independent of the ritual leader's involvement. The women, mainly married women, imitate the behavior of men on occasions of childbirth and sickness of cattle. On these occasions, the reversal of roles and the rituals that follow are supposed to "dance away" or "throw away" the ritual contamination and restore the region to a state of ritual purity. Usually it is the responsibility of men to ensure success in childbirth, child development, and cattle herding. Unusual occurrences, such as the birth of twins, breech delivery, or cattle sickness, make the women "active agents." Men assume a passive role on these occasions. Participating women do not cohabit with their husbands; they function as men, doing the jobs of men. Their social position changes; ritually they are males and are sacred (transitional state or *marge*, following van Gennep's classification). They alone have the power to remove the contamination or evil responsible for the changes that necessitated the performance of the ritual in the first place. The burlesque performance ends with the removal of contamination.

Rigby focuses upon symbol and meaning, in contrast to Gluckman's theory, which focuses upon authority (structural) relationships that are reversed as a mark of protest. In other words, Rigby's analysis is an interpretation of operational (pragmatics), positional (syntactics), and exegetical (semantic) meanings of the "dual symbolic classifications obtaining in Gogo social and value categories." Because of dualistic notions of cognitive categories, people assume that through the reversal of oppositional social categories they could manipulate the natural categories. Unusual happenings are natural disasters (i.e., reversed from what ought to be), but these natural disasters can be set right, the people believe, by a temporary reversal of the oppositional social categories, and thereby what is reversed already is re-reversed and thus brought back to its original state.

Rigby states (1968: 170):

> In fact, it is not necessary to postulate equilibrium and social cohesion as the functional roots of social structures when attempting to find structural explanation for role reversal rituals. Instead, we must attempt to establish a relationship between categories of meaning on all levels, exegetical, operational, and positional, expressed in ritual, and the structural categories (the categories of persons and their interrelationships) relevant to the rituals. In order to do this, the structural principles underlying the symbolic and social orders must be isolated. Their structural interrelationship may then be established.

Victor Turner (1969) describes in detail a curative ritual called *Isoma*, which is practiced among the Ndembu of eastern Africa. The Ndembu follow matrilineal social structure and practice virilocal residence. Ethnographies that deal with similar cultural formulations of social organization report stress and conflict within the society; the Ndembu are no exception. The *Isoma* curative ritual is oriented toward symbolically expressing the obligations of women who participate in the matrilineal and virilocal arrangement. The ritual reminds the women that their primary loyalty is to their matrikin. "In brief, the whole person, not just the Ndembu 'mind,' is existentially involved in the life or death issues with which Isoma is concerned" (Turner 1969: 43). Among the Trobriand islanders who practice matrilineality and virilocality, there is a rule that boys, on reaching puberty, leave the father to live with matrikin, usually the uncle. Since the Ndembu do not have this system, the locus of children is ambiguous and is a problem. Both the fathers and the matrikin would like to have the children with them. Since the ties between mother and children are close, usually both the children and the mother leave the husband's village at the end of her reproductive cycle. The departure usually also marks the end of the marriage. The contradiction is that if the lineal continuity is to be safeguarded, marriage continuity is not possible. Marriage discontinuity is essential for lineage continuity. However, the ideal norm is that a woman must please her husband and bear children. When she does this, however, she neglects her kin.

When a woman is barren or when she suffers a miscarriage, the spirit responsible is a lineal ancestor. This implies that a woman must have emotional and intellectual attachment only with her matrikin. But she can increase the matrikin only by pleasing her husband and having children. Symbolically, however, the lineal ancestors can prevent this. When she does not have children, she fails her matrikin. This is attributed to her forgetting her obligations to the lineal ancestors who were punishing her, and to her making her remember her lineal ancestors. Barrenness is the method by which a woman is kept aware of where her loyalties should be.

Isoma is both a curative rite and a curative cult. The membership of the cult is composed of former patients and men matrilineally related to former patients. Because cult membership is not restricted to a lineage or village, the cult cuts across lineage and village and is a community of the afflicted. The doctors are women, but the senior doctor is a man, which fits with the common system, wherein men hold authority although the society may be matrilineal.

Turner's method is different from that followed by most anthropologists, who seek from the informants the contents of myths and then try to explain rituals in terms of the myths. The Ndembu, according to Turner, have few myths but have an abundance of interpretations for rituals. Thus, Turner begins with the rituals, and identifies the basic units of the ritual—symbols. Every item in the ritual is a symbol—it stands for something else. A ritual symbol is called by the Ndembu *chijikijulu*, which means both a blaze and a beacon. *Chijikijulu* connects the known and the unknown; it makes known the mysterious and the dangerous.

The name *Isoma* is derived from a word that means "to slip out of place or fastening." A woman caught in *Isoma* is one who has miscarriages and therefore the child slips out. The word from which the term *Isoma* is derived also means "to leave one's group." A woman who is caught in *Isoma* is one who failed to remember her matrikin. The patient's condition is referred to sometimes as *lufwisha*, which is derived from a word that means "to lose children." The spirit of *Isoma* can appear in dreams, although in different forms (as masked beings). This symbolism represents the spirit (*Mvwengi*) who embodies masculine power and is dangerous to women. The Ndembu believe that it is not a male spirit who afflicts women but a female ancestor masquerading as a male. It may be that a barren woman is symbolically a male.

Although the implicit function of *Isoma* ritual is to create harmony in consanguineal and affinal relationships, the ritual is performed to rectify or pacify the cause of barrenness or miscarriage. The cause is the spirit, but the spirit is activated by a curse (witchcraft) that aroused the afflicting spirit, or by sorcery. A living relative could activate the spirit through a curse. Thus, performing *Isoma* not only pacifies the spirit but also counteracts witchcraft. The rites are performed near the place where matrikin live. During the period of the ritual, virilocality is changed to uxorilocality.

The diviner decides whether the rite is to be performed at the hole of a giant rat or the burrow of an ant-bear. The holes are blocked, representing fertility, which is symbolically blocked by the spirit. The rite symbolically opens fertility. The diviner finds out whether the spirit had manifested itself as a rat or an ant-bear. The rite must be performed near the river, a usual site for the performance of witchcraft and sorcery. The doctors collect medicines from the bush while the patient is secluded in a hut built by her husband. The patient is like an initiate who, after going through the ritual, can once again become a fertile woman.

The husband supplies a red cock, the matrikin a young white hen. The senior doctor asks the animals to return the woman's fertility. Then a bundle of grass is placed on the top of the closed entrance, and another bundle is placed four feet away. Two holes are dug by hoe, and two fires lit near the second hole. The right-hand side is used by male doctors; the other, called the left-hand side, is used by female doctors. A gourd and roots are placed near the first entrance, representing the patient's body. The holes are dug to about six feet in depth and connected with a hole large enough for a person to go through. The entrance hole is called "the hole of the rat," and the other hole is called "the new hole." The entrance is hot, the other cold.

Certain trees are believed to possess a sacred quality, and medicines are extracted from them after invoking and activating their power. The doctors go to the holes; medicines are pounded and mixed with water. The mixture is divided into two portions, one of which is placed in a potsherd and heated near the entrance hole, while the other is placed in a clay pot and kept near the new hole. The holes represent binary discriminations: heat/cold, tomb/womb, death/life, entrance hole/new hole, red cock/young hen, male/female. The ritual area is encircled by tree branches. The term used by the Ndembu means (1) enclosure, (2) ritual enclosure, (3) fence courtyard, and (4) ring around the moon.

The patient goes through the hole of life and emerges through the hole of death. The senior doctor sprinkles cold medicine and his assistants hot medicine. The husband enters the hole with the patient, stands on her right, and follows her. The patient holds the white hen. The red cock is kept near the old hole (the hot one) for sacrifice. Its blood and feathers are put into the hole after the rite. The white hen represents procreation, and the cock represents maleness.

When the couple comes to the hot hole, the doctors sprinkle medicine and invoke removal of the curse. Then the couple returns to the cool hole, where they are splashed with medicine. They then return to the hot hole. The husband drinks the medicine and goes to the cool hole. Beer is consumed, except by the patient. The husband leads the patient to the hot hole and then back to the cool hole. The patient then leads the husband in the cool–hot circuit. The rite ends with the sacrifice.

The linkage or relationship between the symbols of the sacred other and the symbols of the sacred self is revealed clearly in the analysis offered by Turner. The "objects" used in the ritual share in the properties of the sacred other, and the use of these objects brings the participants into close contact with the sacred other. Turner's semiotic cultural analysis of ritual involves an investigation of the "positional meaning" of the ritual symbols (syntactics), "exegetical meaning" of the ritual symbols (semantics), and "operational meaning" of the ritual symbols (pragmatics). Positional meaning derives from how the symbols are related to one another and their semantic correspondences; exegetical meaning from the interpretations and commentaries of the symbols; and operational meaning from the specific contextual uses of the symbols.

CHAPTER SEVENTEEN
Life Cycle Rituals

RITES OF PASSAGE

In his seminal treatioc *The Rites of Passage,* van Gennep (1960 [1909]) pointed out that the "life of an individual in any society is a series of passages from one age to another and from one occupation to another," and that these passages or transitions from one state to another are marked by special rituals. Rituals are associated with birth, puberty, marriage, and death as well as with exalted occupations and natural or social change. Van Gennep identified three "sub-categories," namely, *rites of separation, transition rites,* and *rites of incorporation,* and suggested that different rituals may focus more on one of the three "rites."

> Rites of separation are prominent in funeral ceremonies, rites of incorporation at marriages. Transition rites may play an important part, for instance in pregnancy, betrothal, and initiation; or they may be reduced to a minimum in adoption, in the delivery of a second child, in remarriage, or in the passage from the second to the third age group. Thus, although a complete scheme of rites of passage theoretically includes preliminal rites (rites of separation), liminal rites (rites of transition), and post-liminal rites (rites of incorporation), in specific instances these three types are not always equally important or equally elaborated. (van Gennep 1960: 11)

Although van Gennep clearly defines his terms and provides us with an insightful understanding of the role of rituals in human life, it is perhaps necessary to clarify some of his concepts. The delineation of separation, transition, and incorporation as specific rites is not appropriate. Every rite of passage has three component parts, of which one or more may have greater or lesser emphasis. The concept of "ceremony" does not enhance our understanding of ritual. Some anthropologists prefer to apply the word *ceremony* to goal-oriented "ritual complexes" such as the "initiation ceremony" and use the term *ritual* to identify a specific act or sequences of ceremony; others use the concept of ritual as a general category and the concept of ceremony as a subcategory of ritual.

Although these distinctions may have some validity, they detract from the fact that the term *ritual* refers to stereotypic, repetitive behavior. Among humans, ritual is symbolic behavior, and the component units of ritual are symbols. Thus, it is more appropriate to theorize that some human rituals convey symbolic messages that are associated with divination, witchcraft, and healing, others with the life cycle of individuals, and yet others with redemption or renewal.

Ritual of any type "separates" the individual from the social roles, fosters the emergence of "liminal ambiguities" with the blurring of social distinctions, and helps to reinforce the social rules through the "reincorporation" of the individual into the old or new social roles with sacred or supernatural affirmation of the rules and roles. Earlier I discussed the contributions of Victor Turner (1969, 1974), who has extended and elaborated the view of van Gennep, particularly with reference to the analysis of the "between and betwixt" or liminal aspect of ritual in which the sacred or supernatural affirmation occurs.

Based on data collected during my fieldwork in 1970, I provide here a brief summary of the rituals associated with the life passages of individuals in a village of southern India. As the village communities of southern India are divided into caste or *jati* groupings (with each group having caste-specific mythologies and rituals), I present information (when necessary) on the differences between and among the caste groups. The caste groups are identified as "non-Brahmins," "Brahmins," "Christians," or "Muslims."

Affluent members of the community performed a specific ceremony for a pregnant woman, called *valaikappu*, usually in the seventh month. On this occasion, women wore several glass bangles "to amuse the fetus with the sound of jingling." A ritual of waving a red-colored mixture of lime and turmeric (*alam*) was performed, and the liquid was placed on the forehead of the pregnant woman by relatives and well-wishers. In the seventh or ninth month of pregnancy, a special ritual called *chimantham* was performed. The woman was seated on a dais in the central place of the house, and *alam* was waved in front of her. On that day the woman was usually returned to her mother's house, where the child was to be delivered.

A midwife or an elderly relative attended the birth. For the first three days, the child was usually given only sugar water, but if the child was very weak, a lactating kinswoman or the mother suckled the child. The mother was given a concoction of various herbs called *kava masala* every day, and she was given a ritual bath on the fifth day. She consumed regular food from that day on and was regularly given a mixture of asofoetida (*perunkayam*) and palm candy (*panankarkankandu*). For the first three months, she was permitted to have only the food that was considered "hot," and ideally she was required to abstain from sexual intercourse during this period.

A naming ritual was performed in the first month, when the father lifted the child and uttered its name before handing it back to the mother. There was no restriction on the frequency of breast feeding; the child was fed when it was restless. At the end of one year, the mother applied a paste of yellow gram, cayenne, or morgosa leaves to her nipples, or tied the nipples with a string, to discourage the child from breast feeding. If there was no later child, weaning occurred at the age of two. Toilet training was done by coaxing and teasing. By the time a child was three, he or she was expected to be toilet trained.

Before the child reached the age of seven, an ear-piercing ritual was conducted by all the non-Brahmin *jati* groups. Elaborate arrangements were made by the child's *ammangan* (maternal uncle). A seance with the family deity was usually held to secure the deity's approval. All the mother's consanguineal relatives (i.e., father's affinal relatives, or *sampanti*) were required to offer gifts (*moy*). Hair was shaved from the head by a special barber, and piercing was done by a ritual goldsmith. A Brahmin priest was not required in this ritual.

An elaborate female initiation ritual was performed by all the non-Brahmin *jati* groups. The female child was usually isolated for seven, nine, or eleven days. The *ammangan* (mother's brother) bore all the expenses connected with the purificatory ritual for her acceptance into the household. A seance with the family deity was held, and a special *alam* ritual for the girl was performed. A Brahmin priest was not required in this ritual.

Brahmin *jati* groups performed a male initiation rite called *upanayanam*, at which time a thread was worn by the male child as a mark of his becoming a "twice-born" and was permitted to acquire secret formulae of the Brahmanical tradition.

Among non-Brahmins, preferential mates were cross-cousins, and the marriage was generally performed at the bridegroom's residence. Marriage was preceded by a ritual called *nichayartam*, at which time the terms of exchange of gifts for the bride and groom were decided. Three, five or seven days before the marriage ritual, a long pole (*pantal kal*) was planted, and a special ritual was performed. On the day preceding marriage, a special ritual called *nalangu* was performed that involved ritual bathing, particularly of the bridegroom. *Ammangan* (maternal uncle) and *attay* (paternal aunt) had special privileges in this ritual. During the marriage ritual, the bridegroom tied a turmeric-stained string (*thali*) around the bride's neck. Most *jati* groups employed a Brahmin priest for the marriage ritual.

Both burial and cremation occurred. Adults were usually cremated. A mortuary ritual called *punniatanam* or *kariam* was usually performed on the first, seventh, eleventh, and sixteenth days after death. A Brahmin priest was invited by most *jati* groups to purify the house.

Christians differed from the Hindu *jati* groups only by employing the Christian priest to officiate over the ceremonies and by having a naming ritual in which a godmother had special responsibility for the child. The dead were always buried.

Muslims had adapted most of the Hindu rites but performed the Muslim ceremonies also and employed the Labbay Muslim priests. The most characteristic adaptation of a Hindu ritual by the Muslim was the performance of the female initiation ritual, which the Labbay Muslim priests did not consider important.

The Muslims had an elaborate naming ritual. Soon after the child was washed, a Labbay Muslim priest or elder touched the ears and forehead of the child and recited scriptures before pronouncing the names of the saints selected by the family. The child's name of reference and address was, however, given on the seventh day. An ear-piercing ritual was restricted to females. An elaborate initiation rite called *katana*, or *sunnathu* (cutting), *Kalayanam* (marriage), was performed for boys, during which the foreskin of the penis was removed. Marriage was a contract that the *kazi* (Muslim register) confirmed, and divorce was permitted with the approval of the *kazi*. A man was required to pay a dowry (*mahar*), and the marriage ritual (*nikka*) was held in the bride's house. The father of the bride represented her in the marriage ritual, and either the mother or the sister of the groom represented the bridegroom. Labbay Muslim priests buried their dead within the compound surrounding the mosque. The dead of other Muslims were buried in a Muslim cemetery.

It is important to discover how certain types of rituals and messages are symbolically linked with other aspects of the societies. Are rituals associated with birth such as *couvade* (male simulating pregnancy and birth) historical aberrations (acquired through diffusion), or can we say that certain types of elaborate birth rituals are associated with certain cosmogonic beliefs and kinship concepts that affirm the child's link with the cosmos and the father? Are puberty rituals more important in certain types of societies? Are male pubery rituals much more common in secretive, male-oriented cultural traditions (where the "sacred knowledge" is transmitted to the male during the puberty ritual)? Are marriage rituals more elaborate in societies that do not uphold divorce? Are mortuary rituals more elaborate in societies in which the dead ancestors—ghost, souls, spirits, and so on—are symbolically linked with cultural formulations about health and prosperity?

In the next two sections I discuss briefly the theoretical implications of explaining puberty rituals as either affirmation of male social roles or as psychological expressions of male sexual ambiguity.

RITUAL AFFIRMATION OF MALE SOLIDARITY

In what follows I present a discussion of Frank W. Young's (1965) book *Initiation Ceremonies: A Cross-Cultural Study of Status Dramatization*, which evaluates psychologically oriented explanations of initiation rituals and presents instead a sociological theory.

The hypothesis postulated by Young is that societies which emphasize cooperation and are cohesive (have solidarity) dramatize elaborately the status changes because in those societies members are required to have a clear definition of their roles. His book attempts to answer (using cross-cultural data contained in the *Human Relations Area File*) the question of whether there is a positive relationship between social solidarity and initiation rites and attempts "to test the hypothesis that the degree of solidarity of a given social system determines the degree to which status transition within it will be dramatized" (Young 1965: 1).

Young found it unnecessary to include under the category of "initiation rites" sporadic rituals of initiation such as marriages and funerals and other discontinuous rituals in human life. The degree of dramatization was measured (scaled) for fifty-four societies. Sixty percent showed no dramatization of sex role in male initiation, and 42 percent had no dramatization for females. But male initiation was found to be "more elaborate or intense than those for females." The elaborateness was scaled on the basis of activities such as exchange of gifts, change in names, special dress for the initiates and officiates, and the emotional or affective response of the people. The degree of dramatization was scaled by indicators such as duration and group participation. It turned out that in male initiation the community as a whole was involved—in contrast to female initiations, wherein only females were involved.

Solidarity is greater in a group when it sets itself apart from other members of the society. If men form a group, they will have an "audience" of women and children. Following Goffman's (1959) theoretical scheme, Young interprets male initiation as a boy gaining entry to the universe of adult males. It is not merely a matter of the boy internalizing the norms of a new role or situation; he is required to present a new self to the audience. As he enters the "backstage" of the in-group (adult males), a new perspective of the solidarity group as well as the audience opens up to him. The greater the solidarity of the group, the greater would be the institutionalized means of gaining entry. The theme of male solidarity is given expression in the ceremony. The group realizes the threat involved in opening its doors, but the impact of the ceremony is supposed to sensitize the initiate to the group's distinct place in social schema.

According to Young, theorists like Whiting (1961) and McClelland (1961) emphasized the personality determinants of group expression. Whiting postulated that initiation ceremonies resolved a conflict situation that arose from a boy's initial close association with his mother and the later requirements of adulthood. The basis of such a theory was that child-rearing practices determined social tendencies. In contrast to a psychological explanation, Young theorizes that institutionalized male solidarity resembles corporate units: "[S]olidarity develops when all the adult males are expected to participate in an activity that has stabilized to the point of maintaining barriers to outside perception, either in the form of a building or by way of taboos against outsiders." In some instances masculine symbols are employed to denote the exclusiveness of the group. But the most common indicators are religious separation, hierarchy within the group, preparedness to meet outside threat, and boundary. In exceptional cases initiation ceremonies are performed in the absence of solidarity groups, and such ceremonies are not performed even when solidarity groups exist. However, when "male solidarity is more institutionalized, the elaboration of initiation ceremonies increases" (Young 1965: 64–74).

Young suggests that Whiting's coding was biased in favor of viewing mother–son sleeping arrangements as existing in societies even when the data did not explicitly state such an occurrence. Whiting ignores the custom in which girls also sleep with their mothers. According to Young, Whiting's inference that male envy leads to the expression of the desire for identification with the male group is merely a speculation. The predictive power of Whiting's theory arises not from the reasons he gives but because the ceremonies reflect social solidarity.

THE SYMBOLIC TRANSFORMATION OF BIOLOGICAL IDENTITY

Mutilation of the body during initiation rituals is widespread: circumcision, subincision, perforation of the nasal septum, scarification, removing a tooth, and other emblematic signs of maturity (or becoming an adult) occur in many societies. Anthropologists and anthropologically oriented scholars have long speculated on the reasons for the performance of such acts. They agree that the performance is a signification of transforming social identity, often to denote and connote the acquisition of a sacred social identity; but there is very little agreement on why particular types of mutilation occur.

The believers or the participants themselves may have differing explanations for the same type of mutilation. For example, Jews and native Australians, who practice circumcision (cutting the foreskin of the penis), differ in explaining why it is done; and the practice of subincision (splitting the penis through opening the lower part), which occurs in native Australian societies and New Guinea societies, has different meanings for different groups. Scholars also differ in explaining these ritual customs: Some scholarly explanations correspond to the emic (native) formulations. For example, some groups believe that subincision provides boys with a vulva, an explanation similar to that of Bruno Bettelheim (1954), and some groups believe that subincision represents the formation of androgynous unity or totality, an explanation which is similar to that of Mircea Eliade (1954). Bloodletting through subincision and ritual bloodletting in general have been interpreted as either imitating menstruation or as symbolically removing female blood from the male. Beliefs and rituals of this nature may have spread historically, and it is also likely that different cultural traditions might have evolved these customs independently. It is worth noting that the British social anthropologist Mary Douglas (1966) explains subincision in the Arunta cultural tradition (of Australia) as the splitting of the penis into two halves to represent symbolically the symmetry of the two groups that make up the social universe of the Arunta. But not all groups with the moiety system (division of groups into two halves) have the ritual of splitting the penis.

Because the ritual acts of circumcision and subincision have acquired theoretical significance for understanding the nature of initiation ritual, I will describe briefly the male initiation ritual among the Arunta and discuss the views of Bruno Bettelheim and Mircea Eliade. (See W.E.H. Stanner's book *On Aboriginal Religion* [1963] for a description of the religious practices of Australian tradition.)

The Arunta have an extremely elaborate male initiation ritual. Actually, a boy is initiated into adulthood by participating not just in one but in four rituals. These rituals constitute a ritual-complex that is the central religious aspect of the Arunta cultural tradition: Through the series of four rituals, boys are socialized into the Arunta sacred lore and are initiated into the secret knowledge of the *churinga* (totemic representations). Girls, on the other hand, are initiated into adulthood in a simple manner.

When the boy is about ten, his nasal septum is perforated, and he is tossed into the air and painted with white and red substances. This ritual signifies that he can participate in the adult activities of males. When the boy is about fifteen, boys of the same age group are taken to a secluded place where they are taught the sacred lore for a minimum of three days. During this ritual seclusion, they are circumcised, and the scalp is bitten by the male adults to let the blood flow in large amounts. After the boys recover, they are taken once again to the secluded place, and the ritual of subincision (slitting open the bottom of the penis to expose the urethra) occurs. Before and after this ritual, boys are taught the meaning of *churinga* images (totemic objects of the Arunta). The fourth or final ritual of initiation is called *engwura*, which may continue for several months. Males re-open their healed penises to let blood flow, endure ordeals by fire, and participate in elaborate singing and reciting of the sacred lore. Boys acquire sacred names (which are kept secret) and are declared to be adult males, or those who are the guardians of the sacred tradition.

Bettelheim (1954) in his book *Symbolic Wounds: Puberty Rites and the Envious Male* presents the following hypothesis: Circumcision is a kind of fertility ritual that communicates messages about copulation and procreation; circumcision marks the beginning of being able to create new life, and the assumptions about human fertility are the central aspect of the initiation ritual. One of the reasons for having male initiation rituals is to assert that males also can create or have children. Males are envious of their being unable to give birth physically, and therefore they symbolically assert their role in fertility or procreation. In cultural traditions with little understanding of the male role in conception, there is likely to be more rituals which assert that males are involved in procreation.

According to Bettelheim, subincision signifies that males also have sexual organs to procreate like women. Because women menstruate, because menstruation stops when a woman is pregnant, and because women do not generally have children after menopause, males enact menstruation by periodically opening their penis wounds, and they stop the bleeding to symbolically enact their capacity and role in child-bearing. Circumcision is a substitute for menarche, and subincision is an additional effort to acquire the sacred power for giving birth or procreating.

Mircea Eliade (1958) in his book *Rites and Symbols of Initiation: The Mysteries of Birth and Rebirth* makes the following observations about the ritual act of subincision as signifying blood symbolism:

> . . . the primary purpose of initiatory subincision appears to be obtaining fresh blood. Throughout the world, blood is a symbol of strength and fertility. In Australia as elsewhere, the novices are daubed with red ocher—a substitute for blood—or sprinkled with fresh blood. Among the Dieiri, for example, the men open veins and let the blood flow over the novices' bodies to make them brave. Among the Karadjeri, the Itchumundi, and other Australian tribes, the novice also drinks blood; and the same custom is found in New Guinea where the explanation given for it is that the novice has to be strengthened with male blood because the blood he has had so far was entirely his mother's. (Eliade 1958: 26–27)

Eliade (1958: 26) also notes that subincision may symbolically represent the acquisition of a vulva by the male (as some Australian tribes believe) and thereby symbolically assert the male sacredness of androgynous unity. "The androgyne is considered superior to the two sexes just because it incarnates totality and hence perfection. For this reason we are justified in interpreting the ritual transformation of novices into women—whether by assuming women's dress or by subincision—as the desire to recover a primordial situation of totality and perfection."

ESCHATOLOGICAL RITUALS

Rituals associated with beliefs concerning "afterlife" are nearly universal. The cults of the dead in a number of African, Asian, Amerindian, and Oceanic societies have been recorded by anthropologists. Most Christians are at least familiar with the ritual of All Soul's Day. Some societies have very elaborate rituals associated with deceased ancestors, who are invited to participate in the affairs of the living; some societies have elaborate rituals to exclude the spirits of the dead from any involvement with the living.

Mortuary or funeral rituals vary in their characteristics and durations: Some groups have several weeks or months of ritual mourning and taboos, and some groups have almost no mourning period or taboos associated with death. Western societies as well as Chinese, Japanese, and a few other societies have the ritual of burial; Hindu societies and some Native American societies have the ritual of cremation; some African and Asian societies have the ritual of placing the corpse out in the open either for vultures or wild animals to eat or for the body to be destroyed.

The Konyak Nagas of the India–Burma region have a custom of placing the corpse on a specially built platform (near the houses) for it to decay. Food offerings are made to the corpse; on the sixth day, the skull is wrenched from the body, and the putrefying brain is removed. The cleaned skull is kept in the house, and the skull-less corpse is left on the platform to decompose. The skull is periodically given food for three years. The Konyak believe that the soul resides in the skull, although the individual's "personality" has left this world and resides in the land of the dead (see Furer-Haimendorf 1969).

It is not uncommon to have two or more separate rituals (separated by weeks or months) for the dead. For example, the Kota tribe of southern India has two rituals for the dead, one called Green Funeral, which is performed soon after death, and the other called Dry Funeral, which is performed once a year, or once in two years, as a collective ritual for all Kota who have died during the previous one or two years (Mandelbaum

1954). The Huron of North America had a ritual for the dead called the Feast of the Dead that was performed every ten or twelve years. Fagan (1984) interprets this ritual as the most important ritual to promote unity within the tribe and harmonious relationships with neighboring tribes.

> The Feast of the Dead lasted for about ten days. The first eight were spent collecting bodies from local cemeteries for reburial. All corpses except the most recently deceased were stripped of flesh and skin and the robes in which they had been buried, which were burned. The washed and cleaned bones were wrapped in new beaver skins and placed in decorated bags. Then the families feasted and celebrated the dead. On the appointed day, processions of mourners carried the dead to the village where the ceremony was to be held. Gifts were exchanged and friendships affirmed at each settlement along the way. (Fagan 1984: 200–201)

Eschatological beliefs and ritual are symbolically linked with social order. Broadly speaking, four types of such beliefs and rituals can be identified: (1) formulations of afterlife that promise rewards in heaven or paradise for good conduct in this life, as in Christian or Islamic orientations; (2) formulations to justify one's social situation with reference to one's actions in a previous life, as in Hindu–Buddhist orientations; (3) formulations of ghosts or spirits or the dead that serve as vehicles for the projection of hostility and contribute, indirectly, to social harmony among the living, as in Ifaluk society; and (4) formulations of how the spirits of the deceased ancestors continue to regulate the conduct and economic prosperity of the descendants, as in Chinese society.

Francis L.K. Hsu (1967) has given a detailed description of the rituals associated with deceased ancestors. In the traditional Chinese society, the living are "under the shadow of the ancestors." Every household has a family shrine, in which is kept a wooden tablet for each ancestor with his or her age at death recorded. Periodic rituals, including offerings of food, are performed in the shrine; in addition, rituals are performed for the deceased ancestors at the graveyard and at the clan temple. The Chinese conceptualize the existence of a spiritual residence and a worldly residence for the spirits. Spirits need periodic, ritual sustenance from the living and will in turn help the living. The continuity of human life is conceptualized with reference to the ancestors: The living father and son are identified lineally with the deceased ancestor, and just as the father is required to perform rituals for his deceased father and ancestors, the son will be required to perform rituals for his deceased father and ancestors. Hsu notes that the deceased ancestors live among the descendants "not only biologically, but also socially and psychologically." The success of the descendants is attributed to the deceased ancestors, and the ritual glorification of the dead affirms the familial, economic, social, and political ideals of the Chinese.

CHAPTER EIGHTEEN
Rituals of Social Renewal

CALENDRICAL AND CYCLICAL RITUALS

Anthropological classifications of rituals often distinguish between "crisis rituals" that occur in response to an individual's transition(s) (such as birth, puberty, marriage, parenting, sickness, and death), and "cyclical rituals" that occur seasonally or periodically, with the involvement of the entire community. Crisis rituals may also involve the community, but the involvement of the community is more like a support group for the "individual," and the participants in the crisis rituals can expect similar social affirmation for themselves when their time comes. Cyclical rituals, on the other hand, are performed for the welfare of the society as a whole, or for particular groups, whose continuity transcends the life of the individual. Cyclical or seasonal rituals of this kind may have a fixed, calendrical date that occurs once a year, or they may be rituals that are performed communally every day, every week, or every month. Some cyclical or seasonal rituals occur on a regular basis, but with no specific calendrical date, and some rituals associated with individuals (such as initiation or death) may have a collective, cyclical orientation with an annual ritual for all the initiates or for all the dead.

For analytic purposes, it is useful to have a category called "rituals of social renewal" to identify all the cyclical or seasonal, communal rituals and to have the following subcategories.

Rituals of Social Renewal

Annual rituals of social renewal—for example, Thanksgiving, Christmas, Easter, All Saints' Day, Ramadan (Islam), Deepavali (Hindu Festival of Lights), Pongal (Tamil harvest festival), Winter Solstice (many Native American cultures)	Weekly or monthly rituals of social renewal—for example, sacred days such as Friday (Islam), Saturday (Jewish), Sunday, Full Moon (Islam, Hindu)	Noncalendrical but cyclical (repetitive) rituals of social renewal—for example, Sun Dance (Indians of North America), Graveyard Rituals (Chinese and other cultures)

The term *social renewal* is an appropriate concept to identify these rituals because all of them affirm group orientations and help redefine or reaffirm the commitments of the individual to the "community of believers," even when particular individuals who participate in them may have different personal objectives. They communicate messages that make the society sacred or supernatural, and they promote formulations of the sacred self in the individual that correspond to the sacred others who are propitiated or invoked in the ritual.

The previous chapter pointed out that the concept of "rites of passage" has been used to discuss the nature of all rituals, including what has been identified in this chapter as rituals of social renewal. The concept of rites of passage correctly identifies the processual structure of all rituals: separation of the participants from society; a temporary stage of transition or liminality in which the participants are unified into a socially undifferentiated community; and the re-entrance or incorporation of the participants back into the social roles. But because van Gennep discussed the concept with reference to the "passages" of individuals from one stage or status to another and suggested that different rituals focus on one or more of the three aspects (separation, transition, and incorporation) of ritual, the use of the concept tends to be limited to "life cycle rituals" (as discussed in the previous chapter). I have suggested that classifications of rituals into different categories can be misleading because they overlap considerably, and because cultural traditions vary in their delineation of boundaries that mark the rituals as individual-crisis ritual or as communal-seasonal ritual.

RITUAL AFFIRMATION OF SOCIAL
AND SELF COHERENCE

Life cycle rituals have reference to the life of an individual and signify universal experiences of humankind. In contrast, rituals of social renewal have more of a specific, contextual significance in the sense that societies identify certain historical events or values as the focus of the rituals. In this respect, rituals of social renewal have "nationalistic" overtones and are often vehicles to maintain cultural boundaries.

Most social renewal rituals have their origins in religious, political, or ethnic histories. Exceptions are rituals of social renewal that have referents in natural or biological attributes such as "solstice rituals" and "fertility rituals" that are linked with the planting and harvesting of food crops and changes in the seasons (winter or summer) or astronomical signs.

In the United States, the ritual of Thanksgiving has special historical and cultural significance. Although Thanksgiving rituals are performed in other countries also, the American Thanksgiving affirms certain conceptions of America and the American self. Likewise, although Christmas and Easter are annual rituals that are important to all Christians, their significance must be understood with reference to the denominational differences and the cultural significations of those rituals. Roman Catholic cultural traditions have emphasized the importance of rituals associated with All Saints' Day; and there are several other social renewal rituals, linked with Christianity, that have greater cultural relevance in Catholic countries. The sabbath (day of sanctity and rest) may serve as a day for ritual expression of the moral and social values in Islamic, Judaic, or Christian religious traditions, but the expression of the values reflects the cultural tradition: Islam has a different history of religiosity in Morocco and Indonesia; Christianity has a different history of religiosity in Mexico and the United States; the sabbath in Morocco reflects Moroccan culture; the sabbath in the United States reflects American culture. There are innumerable Hindu rituals of social renewal, but their significance and use vary from region to region and from group to group.

The foregoing examples are not meant to be an exhaustive or comprehensive survey of the significance of social renewal rituals. These examples suggest that the rituals have specific cultural significance and are expressive of the values, historical events, and group identities. Thus, although the rituals occur universally and are characterized by the existence of certain common features, it is important to interpret them within their cultural contexts in order to understand their significance. A brief discussion of the Sun Dance ritual illustrates this point more fully.

The Sun Dance ritual is an important ritual of social renewal in many North American Indian societies, but its cultural significance and interpretation vary. The Crow Indians believed that "the essence of the ritual lies in the vision-quest of a mourner thirsting for revenge" (Lowie 1924: 275). The Comanche Indians held their last Sun Dance in 1978: They believed that the ritual was performed to enhance the supernatural power of participants, particularly that of the medicine men; "Every dance originated in a supernatural sanction received by some medicine man" (Linton 1935: 420). The Lakota Indians of the Rosebud reservation of South Dakota have been debating whether there should be a uniform, standardized Sun Dance ritual ideology, or whether the ritual may be performed in any culturally relevant manner. The following two quotes taken from Grobsmith's (1981) description of the Sun Dance among the Lakota show that the ritual has undergone changes in several respects and that much controversy surrounds the interpretation of its significance to the participants and the groups as a whole.

Before the twentieth century, the Sun Dance was considered a drama enacting the symbolic capture, torture, and release of the enemy. Young men went though the Sun Dance annually to demonstrate their bravery as though they themselves had been captured and tortured, finally struggling to obtain their freedom. The practice of piercing the flesh of the individual by thongs attached to ropes tied to the Sun Dance pole and the subsequent breaking free certainly does bring to mind the traditional imagery. People on the reservation no longer give this explanation for the Sun Dance; in fact many do not even know of it. (Grobsmith 1981: 70)

There have been several types of Sun Dance endurance and ordeals. In some rituals the dancer gazed at the sun for a whole day; at other rituals the dancer was either pierced with skewers or suspended in the air hanging between poles with the skewers. As noted earlier, controversies often surround the adoption of what is regarded as the correct form of Sun Dance ritual.

Although the Sun Dance is the most sacred and elaborate of Lakota rituals, there is often disagreement among reservation residents as to whose form of performance is correct, whose is too commercialized, or whose is most sacred. Because of this local disagreement, some Sun Dances are poorly attended. Different factions sponsor their own Sun Dance, so there may be as many as three or four in a given summer. This is not surprising since there is considerable variability in the style of each medicine man. (Grobsmith 1981: 74)

Among the Cheyenne of Oklahoma, Sun Dance is second to Arrow Renewal in importance. "The central theme of the Cheyenne Sun Dance is world renewal" (Hoebel 1978: 18). Sun Dance among the Cheyenne involved extensive self-torture—"hanging from the center pole" held by skewers pierced through the skin on the chest. Hoebel (1978: 23) notes that "self-sacrifice does not contribute to the earth-renewal purposes of the Sun Dance, nor is it done on behalf of the tribe as a whole. It may be vowed to help cure a relative or to avert danger in war. Or it may be undertaken as a result of a dream."

Sun Dance ritual in the contemporary Shoshone and Ute societies is performed without the acts of gazing at the sun or "hanging from the central pole." Jorgensen (1972) observed the ritual as it was performed in different places, and along with information gathered from the informants, he has given us a detailed description of the native (emic categories) interpretations of the ritual as well as the ritual's historical and cultural significance for the Shoshone and Ute Indians. Sun Dance defines the relationship between humans and nature, between the individual and group, acquisition of supernatural power by the individual, and the use of the power for healing and social purposes. Sun Dance ideology holds that everything in nature, both inanimate and animate, participates in supernatural power; life is made possible and is continued with the fusion or synthesis of the complementary but opposite aspects of power. Sun Dancers synthesize hot/dry and cold/wet aspects of the power and thereby increase their own supernatural power. A dancer, in exhaustion, may become unconscious, but from the cultural perspective the dancer is knocked down by the Buffalo, a repository of enormous power, and has a vision. Through this the dancer is "shamanized"; he learns new songs and different ways of using the supernatural power and becomes a shaman with the power to heal the sick. Thus, the power acquired in large amounts has relevance and meaning only in the social context; power has to be used to heal the sick and to contribute to the prosperity and well-being of the group.

In Jorgensen's (1972) view, Sun Dance ritual has developed as a religious movement, focusing on redemption or bringing about an inner change in the person to foster the development of peaceful and harmonious coexistence with nature and the group. On the one hand it teaches that all energy comes from nature and that the sun is the greatest source of this power; without the power nothing can exist. On the other hand, the ritual teaches that an individual can pursue and capture more power than is necessary for life; this excess power, however, must be used for social purposes and not merely to meet one's selfish desires.

Sun Dance ritual is also a religion, with an elaborate cosmology, cult of shamanistic healers, priesthood, and sacralized social values. The ritual unifies the group; provides the participants with a coherent, meaningful system of beliefs concerning life and the universe; and enables the participants to acquire the shamanistic and priestly sacred selves.

I present below some more examples of social renewal rituals that illustrate the wide range in types of rituals that can be included in the category of rituals of social renewal.

The Swazi of southern Africa have an annual ritual of kingship that lasts for about three weeks each year. It is called the *Newala* ritual. Kuper (1986: 75) notes that "The Newala symbolizes the unity of the state and attempts to maintain it."

The Hutterites in North America have a church ritual every evening in which recitation of Biblical verses occurs. The ritual emphasizes the need for spiritual life and order, but as Hostetler and Huntington (1967: 35–36) note, "The church service reinforces the basic pattern of Hutterite life and simultaneously gives relief and depth by setting the sacred against the secular. . . ."

The Konyak Nagas (of the India–Burma border region) had a custom of social renewal that required "head-hunting." Warriors hunted for a head in enemy villages and brought it to their village to perform a ritual for affirming the values of the community. Furer-Haimendorf (1969: 99) notes that "Konyaks were firmly convinced that the capturing of heads was essential for the well-being of a village and that a community which failed over a period of years to bring in a head would suffer a decline in prosperity."

The bear ritual among the Ainu begins with the capturing of a bear cub, raising it (as a "grand-child"), slaughtering and consuming it ritually when the bear is a year and a half in age. A special ritual called *kamuy oka inkara* (which means "seeing the deity off") is held by the host family (i.e., the family that raised the cub). People from all the Ainu settlements participate in this ritual. Ohnuki-Tierney (1974: 92) notes: "While all other Ainu rituals are held by individual family or by an individual shaman, the bear ceremony involves not only all the members of the settlement but those from numerous other settlements. It thus provides one of a very few occasions for people from distant settlements to gather, renewing old ties and creating new ones. . . ."

PART FIVE

Conclusion: Anthropology and the Study of Religion

CHAPTER NINETEEN
Changing Perspectives in the Anthropological Study of Religion

EVOLUTIONARY TYPOLOGIES IN THEORIZING ABOUT THE NATURE OF THE SACRED OTHER AND THE SACRED SELF

Historically, many controversies and debates in the anthropological study of religion resulted from two fallacious assumptions: (1) the belief that "natural" or "elementary" forms of religion were found in "primitive" or non-Western cultures, and (2) that a religious form "discovered" or found in one primitive culture could be used to make general statements about the evolution and function of a particular type of religious institution.

Because of the foregoing assumptions, certain religious forms found in Siberian, North American, and Oceanic cultures acquired anthropological significance as the fundamental or elementary aspects of primitive or archaic religion. For example, terms such as *shaman*, *mana*, *tabu*, and *totem* became anthropological concepts to identify the relationship between certain types of religious phenomena and certain stages of mental and cultural development. A characteristic feature of anthropology had been to render the emic (native, cognitive) categories of non-Western cultures into etic or scientific categories of anthropology with the notion that the cultural categories of the non-West revealed to science the beginnings of religion or other institutions.

The word *shaman*, taken from the Tungus language, literally refers to the ecstatic, ritual specialist who has the capacity to undertake journeys to the world of spirits and to commune with (and seek the assistance of) spirits. Anthropologists used it as a concept to identify a variety of ritual specialists such as "medicine men," "sorcerers," and "spirit mediums." The concept of shaman was used also to formulate a theory that shamanism constituted the archaic or primordial form of religion, which was magical in orientation. This evolutionary typology led scholars to identify parallels in the existence of shamanistic types of practices or "magical" rituals (such as divination and healing) in different parts of the non-Western World.

Robert Codrington's (1891) description of beliefs in supernatural power (*mana*) became the basis for Robert Marett's (1909) theory that such a belief was the earliest form of religion. It was not recognized that beliefs in supernatural power occurred in a number of different places with different meanings. The term *mana*, an Oceanic word for sacred power, has multiple contextual meanings; in Melanesia, mana had no specific association with political authority, but in Polynesia *mana* was linked with the political authority of chieftains and nobles. The word *tabu*, another Polynesian term, which referred to various ritual avoidances and prohibitions that were indirectly related to *mana*, acquired anthropological significance to theorize about the nature of magic. *Mana* and *tabu* types of beliefs and practices were identified as an early form of magical orientation in the evolutionary typologies of many anthropological studies.

In one of the most misleading theoretical interpretations of religion, the Ojibwa term *totam*, which had a specific and limited meaning of a guardian spirit in the form of an animal, was anthropologically transformed into a general concept and theory to define and illustrate the characteristics of primitive religion. Totemism became a subject of much controversy in the late nineteenth and early twentieth centuries; religious phenomena such as the belief in guardian spirit, the worship of animals, objects and plants (designated as sacred), as well as the identification of individuals and groups with reference to animals, became classified as totemism.

The foregoing examples of the use of particular ethnographic data to formulate general theories of religion illustrate that anthropological typologies and classifications have the potential to distort our understanding of cultural reality. It is important to keep in mind that typologies are our constructs (cultural and/or scientific) for identifying the existence of similarities and differences in phenomena; they do not explain the causes for the similarities and differences (unless they are associated with theories).

Nineteenth- and early-twentieth-century anthropologists linked their typologies with unproven and empirically unverifiable theories of mental and cultural evolution and erroneously presented examples of racial types, kinship types, and religious types as demonstrating the operation of an evolutionary, natural law of the mind and culture. Certain racial, kinship, and religious types were identified as more advanced than others, and a logical construct of the hierarchy of types was mistakenly conceptualized as empirical evidence of evolutionary progress; "higher" racial, kinship, and religious types were explained as the product of superior biological and mental characteristics. It was generally assumed that the lowest level of biological/mental development produced the "savage" or "primitive" cultural phenomena such as *mana, tabu,* totemism, and magic; at a slightly higher level of "barbaric" development, cultural phenomena such as polytheism occurred; and at a still higher level (identified as civilization), phenomena such as monotheism emerged. Compounding these errors was the fallacy of correlating the primitive cultural phenomena with dark-skinned racial types, and the advanced cultural phenomena with white-skinned racial types.

Needless to say, the evolutionary typologies and explanations served an important ethnocentric function in the Western intellectual tradition. However, it must be pointed out that typologies and classifications have an important function in all human discourse (both scientific and cultural), and as long as we do not confuse logical constructs and ontological realities and do not reify our constructs, typological models can be used fruitfully in the anthropological study of religion. In other words, the baby should not be thrown out with the bath water. Typologies and classifications can also serve as scaffolding to construct theoretical edifices.

THE IDEAS OF PROJECTION AND FUNCTION IN THEORIZING ABOUT THE NATURE OF THE SACRED OTHER AND THE SACRED SELF

The ideas of projection and function are either implicit or explicit in most anthropological theories explaining the origins of religion. Ancient Greek and Roman philosophers as well as many late-nineteenth- and early-twentieth-century scholars such as Max Muller, Edward Tylor, Sigmund Freud, and Emile Durkheim theorized that humans project their known experiences into the outer world and create models of the unknown, using known or knowable models. These scholars differed in their conceptions of what exactly was projected and why projection was necessary. Max Muller theorized that the projection of human attributes onto natural phenomena, or anthropomorphism, resulted from underdeveloped cognitive skills for abstraction; Edward Tylor suggested that religion originated in an erroneous projection of intra-psychic (psychological) experiences such as dreams or visions. Sigmund Freud theorized extensively about how inner feelings and drives are projected onto the outside, to other peoples and supernatural entities. According to Freud (1938: 857), "The projection of inner perceptions to the outside is a primitive mechanism which, for instance, also influences our sense-perceptions, so that it normally has the greatest share in shaping our outer world." Freud's discourse on projection contributed to the theoretical view of religion as a "projective system." Emile Durkheim viewed the sacred as the projection of the important social/moral values of the society. Religion was, in the views of these scholars, deification or worshipping of one's own psyche or society. A similar perspective, in a humanistic framework, was forcefully presented by Ludwig Feuerbach in 1841 in his work *The Essence of Christianity*. He theorized that "Man projects his nature into the world outside of himself before he finds it in himself" (Feuerbach 1957: 11).

Explanations that religion is a derivative of other institutions or that it corresponds to the prevailing social structure incorporate the idea of projection to denote the foundation of religion. Religion, in such explanations, is seen as the symbolic representation of the concrete reality of human experience. Norbeck (1961; 1974: 20) has been explicit in suggesting that religious creations are modeled after experience and that religion is a "projective creation of man that reflects himself and the world of his experience." Psychological anthropologists such as Melford Spiro (1952: 196) and Morris Opler (1936) have long theorized about religion serving as a channel to displace anxiety and aggression and thereby functioning to help human beings adjust and become integrated in society. Malinowski's (1925, 1954) "biopsychological functionalism" and Radcliffe-Browns (1939, 1952) "social structural functionalism" shaped the development of social anthropology. In social anthropology, religious beliefs and practices were conceptualized as institutions that contributed to meet the needs of the individual or the society; it was theorized that religious institutions functioned to maintain the equilibrium of the individual and the society, promoting the well-being of individuals and the integration of society. Most of the functionalist explanations were teleological or tautologous (or both), and their theoretical importance was limited. However, it can be said that if the ideas of projection and function are applied in a broad, general manner, all human activities (thinking and behavior) have projective and functional aspects.

In an article entitled "A Cognitive Theory of Religion," Guthrie (1980:

181) suggests that anthropomorphism "is common in the cognition of daily life and universal in religion." He notes that:

> (1) people hold religious beliefs because they are plausible models of the world, apparently grounded in daily experience; (2) religion may be defined as systematic application of human-like models to non-human, in addition to human, phenomena (e.g., in the discovery of "messages" in plagues and droughts as well as in human language); and (3) since all models, religious or secular, depend on analogy and metaphor—whether or not they also depend on logic—there is no fundamental disjunction between religious and non-religious modes of thought, despite their differences in content. The relation of religious to nonreligious thought is one of similarity of form and continuity of substance.

To argue that religion and science are rooted in cognition is the same as arguing that culture is rooted in cognition, a pan-human activity of creating and organizing the world; but the control that human beings establish through such a mechanism has different consequences. In science, the controlling effort results in an approximation of the world for predictable, practical ends. In religion, such an effort provides the believers with coherence, meaning, and integration of the symbolic self.

Human beings project their psychological and social experiences in formulating the attributes of the symbols of the sacred other (deities and metaphors of spirituality). But these symbols also possess attributes that are not purely psychological or social in the sense that they represent the fusion of the unknown and the known, the empirically verifiable and unverifiable; and as O'Flaherty (1973) has pointed out, gods, goddesses, and spirits often dramatize the extremes and extraordinary, superhuman proportions. For example, the Hindu god Siva is an "erotic ascetic." He is ithyphallic at the same time that he is a celibate yogi. He is both a symbol of cosmic destruction and cosmic creation. He has human and nonhuman forms. The use of the symbol Siva, who is sacred and superhuman, produces a sacred self capable of comprehending and coping with various contradictions of human life in Hindu culture.

Although projection is universal in cognition, both scientific and religious, the use of projective representations in religion is different from that of science. In religion, the construction and maintenance of the symbolic self as sacred are the fundamental factors, and this serves as a device to keep the symbolic self integrated, providing coherence and meaning. As George H. Mead (1913: 379) notes: "The fundamental difference between the scientific and moral solution of a problem lies in the fact that the moral problem deals with concrete personal interests, in which the whole self is reconstructed in its relation to the other selves whose relations are essential to its personality."

EXPLANATION AND INTERPRETATION
OF THE SYMBOLS
OF THE SACRED OTHER
AND THE SACRED SELF

Several anthropologists have voiced concern over the "inadequacy" of anthropological explanations of religion and have suggested that the study of religion is theoretically stagnant. For example, Clifford Geertz wrote in 1966:

> Two characteristics of anthropological work on religion accomplished since the second world war strike me as curious when such work is placed against that carried out just before and just after the first. One is that it has made no theoretical advances of major importance. . . . The second is that it draws what concepts it does use from a very narrowly defined intellectual tradition.

Paul Heelas (1977) has been more direct in identifying the reasons for theoretical inadequacy in the study of religion. He notes:

> In the last fifteen years or so, it has become increasingly apparent that traditional, positivistically inclined anthropology has not been able to cope satisfactorily with the demanding task of offering new insights into the nature of religious phenomena. Positivism has proved to be inadequate for three main and interrelated reasons: theoretical stagnation, neglect of meaning, and neglect of intra-religious explanations.

August Comte (1788–1857) promoted the view that the scientific or positivistic stage was the culmination of the human mind developing from its primitive or theological stage to the civilized or positivistic stage. Comte believed that it was necessary to constitute a "religion of humanity" that would reflect the scientific worldview. He sought to bring about a congruence between the scientific knowledge of the world and the social conventions of the Western tradition. He perceived that a disjunction existed between the knowledge of the world, which was derived through science, and the knowledge of humankind, which was promoted by Christianity, and he tried to reconcile the contradiction by having sociologists serve or officiate as priests of the universal church of humankind. Comte believed that because these priests would have the scientific understanding of the world they would not seek to maintain an archaic theological worldview of humankind. Comte's narrow view of science stood in the way of his applying or using symbolic analysis for an understanding of cultural formulations.

I share the theoretical position of Florian Znaniecki, who eloquently formulated the humanistic, scientific study of culture in several books. As Bierstedt points out, "he developed the view that all knowledge, including scientific knowledge, is a product of the sociocultural situation in which it arises" (Bierstedt 1969: 34). In his book *The Method of Sociology* (1934), Znaniecki clearly formulated the distinctive features of the cultural sciences such as anthropology and sociology.

> In a word, the data of the cultural student are always "somebody's," never "nobody's" data. This essential character of cultural data we call the humanistic coefficient, because such data, as objects of the student's theoretic reflection, already belong to somebody else's active experience and are such as this active experience makes them. (Znaniecki 1934: 36)

The fundamental difference between the study of physical phenomena and cultural phenomena is in the fact that the study of cultural phenomena is the study of knowledge and meaning. In other words, the scientific study of culture is an inquiry into how people have created an understanding of their world of experience. Thus, anthropological inquiry is a search for an understanding of understanding(s). We explain and interpret how people create, maintain, evaluate, and dramatize their understanding. This mode of inquiry involves the analysis of the different levels of cultural reality and is much more complex than the method of formulating hypotheses to test the existence of cause-and-effect relationships.

Hypothesis testing is a valid method, perhaps a necessary method, but is not sufficient to acquire an understanding of how cultural universes are created and maintained. Semiotic cultural analysis, as I see it, is an all-inclusive technique that does not restrict anthropological inquiry to any particular kind of approach such as cultural materialism or cultural idealism. In semiotic cultural analysis we try to understand the structure and meaning of representations as well as the representations of these representations at different levels. In short, semiotic cultural analysis explains and interprets symbols at multiple levels of their construction and usage.

The recent shift in anthropology from a narrow positivistic ideology to a semiotic and hermeneutical or interpretive understanding has promoted the anthropological study of religion as cultural construction of the sacred other and the sacred self and has contributed to an understanding of religious phenomena in terms of how they are used to create order, control, meaning, organization, boundaries, and so on for the maintenance of the coherence and integrity of the symbolic self. The study of the relationship between religion and the symbolic self and the study of how or why the symbolic self is related to religious phenomena in a certain manner in a given historical period make the anthropological study of religion a theoretically and methodologically distinctive approach to the understanding of religion.

Horton (1968) in his stimulating essay "Neo-Tylorianism: Sound Sense or Sinister Prejudice" argues that the rationalist or intellectualist approach to religion has merit; just as the historian of science can show

how Western society progressively discarded an animistic or religious worldview and acquired a scientific worldview, anthropologists should not be worried about showing that the worldview of preliterate peoples is often based on erroneous or false assumptions about nature. Horton's major contribution is in emphasizing that the accepted scientific worldview of today will probably be discarded in the future: Science, as Thomas Kuhn has shown, does not necessarily progress in a linear fashion, eliminating error and arriving at truth, but is itself shaped by paradigmatic frameworks of culture that help us understand and explain phenomena, and there is no certainty that these frameworks will last forever. Thus, it is important to realize that people make mistakes in cognition, and neither preliterate nor literate societies are immune to this fact. Thus it may be valid to state that some societies have greater scientific knowledge than others, with techniques of controlled experimentation, more sophisticated systems of developing new knowledge, and better procedures for discovering the principles of nature.

But the presence or absence of scientific techniques and knowledge is unrelated to the existence or non-existence of religious knowledge of the world and humans' place in the world. The relevance of religious knowledge is integration of the symbolic self through linking the symbolic self and the sacred other, and religious knowledge coexists with scientific knowledge: People may scientifically understand dreams (Freud, for example, has his counterparts in preliterate societies), or the medical cause of smallpox, but the scientific discoveries of the nature of dreams and smallpox do not eliminate symbols or representations of self integration and do not eliminate existential and cultural contradictions. Science has succeeded in eliminating religious explanations in many areas, such as shamanistic medical practices, but it does not eliminate religion from culture because religion deals with a dimension of culture that is concerned with symbolic self integration, coherence, meaning, and so on.

The symbols of the sacred other or the sacred self cannot be comprehended through Aristotelian logical premises (all A are B; all B are C; therefore all A are C) and the principles of identity (A is A), contradiction (A cannot be both A and not A at the same time), and the excluded middle (A must either be A or not A). The valid deductions and inferences for comprehending the symbol of Siva are in the Hindu cultural structures of significances and meaning, not in the mathematical rules of deduction and inferences. Hindus use Siva as a metaphor to organize their symbols of self integration, and this organization occurs in relation to culturally created anxieties, oppositions, and conflicts. Siva cannot be understood without his mediating metaphorical function, and those who use him as a metaphor manifest a symbolic self that relates with everything of significance for human existence in a structurally coherent manner, as such a symbolic self as is considered appropriate in Hindu culture.

As Leach (1976: 69–70) has pointed out, "When we are engaged in an ordinary technical action we take it for granted that if an entity A is distinguished from an entity B, it cannot simultaneously be held that A and B are identical. In theological argument the opposite is the case. . . .

> Christianity affords some of the very striking examples: the concept of the Virgin-Mother of God is one; the proposition that God the Son is "begotten" of God the Father, even though God the Father, God the Son, and God the Holy Ghost have been one and the same and identical from the beginning, is another. Admittedly even devout Christians have great difficulty in "understanding" such mysteries, but it cannot be argued that just because religious propositions are non-logical (in the ordinary sense) they must be meaningless.

THE ANTHROPOLOGY OF RELIGION AND THE HISTORY OF RELIGION

In the early 1980s, I attended a conference that was held in connection with the opening of a new doctoral program in the Department of Religion at a leading American university. Two of the distinguished panelists were anthropologists—a British social anthropologist (an Englishman) and an American cultural anthropologist (an African-American). The British social anthropologist denounced the theoretical contributions of most anthropologists as useless and praised theological scholarship on religion. The American cultural anthropologist spoke on the theoretical changes that occurred in the field of anthropology, how beliefs and actions evolve around changing sociopolitical factors, how certain peoples and cultures (like his) were made into objects of study by anthropology, and how a phenomenological/historical approach could serve to enhance the scholarly contributions in both the anthropology of religion and the history of religion.

The British social anthropologist proclaimed that Emile Durkheim was a "brilliant failure" because religion cannot be reduced to society, and "sociological interpretations of religion are therefore necessarily false"; A.R. Radcliff-Brown, he continued, lacked originality and had probably stolen ideas and data from his students; Bronislaw Malinowski was confused in being unable to make a distinction between explanation and description; E.E. Evans-Pritchard revolted against Radcliffe-Brown's positivistic approach for personal reasons and adopted a hermeneutical approach because of his conversion to the Roman Catholic faith; Victor Turner's analysis of religious symbols had not advanced much beyond that of Saint Ambrose of the fourth century A.D.

After having judged his colleagues, the British social anthropologist said that in anthropology we have "a theory of mistakes" and "only hindsight," meaning that our understanding comes from knowing what we have done wrong; that social anthropology was, in fact, involved in the study of meaning and interpretation so that it would be valid to discard the prefix *social* and call the discipline "semantic anthropology," and that he was happy to be called a "semantic anthropologist."

Our "semantic anthropologist" proceeded to say that he had more in common with theologians, that he seldom discussed anything with his fellow anthropologists, but had very rewarding discourse with Biblical scholars who were versatile with several languages (including Greek, Hebrew, and Latin) and had an excellent understanding of "what happened in history." It was apparent to him (he noted) that, with the exception of himself and three other anthropologists (whose names or nationalities he did not reveal), anthropologists lacked the necessary training in historical scholarship and language competence that theologians possessed, a fact that, according to him, made the theologians great semantic anthropologists. He asserted that the anthropology of religion ought to be the "theology of religion," by which he probably meant that the concern of the anthropology of religion ought to be the study of beliefs in God and spiritual beings in their religious contexts.

A Biblical scholar in the audience responded by saying that theologians were critical of themselves and their scholarship, with the assessment that theologians lacked necessary historical scholarship and language competence that other humanists had, and that theologians were moving closer toward using sociological and anthropological analysis and less of historical and semantic analysis.

Bereft of the pomposity of his pronouncements, the semantic anthropologist's views are significant: The dialogue between the anthropologists of religion and historians of religion will enrich both fields. Anthropologists in the twentieth century spent many years focusing their study of religion on descriptions and comparisons of non-Western religions. This led to the emergence of a kind of ethnography-centrism, with many anthropologists engaging in a discourse on phenomena without being sensitive to the philosophical and historical scholarship of their times or societies. Historians of religion were concerned primarily with the description and interpretation of the development of particular world religions, and this led to a kind of library-centrism, with many historians not being sensitive to how religion was conceptualized and experienced by people with no written records.

In recent times a shift in focus has occurred, with historians of religion undertaking field research, and anthropologists of religion undertaking library research: New disciplinary orientations in both fields have emerged, promoting an interpretive or hermeneutic understanding of the use and cultural significance of religious ideas and symbols. There is a growing recognition in both fields that religious beliefs and practices require detailed, "thick" description in their historical and ethnographic contexts as well as interpretations and explanations that would reveal their underlying structures of meaning and universal themes.

It has taken about a century to realize the significance and importance of the foregoing perspective on religion. William Robertson Smith, the historian of religion (who was a scholar of Biblical criticism and "semitic" languages and religions, as well as a minister of the Scottish Free Church), saw clearly the need to combine historical and anthropological scholarship on religion, and he consequently undertook anthropological fieldwork, an activity that his anthropological colleagues did not emphasize at the time. Robertson Smith was stripped of his clerical function and also lost his position at the University of Aberdeen for offering scientific interpretations of Biblical rituals.

A characteristic feature of Robertson Smith's scholarship was his emphasis on the study of the function of rituals. He sought to understand how rituals functioned in their cultural contexts and interpreted their origin and meaning. Most of the scholars of his era were too preoccupied with the study of myth to understand primitive or archaic religion (for example, Max Muller and James Frazer); in contrast, Robertson Smith argued that the study of ritual would reveal the foundations of primitive or archaic religion. Warburg (1989: 53) correctly points out that "Robertson Smith's most decisive contribution to the study of religion is without doubt his discussion of the relationship between cult and myth" as he was of the view that "in antiquity it was the religious practice which constituted the firm and most invariable part of religion."

It is curious that the anthropologist who has contributed significantly to the current discourse on structure and meaning emphasizes the study of myth rather than ritual, and comparative analysis rather than fieldwork. Claude Levi-Strauss's "semiology" is devoted to unraveling the cultural unconscious through the study of mythical, totemic, and kinship structures that are produced by the "savage" or "raw" mind. Although he focuses on the study of the operation of binary structure and the structural transformations in different ethnographic contexts and identifies such a study as uniquely anthropological, he is also very sensitive to the role of historical scholarship in understanding cultural phenomena. For example, he notes:

> . . . anthropology cannot remain indifferent to historical process and to the most highly conscious expressions of social phenomena. But if the anthropologist brings to them the same scrupulous attention as the historian, it is in order to eliminate, by a kind of backward course, all that they owe to the historical process and to conscious thought. . . . [T]he famous statement by Marx, "men make their own history, but they do not know that they are making it," justifies, first, history and, second, anthropology. At the same

time, it shows that *the two approaches are inseparable* [emphasis mine]. (Levi-Strauss 1963b: 23–24)

In the 1950s Mircea Eliade noted that historians of religion had adopted two distinguishable types of methodologies: "One group concentrated primarily on the characteristic *structures* of religious phenomena, the other chose to investigate their *historical context*. The former seek to understand *the essence of religion*, the latter to discover and communicate its history" (Eliade 1957: 232). Anthropological scholarship on religion can contribute to an understanding of how human beings structurally and historically create, maintain, and transmit symbols of the sacred other in relation to the symbols of the self.

It is not enough to state that religious beliefs and practices are rooted in the archaic, historical past and embodied in the unconscious structures of the mind. Formulations such as eternal forms or ideas (Plato), proto-myths (Dumezil), archetype (Jung), and science of the concrete (Levi-Strauss) may provide us with logical models for the coherence of *our* symbolic selves; but anthropologists must also seek to shed light on how such a coherence of symbolic selves is achieved in *different* cultural traditions.

A purely structural analysis is not adequate for an understanding of why the Shiite Muslims, Cheyenne Indians, or Arunta Australians practice certain types of body mutilations—all of which are manifestations of merging the symbolic self and the sacred other. By the same token, a purely historical analysis is not adequate for an understanding of the mechanisms of communication between the symbolic self and the sacred other. Just as human life is a composite of structural and historical dimensions, the study of cultural phenomena must combine structural and historical analysis. The disciplines of anthropology and history are therefore interdependent scholarly pursuits for an understanding of the cultural creation, maintenance, and transmission of the relationship between the symbolic self and the sacred other.

CHAPTER TWENTY
The Past and Future of Religion
in the Anthropological Context

THE TENSION BETWEEN
ANTHROPOLOGY AND RELIGION

Both religious and anthropological knowledge often expresses (and is shaped by) the intellectual and material concerns of a society of a particular historic period. Although anthropological and religious systems may acquire a measure of intellectual autonomy, as in the instances of academic anthropology and theology, they are culturally embedded and are linked with other institutions. The questions that theologians and anthropologists raise as well as the teachings of religion and anthropology may, in fact, reflect the cultural contradictions and resolutions of particular societies. As Geertz (1968: 398) notes, "The questions that anthropologists have pursued among exotic religions have arisen from the workings—or the misworkings—of modern Western society, and particularly from its restless quest for self-discovery."

Because both anthropology and religion are concerned with asking and answering questions about the nature of humankind, unless there is a mutual recognition that they conceptualize humankind differently, and therefore *ask and answer different kinds of questions about the nature of humankind*, there can be tension or conflict between anthropologists and re ligionists. On the other hand, religious orientations frequently internalize anthropological findings in creating coherent religious worldviews, and anthropological orientations frequently coexist with religious worldviews without any opposition. Needless to say, the teaching of anthropology occurs most effectively in cultural contexts that promote free inquiry and critical thinking, wherein a scholar can investigate the sources of knowledge without fear of losing his or her life or livelihood, and without a priestly or political hierarchy of censors defining the nature of knowledge and defining what can and cannot be taught.

In the eighteenth century, scholars such as David Hume (1711–1776) distinguished between "natural" and "prophetic" religions and dismissed religion as irrelevant by explaining that natural religion was rooted in irrationality, ignorance, and fear. In the nineteenth century, this discourse on religion was used to emphasize the dichotomy between "primitive" and "civilized" peoples; anthropological formulations sought to illustrate how religion developed during the primitive mental and cultural stages of humankind and how it progressed to acquire a monotheistic orientation in later advanced, civilized stages. Anthropologists such as Edward Tylor (1832–1917) and James Frazer (1854–1941) predicted that humankind would not need religion in the future—science would provide all the explanations, and society would be maintained by rational institutions. The rise of the discipline of anthropology was viewed by many as a sign of the decline of religion in human affairs. Anthropology was used by some to show how early humankind lived in a world of conflict, chaos, and suffering: The existence of body mutilations in rituals (such as occurred in the Sun Dance among the Plains Indians) was seen as an example of the neurotic or pathological condition of primitives and savages.

But romantic and idealist philosophers such as Friedrich Nietzsche (1844–1900) bemoaned the loss of meaning in a world that was demystified by science, and he identified meaninglessness, individualism, and chaos as characteristics of the modern Western world. Nietzsche proclaimed that God was dead, by which he meant that there was an acute cultural and moral crisis in the West brought about by the death of tradition. Nietzsche's views clearly exemplified the ambivalence of many German intellectuals: Nietzsche distrusted the validity of all religions and was extremely hostile toward Christian religious principles, but at the same time he felt that science had not and could not provide meaning for human existence. (A similar revolt against both science and established religion exists in contemporary Western society: Nietzsche glorified the individualistic, Dionysian "superman" as the man of knowledge and action who would liberate humankind from the shackles of both science and established religion; later, I discuss how, in contemporary Western society, there are some scholars who glorify the shaman as the intellectual hero who would liberate the self from the cultural bondages and blinders that are believed by them to be sustained by science and established religions.)

The rationale for the study of natural or primitive religion was formulated as a theological necessity by William Robertson Smith (1846–1896), who theorized that there was a basic difference between heathenism and "positive" religions such as Judaism, Christianity, and Islam but that it was necessary to study heathen beliefs and rituals in order to understand the positive religions. Robertson Smith affirmed the superiority of the Judeo-Christian orientation but was excommunicated by the Free Church, and he lost his teaching position at the University of Aberdeen because he espoused German-oriented Biblical criticism and the study of natural religions. His anthropological fieldwork and library research showed that certain beliefs and practices of Christians were, in fact, beliefs and practices of the tribal cultural traditions, and his discourse of the origins and usages of certain Christian concepts seemed to challenge the fundamentalist Christian perspective that propagated Christian beliefs and practices as divine manifestations. The following quotation from Robertson Smith's book *The Religion of the Semites* (1889) contrasts prophetic and natural religions:

> Judaism, Christianity and Islam are positive religions, that is, they did not grow up like the systems of ancient heathenism, under the action of unconscious forces operating silently from age to age, but trace their origin to the teaching of great religious innovators, who spoke as the organs of a divine revelation, and deliberately departed from the traditions of the past. Behind these positive religions lies the old unconscious religious tradition, the body of religious usage and belief which cannot be traced to the influence of individual minds, and was not propagated on individual authority, but formed part of that inheritance from the past into which successive generations of the Semitic race grew up as it were instinctively, taking it as a matter of course that they should belief and act as their fathers had done before them. The positive Semitic religions had to establish themselves on ground already occupied by these older beliefs and usages; they had to displace what they could not assimilate, and whether they rejected or absorbed the elements of the older religion, they had at every point to reckon with them and take up a definite attitude towards them. No positive religion that has moved men has been able to start with a tabula rasa, and express itself as if religion were beginning for the first time; in form, if not in substance, the new system must be in contact all along the line with the older ideas and practices which it finds in possession. A new scheme of faith can find a hearing only by appealing to religious instincts and susceptibilities that already exist in its audience, and it cannot reach these without taking account of the traditional forms in which all religious feeling is embodied, and without speaking a language which men accustomed to these old forms can understand. Thus to comprehend a system of positive religion thoroughly, to understand it in its historical origin and form as well as in its abstract principles, we must know the traditional religion that preceded it. (Robertson Smith 1889: 1–2)

Robertson Smith's studies established a new anthropological perspective on the study of religion. As opposed to the "rationalist" and other psychological theories of religion that were popular among the anthropologists of the eighteenth and nineteenth centuries, Robertson Smith offered a "symbolic"/sociological theory of religion. This difference had a profound significance for all future studies: The rationalists, in general, believed that religion was an irrational phenomenon that was bound to vanish in a rational society; the symbolists (like Robertson Smith and Emile Durkheim as well as the German historicists, phenomenologists, and theologians) believed that religion served an important integrative (or symbolically unifying) function in society and investigated the role of nonrational, emotional, and sentimental aspects in culture and society. The symbolists focused on the analysis of communicative or symbolic rationality (as opposed to the technological or scientific rationality) for understanding the role of religion in human life.

My study of religion is a contribution toward an understanding of religion as a cultural or symbolic system, and I have offered interpretations to show how and why symbols of sacred others are created and used in the transformation of human identity into supernatural (sacred) identity. I have also formulated in this book an anthropological approach to the study of religion within the semiotic framework of culture and self. I have suggested that the representation of the self as sacred or supernatural occurs in relation to cultural formulations about the existence of sacred or supernatural others. An analysis of the relationship between the symbols of self and the symbols of the sacred other shows that sacredness of the symbolic self is achieved in two ways, namely, through the merging or union of the symbols of the self and the symbols of the sacred other, and through the positive or negative approximation of the symbols of the self and the symbols of the sacred other. Through the former type of relationship, shamanistic sacred selves are produced, and such an orientation helps to cope with anxiety, stress, and other predicaments. Through the second type of relationship, priestly sacred selves are produced, and such an orientation helps to maintain the mythological charters of everyday social life. This difference is important for the maintenance of the integrity or coherence of the *symbolic* self because cultural modes of life have to deal with both chaos and order. Symbols of the sacred other are created, maintained, and used to synthesize and fuse the experiences of different domains, and they serve as powerful cognitive and affective models to represent the symbolic self as sacred; as having the capacity to cope with the natural realities of suffering, death, inconsistencies, conflict, and so on; as well as to affirm social institutions and structures.

As Peter Berger (1969) notes, humans often encounter chaos and meaninglessness that could destroy culture and in turn humanity. Non-human animals in their death or suffering do not have to cope with these problems because they do not live in a created cultural reality. Humans conceptualize about imponderables, uncertainties, suffering, and death and ask why these things exist; they have to create personally meaningful systems in terms of such conceptualizations. By having a sacred or super-natural protective cover, the cosmic order and the cultural order are af-firmed, and the integrity of the symbolic self is kept intact or coherent despite the experiences of disorder, suffering, etc. And as Clifford Geertz (1969) points out, sacred symbols fuse people's conceptions of orderly cos-mos and group values as well as synthesize experiences of different do-mains and facilitate an understanding of the relationship between the known and the unknown.

The conclusions of Anthony Wallace and Clifford Geertz (two Ameri-can anthropologists who have specialized in the study of religion and have written extensively on the analysis of religion) about the future of religion are worth repeating here because they indicate how different anthropologi-cal perspectives can lead to different conclusions. Anthony Wallace pro-motes positivistic anthropology and offers a psychological analysis of re-ligion. Clifford Geertz promotes interpretive anthropology and offers a symbolic analysis of religion.

Wallace (1966: 265) suggests

> as a cultural trait, belief in supernatural powers is doomed to die out, all over the world, as a result of the increasing adequacy and diffusion of scientific knowledge and of the realization of secular faiths that supernatural belief is not necessary to the effective use of ritual. The question of whether such a denoument will be good or bad for humanity is irrelevant to the prediction; the process is inevitable.

On the other hand, as Geertz (1969: 2–3) points out,

> Whatever the ultimate sources of the faith of a man or group of men may or may not be, it is indisputable that it is sustained in this world by symbolic forms and social arrangements. What a given religion is—its specific con-tent—is embodied in the images and metaphors its adherents use to charac-terize reality. . . .

It appears to me that both religion (or theology) and anthropology will continue to exist in different guises because humans live in and with a *created* cultural reality and with *culturally created* (symbolic) selves. Humans use, create, and recreate cultural formulations of what is human, why there is suffering and injustice, why there is sickness and death, and why there is a discrepancy or disjunction between the ideals and actual experi-ences. As the following quotations suggest, the future of anthropology and religion is not predicated upon whether science has the answers about the universe and humankind: Both anthropology and religion, in the final analysis, are concerned with formulations of the self (human identity) and meaning; religion defines the self with reference to the sacred other, and anthropology defines the self with reference to the human other. The following statements by Nobel Laureate Peter Medawar (on religion) and the French anthropologist Claude Levi-Strauss (on anthropology) are worthy of serious consideration and reflection:

> It is not to science . . . but to metaphysics, imaginative literature or religion that we must turn for answers to questions having to do with first and last things. Because these answers neither arise out of nor require validation by empirical evidence, it is not useful or even meaningful to ask whether they are true or false. The question is whether or not they bring peace of mind in the anxiety of incomprehension and dispel the fear of the unknown. The failure of science to answer questions about first and last things does not in any way entail the acceptability of answers of other kinds; nor can it be taken for granted that because these questions can be put they can be answered. So far as our understanding goes, they can not. (Medawar 1984: 60)

> What we call Renaissance was a veritable birth of colonialism and anthropology. . . . Our science arrived at maturity the day that Western man began to see that he would never understand himself as long as there was a single race or people on the surface of the earth that he treated as an object. Only then could anthropology declare itself in its true colours: as an enterprise reviewing and atoning for the Renaissance, in order to spread humanism to all humanity. (Levi-Strauss 1967: 52)

> [The place of the anthropologist is] with "the others," and his role is to understand them. Never can he act in their name, for their very otherness prevents him from thinking or willing in their place: to do so would be tantamount to identifying himself with them. (Levi-Strauss 1968: 385)

THE CULTURAL ROOTEDNESS OF ANTHROPOLOGY

History—the record of cultural boundaries between and among various individuals and groups—shows that cultures are created and re-created with old and new symbols to constitute viable symbolic self-configurations. Anthropology is part of this historical-cultural flow of constituting symbolic self-configurations. In other words, anthropology is a cultural system related to other cultural systems and is involved in the creation and re-creation of symbolic self-configurations.

Looking back at the history of anthropology, it is evident that anthropology is culturally embedded in the context in which it is used to engage in a discourse on humankind. The data on other peoples (which anthropologists collect) communicate significant messages to the audience of the anthropologist, usually the group to which the anthropologist belongs; and thus anthropology serves the intellectual concerns and needs of the people who use this information about other peoples.

An example of the cultural rootedness or embeddedness of anthropology is the contemporary anthropological interest in shamanism.

During the past three decades, there has been a gradual change in Western societies, particularly in the United States, from a rejection of shamanism, witchcraft, and sorcery as fallacious, pseudo-scientific orientations to interpreting them as examples of the spirituality of humankind. In regions such as California, there have emerged dozens of spiritualist and healing cults that incorporate shamanistic rituals. A few anthropologists have also become involved with these cults, and anthropologists such as Carlos Casteneda have written several books on shamanism and sold millions of copies, capitalizing on this shamanic revival and, in turn, propagating the idea that there is a separate, spiritual reality that can be perceived and comprehended through shamanistic techniques. The current interest in shamanism (and the attempts to glorify the shaman as possessed of qualities to "scientifically" explore the "mysteries" of the universe and humankind) can be interpreted and understood with a historical study of the intellectual currents and cult activities in Western civilization.

As I mentioned earlier, the scholars who theorized about the nature of humankind and religion in this eighteenth century were, by and large, rationalists and empiricists, committed to a psychological worldview; they viewed religion as an irrational, irrelevant reality that stood in the way of progress and rational discourse on humankind. The late-nineteenth-century scholars had a biopsychological worldview, and many of them assumed that rational knowledge progressed in relation to the manifestations of superior biological and mental characteristics. The symbolic/sociological/phenomenological perspective on culture was a reaction against the mentalism and biologism of the eighteenth and nineteenth centuries.

The shaman and shamanistic phenomena (generally identified in the eighteenth and nineteenth centuries as sorcerer and magical phenomena) were considered by the eighteenth- and nineteenth-century scholars as dangerous charlatans and superstitions of primitives or savages who had not yet acquired scientific knowledge to explain mental, social, and physical processes. Religion was conceptualized as more advanced supernaturalism than shamanism and was considered less harmful. The nineteenth-century interest in spiritualist cults (as evidenced by the success of the Russian psychic/spiritualist Madam Blavatsky and the American psychics the Davenport brothers, and as evidenced in some of the writings of Arthur Conan Doyle and Alfred Wallace) was seen by anthropologists such as Edward Tylor as a dangerous glorification of irrational superstitions that had not yet been totally eliminated from Western civilization. There was a fear that the interest in spiritualist cults could lead to the reemergence of a magical worldview and the reenactment of the "witch craze" of the sixteenth and seventeenth centuries.

The symbolists of the late nineteenth and early twentieth century such as Robertson Smith and Emile Durkheim also distinguished two types of supernatural orientations, namely, magic and religion. They identified shamanism as a magical approach and characterized it as "anti-social" because of its apparent lack of concern for or involvement with moral and social conventions. Shamanism, in their view, was an individualistic and destructive form of supernaturalism. These scholars asserted the importance and significance of religion in relation to its social and intellectual integrative functions, and they did not see a conflict between religion and science; they believed in the need for and coexistence of religion and science and sought to eliminate shamanistic superstitions, identifying them as pseudosciences.

Today, in many Western societies, such as the United States, we see the existence of a revolt against both science and established religions. This revolt has, in some intellectual circles of the Western tradition, become linked with mystical-psychological reductionism, as such a reductionism is formulated in "transpersonal sciences" such as "transpersonal psychology" and "transpersonal anthropology": "Transpersonal science" affirms and refers to the existence of a spiritual reality by conceptualizing the individual as a psychic system that transcends culture and society. Grof (1988: 37–38), a transpersonal psychiatrist, delineates transpersonal phenomena as follows:

> Experiential sequences of death and rebirth typically open the gate to a trans-biographical domain in the human psyche that can best be referred to as *transpersonal*. The common denominator of the rich and ramified group of transpersonal phenomena is the subject's feeling that his or her consciousness has expanded beyond the usual ego boundaries and has transcended the limitations of time and space.

Many transpersonal psychologists and anthropologists are affiliated with psychologically oriented mystical cults that are often referred to as "new age" or "human potential" movements. Transpersonal psychologists and anthropologists seem to have found in shamanism and in oriental mysticism (such as Lamaism, Tantrism, Yoga, and Dao) a "scientific approach" to the understanding of the universe and of human potentiality and spirituality.

The cultural embeddedness of transpersonal anthropology and new-age movements may be analyzed in relation to certain intellectual developments in Western society. In the middle of the twentieth century, the revolt against positivist science acquired multiple intellectual forms and currents, and ideas such as progress and scientific rationality looked odd in the face of the death and destruction caused by World War II and the existence of racism and other forms of cruelty and oppression in human affairs. One development in this revolt was the elaboration of "existentialist philosophy" and the deification of *angst,* and another development was the strengthening of humanistic approaches in psychology, sociology, and anthropology. Humanistic psychology acquired a close affinity to "counter-culture" move-

ments in Western society, and became a *de facto* "humanistic ethno-psychology" of intellectuals and students who sought alternative lifestyles and
utopian panaceas. Perhaps the best phrase to identify the counter-culture–
oriented humanistic ethno-psychology is to call it *culture-primitivistic-psychological-nativism* because it (humanistic ethno-psychology) promoted cultural
primitivism and psychological nativism. Cultural primitivism has a long
pedigree in Western civilization, going back to the Greeks, with the latest
Western representatives being beatniks and hippies. Psychological nativism
also has a long lineage with Platonic idealism becoming significant among
intellectuals at different times, and in using particular psychological assumptions of Western culture to theorize about human nature (in general).

Culture-primitivistic-psychological-nativism found its greatest syn-
thesizer in Abraham Maslow, who formulated the conception of *Transpersonal Psychology* for exploring "the farther reaches of human nature," or the
final frontier (fourth dimension) of the psyche. This psychic frontier has
been interpreted to mean the "spiritual dimension." Transpersonal psychology acquired intellectual momentum not only through the writings of
Maslow but also with contributions from psychologists such as Carl Rogers
and Rollo May and with discourse and exegetical writings on Eastern mysticism (particularly by those with a psychological orientation, such as Hindu and Buddhist yogas) by new age proponents such as Joseph Chilton
Pearce, Stanislav Grof, and Sheldon Kopp.

The following factors are also important for understanding the cultural significance of the shamanistic self in Western culture: (1) Because the
shamanistic orientation (whether in non-urban, simple societies or in complex, traditional societies) is not directly connected with social order or
moral conventions, it lends itself to the people in contemporary Western
society who reject or deny the validity of social/moral conventions. (2) As
religious orientations such as tantrism promote the use of sexuality in
various esoteric rituals, such orientations appeal to the people who often
seek sexual experimentations and therapies. (3) As shamanistic orientations in general foster the union of or merger between the symbols of the
self and the sacred other, they appeal to those whose symbolic self is not
coherent and who seek symbolic self-coherence, using a guru, a "living
god," or shaman for total merger or union to achieve inner bliss. (4) As
shamanism is involved in providing channels to "see" the world of the
spirits, or the world of the dead, socially disconnected people in Western
society may find in shamanism a kind of connectedness in the spiritual
reality. (5) As shamanism frequently involves the use of psychoactive
drugs, it provides a kind of legitimacy for the use of drugs by those who
desire them. (6) As shamanism asserts the existence of psychic, mystical
power in the universe (and in humans), those who glorify shamanism may,
in fact, be glorifying themselves as having a superior power, and such an
orientation may be used to justify or rationalize their weaknesses and

204 CONCLUSION: ANTHROPOLOGY AND THE STUDY OF RELIGION

failures in the "here and now" world and to proclaim spiritual superiority over those who have succeeded in the "here and now" world.

See the articles by Schultz (1989), O'Hara (1989), Acock (1989), Reed (1989), Thomason (1989), Lawrence (1989), Rosen (1989), and Godon (1989) for illuminating studies on the claims by the proponents and exponents of the new-age movement, and for a historical understanding of how shamanistic beliefs and practices fit into contemporary Western society.

Holger Kalweit (1988: 3) illustrates the culture-primitivistic-psychological-nativism position when he notes that "Perhaps at some point in the near future, when ethnologists acquire detailed data on the psychology of death, thereby emancipating themselves from the state of mere listener to that of a genuine partner in experience, they will no longer misinterpret shamanic experiences as symbolic and cultural artifacts." He also asserts that "The anthropologist who studies the world of the shaman is all too often faced by an impenetrable web of cosmological theories and cultural characteristics, which prevent him from understanding their psychic origin and background. This, we believe, is why we are unwilling to acknowledge the mystical inspiration of the shaman and to put him on a par with other religious mystics." (Kalweit 1988: 241) Kalweit is wrong to assume that scholars are "unwilling to acknowledge the mystical experience of the shaman." Almost all anthropologists consider the shaman a religious mystic. What Kalweit expects the scholars to do is accept the mystical experience not as religious knowledge but as scientific knowledge, and he proposes to redefine what is science or scientific knowledge. Most anthropologists, however, would not refer to shamanistic knowledge as scientific knowledge of the universe, just as most anthropologists would not refer to witchcraft beliefs as scientific knowledge of the universe; and, just as anthropologists study and show how witchcraft beliefs constitute a coherent system for the believers, anthropologists study and show how shamanic beliefs constitute a coherent system for the believers.

On the one hand, the shaman has become the archetype for heroic feats in the world of inner-self explorations, and on the other the shaman is viewed as the guide to undertake journeys to the world of spirits. The shaman not only represents the quest to experience a separate spiritual reality but also embodies spirituality and is considered a master of the laws of the natural reality as well. Shamanistic "death and rebirth," "out-of-body experiences," and "body transformations" or metamorphosis are often presented as documented ethnographies and are analyzed to reveal the symbolic truths contained in them. See Holger Kalweit's book *Dreamtime and Inner Space: The World of the Shaman* (1988) for a description and discussion of how transpersonal psychologists and anthropologists promote shamanic symbology as scientifically significant for revealing the nature of humankind.

The formulation of the shaman as a prototype or archetype, representing "true" knowledge of the universe and humankind, can be interpreted with the model that I have proposed in this book: In situations of stress and anxiety, symbolic coherence of the self is achieved frequently through merger or union with the sacred other. The shaman is the sacred other (spiritual being) for many followers of new-age movements who seek to unite their symbolic selves with representations of the shaman. A new, modern version of the shaman exists in many urban centers of the West. As California is the shaman capital of the modern world, it is appropriate to use the term "California Shaman" to identify the "classic" urban shaman in contrast to the Siberian "classic" shaman. California shamans frequently function as channelers (mediums) for spirits, and as healers, and claim to have spirit allies and to undertake voyages into the spirit world.

It is evident that the proponents of new-age movements promote a new religious synthesis, rather than a scientific understanding of shamanic experiences. As in the case of the prophets of religious movements who emerge in times of stress and anxiety, promising a new and satisfying culture, the new agers promise a utopia of spiritual bliss. This bliss includes astral wanderings (out-of-body experiences) of the self, memories of past lives, seeing one's own development of the fetus, psychic healing of fractured self and the body, and communion with the spirits. It must be pointed out that the new agers' ontological claims of spirituality and the spirit world cannot be empirically verified, just as we cannot empirically verify the ontological claims of other religions: Thus, it is erroneous to claim that new agers have scientifically discovered the spiritual reality of the universe and of humanity. What they have discovered is a particular, cultural formulation of the self as sacred; the sacred self that they formulate is the shamanistic sacred self achieved through the merging of the symbols of the self and the sacred other (i.e., the shaman). It does not make any sense to state that the shamanistic knowledge is scientific knowledge of the universe and of humankind, and that this knowledge cannot be verified scientifically but must be experienced within the paradigm or framework of shamanistic symbology (which is religion).

Students interested in analyzing how shamanism fits in American society may find the short article entitled "Dark Side of the Shaman" by Michael Fobes Brown (1989) illuminating. Brown notes:

> What I find unsettling . . . is that New Age America seeks to embrace shamanism without an appreciation of its context. For my Santa Fe acquaintances, tribal lore is a supermarket from which they choose some tidbits while spurning others. They program computers or pursue other careers by day so that by night they can wrestle with spirit-jaguars and search for their power spots. Yankush's lifetime of discipline is reduced to a set of techniques for personal development, stripped of links to a specific landscape and cultural tradition.
>
> New Age enthusiasts are right to admire the shamanistic tradition, but while advancing it as an alternative to our own healing practices, they brush aside its stark truths. For throughout the world, shamans see themselves as war-

riors in a struggle against the shadows of the human heart. Shamanism affirms life but also spawns violence and death. The beauty of shamanism is matched by its power—and like all forms of power found in society, it inspires its share of discontent. (1989: 10)

Religion and science are cultural systems that produce distinguishable kinds of knowledge about humanity and the world, and neither one is superior to the other. Religious, mythological knowledge and scientific, verifiable knowledge approximate the world of experience with different objectives. The former system of knowledge is centered on affirming the sacredness (supernaturalness) of human identity, and as a result religious formulations are accepted as true without their being subjected to verification; their acceptance is dependent on coherence, meaning, and appropriateness for the believers. The scientific system of knowledge is centered on affirming the existence of an empirically verifiable reality, and as a result scientific formulations are descriptions, interpretations, and explanations of phenomena that can be tested. The former system of knowledge is based on communicative or mythological rationality, and the latter is based on practical or technological rationality.

Cultural traditions are constituted with scientific (technological) and mythological (communicative) rationalities. When an anthropologist studies cultural traditions or cultural systems, he or she examines the significant representations or symbols (which are shared by a group of individuals), their interconnectedness (syntactics), their meanings (semantics), and their use (pragmatics). The anthropologist strives to elucidate the relationship between the symbol and the referent. However, because a symbol is an arbitrary representation of characteristics and meanings, it is necessary to understand the cognitive codes or the *emic* categories that enable the participants in the symbolic systems to perceive and comprehend identities or approximations between the symbols and their referents in a certain manner. But it is possible to distinguish "scientific" symbols that have empirically verifiable referents (even when the representations of characteristics are arbitrary) and "religious" symbols that assert the existence of an empirically unverifiable, spiritual reality.

Although it is possible to keep the boundaries of science and religion distinct, the formulations of these two cultural systems can get incorporated into each other, and their boundaries are often blurred. For example, historians of science have repeatedly pointed out that the scholastic–theological discourse on the rationality of God provided a very important epistemological foundation for the development of modern science. As opposed to the religious–theological view of God as mysterious and capricious, who intervened in human affairs and thereby rendered human life unpredictable, the conceptualization of God as a rational being provided an intellectual basis to theorize that God's creations operate with lawful regularity, which in turn made it possible to engage in research to discover the rational or lawful operation of the world.

Needless to say, religious formulations on the universe and human-kind can promote or prevent scientific research and can incorporate scientific formulations of the universe and humankind. For example, those who followed the creationism "trials" in the United States might have noted that a large percentage of clergymen (some of whom refer to themselves as "deistic evolutionists") did not find in the biological theory of evolution any attempt to discredit the validity of religion. Some in fact argued that scientific discoveries of the physical and biological universe are important facts that would strengthen the religious world view of modern man.

Different civilizations, for different reasons, historically acquire distinguishable types of linkages and separations of religious and scientific systems. For example, in Hindu civilization, the yoga systems of "self-realization" have combined scientific, psychological/biological knowledge and spiritualist or pantheistic orientations, and it is not uncommon to find the existence of a belief that Hindu views on self-realization and the universe are "scientific views" (just as theology in the German tradition acquired acceptance as science). It is also necessary to keep in mind that until the turn of the eighteenth century, most universities in Western societies taught the "sciences" as branches of theology, and often a clear separation of religious and scientific inquiry was not made.

Anthropology is a cultural science, and therefore its methods are similar to those of the cultural sciences such as linguistics and history. Cultural science methodology is not opposed to the positivistic science methods of the physical and biological sciences but is distinguished by its recognition that anthropological data are humanly created cultural systems, and that an understanding of this data requires the study of how the data (conglomerations of cultural systems) are created, maintained, and used. By the same token, it is necessary to study anthropology itself as a cultural system in terms of how and why it is created, maintained, and used. Perhaps no one would deny the fact that anthropology, as a cultural system, responds to changes that occur in a society, and that anthropological foci and research shift in relation to various political, economic, religious, and social factors. If anthropology is shaped by the intellectual concerns of particular societies and periods, and if anthropological explanations change, how valid are the "scientific" statements that anthropologists make about cultural phenomena such as religion? Anthropological statements are scientific when they are and can be subjected to independent verification, and they are open to revision when new information that contradicts earlier statements is made available.

I noted earlier that anthropology is closely related to linguistics and history. It would be helpful to students if we could offer interpretations of cultural phenomena, exploring them anthropologically along with linguistics and historical facts. For example, in discussing important anthropological concepts such as "the psychic unity of humankind" and "cultural relativism," semiotics and historical analysis would add to their clarity. Anthropologists are not alone in promoting discourse on cultural relativism and the psychic unity of humankind. It is not widely known that as early as the sixteenth century, religious leaders espoused some of the ideas that have become important in contemporary anthropology: Many of the Dominican monks of Spain not only were cultural relativists but also fought strenuously to uphold the principle of the unity of humankind and international law and often demonstrated that the characterizations of other peoples as inferior were products of prejudice. In the sixteenth century, Bartolome de las Casas declared that humankind was one and argued that Indian customs must be understood within the framework of Indian culture.

Civilizations go through cycles of upholding human dignity for all and then denying the humanity of the "minorities" or those colonized. In the fifth century B.C. the emperor Darius was a cultural relativist; in his stead came Ayatollah Khomeini with his particular vision of Islam as the truth. The Greeks from about the sixth century B.C. to the first century A.D. fostered freedom of thought without the stifling or constraining power of a religious hierarchy of priests. But during subsequent economic decline, this spark of freedom went out. Western civilization has the security and dominance, which permits discourse on various issues, including the development of a universalistic, nonparochial conception of humankind; but how quickly conceptions of humankind change. When the Americans were afraid of the Japanese during World War II, the Japanese were labeled monsters that should be destroyed. "Anthropologists explained that the Japanese were children, savages, near-lunatics, their character a function of their toilet training, their inferiority complex well justified." (Prescott in the review of the book by J. W. Sower called *War Without Mercy: Race and Power in the Pacific War,* in *Newsweek,* June 30, 1986) Today they are no longer monsters; in the context of a global economy and world trade, American interaction with the Japanese results in their being labeled smart people— and the goals of American interaction are to outsmart them in the arena of technological sophistication.

Human groups have glorified and vilified one another for different reasons, and glorifications and vilifications change in relation to a number of intellectual, economic, and political factors. Today's "Great Satan" is tomorrow's "Great Savior"; yesterday's "evil magician" is today's "shamanistic hero." Anthropology has a responsibility to analyze and interpret the reasons for glorifications and vilifications as well as to examine how and why changes in representations occur. In this sense, anthropology is a kind of cultural analysis whose existence indicates the presence in society of a commitment to free inquiry and critical thinking.

Bibliography

ABERLE, D.F. "A Note on Relative Deprivation Theory as Applied to Millenarian and Other Cult Movements," in S.L. Thrupp, ed. *Millennial Dreams in Action*. The Hague: Mouton and Co., 1962.
——— . *The Peyote Religion Among the Navaho*. Chicago: Aldine Publishing Co., 1966.
ADLER, H.M., AND V.B.O. HAMMETT. "Crisis, Conversion, and Cult Formation: An Examination of a Common Psychosocial Sequence," *American Journal of Psychiatry* 180 (1973).
ALLEN, GRAHAM. "A Theory of Millennialism: The Iruingite Movement as an Illustration," *British Journal of Sociology* 25, 3 (1974).
BABB, LAWRENCE A. *The Divine Hierarchy: Popular Hinduism in Central India*. New York: Columbia University Press, 1975.
BABCOCK, BARBARA A. *The Reversible World: Symbolic Inversion in Art and Society*. Ithaca, N.Y.: Cornell University Press, 1978.
BARBER, B. "Acculturation and Messianic Movements," *American Sociological Review* 6 (1941).
BARNETT, HOMER G. *Indian Shakers: A Messianic Cult of the Pacific Northwest*. Carbondale: Southern Illinois University Press, 1957.
——— . *Being a Palauan*. New York: Holt, Rinehart and Winston, 1960.
BASCOM, WILLIAM. *The Yoruba of Southwestern Nigeria*. New York: Holt, Rinehart and Winston, 1969.
BASSO, KEITH H. *The Cibecue Apache*. New York: Holt, Rinehart and Winston, 1970.
BECK, BRENDA E.F. "The Metaphor as a Mediator Between Semantic and Analogic Modes of Thought," *Current Anthropology* 19, 1 (1978).

BECKFORD, JAMES. "Explaining Religious Movements," *International Social Science Journal* 29 (1977).

BEIDELMAN, T.O. W. *Robertson Smith and the Sociological Study of Religion*. Chicago: University of Chicago Press, 1974.

BELLAH, ROBERT. "Religious Evolution," *American Sociological Review* 29 (1964).

BENEDICT, RUTH. "Religion." In Franz Boas, ed. *General Anthropology*. New York: D.C. Heath and Co., 1938.

BERGER, PETER. *The Sacred Canopy: Elements of a Sociological Theory of Religion*. New York: Anchor Books, 1969.

———. *The Heretical Imperative: Contemporary Possibilities of Religious Affirmation*. New York: Anchor Books/Doubleday, 1979.

BERGER, PETER, AND T. LUCKMAN. *The Social Construction of Reality*. Garden City, N.Y.: Anchor Books, 1966.

BETTELHEIM, BRUNO. *Symbolic Wounds: Puberty Rites and the Envious Male*. New York: The Free Press, 1954.

BIERSTEDT, ROBERT. *Florian Znaniecki on Humanistic Sociology*. Chicago: University of Chicago Press, 1969.

BOARDMAN, E.P. "Millenary Aspects of the Taiping Rebellion," in S. Thrupp, ed. *Millennial Dreams in Action*. The Hague: Mouton and Co., 1962.

BOAS, FRANZ. "The Growth of Indian Mythologies," in Robert A. Georges, ed. *Studies on Mythology*. Homewood, Ill.: The Dorsey Press, 1968 (1895).

———. *The Religion of the Kwakiutl Indians*. New York: Columbia University Press, 1930.

BOCK, PHILIP K. *Rethinking Psychological Anthropology: Continuity and Change in the Study of Human Action*. New York: W.H. Freeman, 1988.

BOURGUIGNON, ERICA. *Possession*. San Francisco: Candler and Sharp Publishers, 1976.

BROMLEY, D.G., AND A.D. SHUPE. *Strange Gods: The Great American Cult Scare*. Boston: Beacon Press, 1981.

BROWN, KAREN MCCARTHY. "'Voodoo,'" in M. Eliade, ed. *The Encyclopedia of Religion*, Vol. 15. New York: Macmillan Publishing Company, 1987.

BROWN, MICHAEL. "Dark Side of the Shaman," *Natural History* 11 (1989).

BURRIDGE, K.O.L. *Mambu: A Melanesian Millennium*. Oxford: Basil Blackwell, 1960.

———. *New Heaven: New Earth, A Study of Millenarian Activities*. Oxford: Basil Blackwell, 1969.

BURHOE, RALPH W. "The Phenomenon of Religion Seen Scientifically," in A.W. Eister, ed. *Changing Perspectives in the Scientific Study of Religion*. New York: John Wiley and Sons, 1974.

CAMBELL, BRUCE. "A Typology of Cults," *Sociological Analysis* 39 (1978).

CAMPBELL, COLIN. "Clarifying the Cults," *British Journal of Sociology* 28 (1977).

CAMPBELL, JOSEPH. *The Masks of God: Primitive Mythology*. New York: The Viking Press, 1959.

———. *The Masks of God: Oriental Mythology*. New York: The Viking Press, 1962.

CANNON, WALTER B. "'Voodoo' Death," *American Anthropologist* 44 (1942).

CARNEIRO, ROBERT L. "Leslie White," in Sydel Silverman, ed. *Totems and Teachers*. New York: Columbia University Press, 1981.

CARRITHERS, MICHAEL, ET AL., EDS. *The Category of the Person: Anthropology, Philosophy, History*. Cambridge: Cambridge University Press, 1985.

CARSTAIRS, G. MORRIS. *The Twice-Born: A Study of a Community of High-Caste Hindus*. Bloomington: Indiana University Press, 1967.

CASSIRER, ERNST. *An Essay on Man: An Introduction to a Philosophy of Culture*. New Haven: Yale University Press, 1944.

———. *Myth of the State.* New Haven: Yale University Press, 1946.

CASTENEDA, CARLOS. *The Teachings of Don Juan: A Yaqui Way of Knowledge.* Berkeley: University of California Press, 1970.

———. *A Separate Reality: Further Conversations with Don Juan.* New York: Simon & Schuster, 1971.

———. *Journey to Ixtlan: The Lessons of Don Juan.* New York: Simon & Schuster, 1972.

CAZENEUVE, JEAN. *Lucien Levy-Bruhl.* New York: Harper & Row, Publishers, 1972.

CESARA, MANDA. *Reflections of a Woman Anthropologist: No Hiding Place.* New York: Academic Press, 1982.

CHAGNON, NAPOLEON A. *Yanomamo: The Fierce People.* New York: Holt, Rinehart and Winston, 1968.

———. *Yanomamo: The Fierce People, 3rd ed.* New York: Holt, Rinehart and Winston, 1983.

CHANCE, NORMAN A. *The Eskimo of North America.* New York: Holt, Rinehart and Winston, 1966.

CHRISTIAN, WILLIAM A., JR. *Person and God in a Spanish Valley.* New York: Seminar Press, 1972.

CODRINGTON, ROBERT H. *The Melanesians.* Oxford: Clarendon Press, 1891.

COHEN, ABNER. "Symbolic Action and the Structure of the Self," In Ioan Lewis, ed. *Symbols and Sentiments: Cross-Cultural Studies in Symbolism.* New York: Academic Press, 1977.

COHN, NORMAN. *The Pursuit of the Millennium.* New York: Harper & Row, Publishers, 1961.

———. "Medieval Millenarism: Its Bearing on the Comparative Study of Millenarian Movements," in S. Thrupp, ed. *Millennial Dreams in Action.* The Hague: Mouton and Co., 1962.

COLLINS, J.M. "The Indian Shaker Church: A Study of Continuity and Change in Religion," *Southwestern Journal of Anthropology* 6 (1950).

CONWAY, F., AND J. SIEGELMAN. *Snapping: America's Epidemic of Sudden Personality Change.* Philadelphia: J.B. Lippincott, 1978.

COURTRIGHT, PAUL B. *Ganesa: Lord of Obstacles, Lord of Beginnings.* New York: Oxford University Press, 1985.

COX, HARVEY. "Eastern Cults and Eastern Culture: Why Young Americans Are Buying Oriental Religions," *Psychology Today* 11 (1977).

CRAWFORD, J.R. *Witchcraft and Sorcery in Rhodesia.* New York: Oxford University Press, 1967.

CRICK, M. *Explorations in Language and Meaning: Towards a Semantic Anthropology.* New York: John Wiley and Sons, 1976.

CROCKER, CHRISTOPHER. "Ritual and the Development of Social Structure," in J.D. Shanghnessay, ed. *The Roots of Ritual.* Grand Rapids, Mich.: William B. Eerdmans Publishing Company, 1973.

———. "My Brother the Parrot," in David Sapir and Christopher Crocker, eds. *The Social Use of Metaphor.* Philadelphia: University of Pennsylvania Press, 1977.

DAUGHERTY, MARY LEE. "Serpent Handling As Sacrament," *Theology Today* 33 (1976).

DAVIS, KINGSLEY. "The Myth of Functional Analysis as a Special Method in Sociology and Anthropology," *American Sociological Review* 24 (1959).

DAVIS, MAY. *Passage of Darkness: The Ethnobiology of the Haitian Zombie.* Chapel Hill: University of North Carolina Press, 1988.

DAVIS, MURRAY S. "'That's Classic!' The Phenomenology and Rhetoric of Successful Social Theories," *Philosophy of Social Science* 16 (1986).

DIAMOND, NORMA. *K'un Shen.* New York: Holt, Rinehart and Winston, 1969.

DIAMOND, STANLEY. "Introductory Essay: Job and the Trickster," in Paul Radin. *The Trickster.* New York: Schocken Books, 1972.

DIRKS, ROBERT. "Annual Rituals of Conflict," *American Anthropologist* 90 (1988).

DOLGIN, JANET L., ET AL. *Symbolic Anthropology: A Reader in the Study of Symbols and Meanings.* New York: Columbia University Press, 1977.

DONNER, FLORINDA. *Shabano.* New York: Dell Publishing Company, 1982.

DOUGLAS, MARY. *Purity and Danger: An Analysis of the Concepts of Pollution and Taboo.* London: ARK Paperbacks, 1966.

———. *Implicit Meanings: Essays in Anthropology.* London: Routledge and Kegan Paul, 1975.

———. "Taboo," in R. Cavendish, ed. *Man, Myth and Magic,* Vol. 20. London: Phoebus Publishing, 1979.

DOW, JAMES. "Universal Aspects of Symbolic Healing: A Theoretical Synthesis," *American Anthropologist* 88 (1986).

DOWNS, JAMES P. *The Two Worlds of Washo.* New York: Holt, Rinehart and Winston, 1966.

DOZIER, EDWARD P. *The Kalinga of Northern Luozon, Philippines.* New York: Holt, Rinehart and Winston, 1967.

DUMONT, L. *Homo Hierarchicus.* Chicago: University of Chicago Press, 1970.

———. "A Structural Definition of a Folk Deity of Tamilnad: Ayenar, The Lord," in W.A. Lessa and E.Z. Vogt, eds. *Reader in Comparative Religion.* New York: Harper & Row, Publishers, 1972.

DUNDES, ALAN. "Earth-Diver: Creation of the Mythopoeic Male," *American Anthropologist* 64 (1962).

DUNN, STEPHEN P., AND E. DUNN. *The Peasants of Central Asia.* New York: Holt, Rinehart and Winston, 1967.

DURKHEIM, EMILE. *The Elementary Forms of the Religious Life.* New York: George Allen and Unwin Ltd., 1915.

EASTWELL, HARRY D. "Voodoo Death and the Mechanism for Dispatch of the Dying in East Arnhem, Australia," *American Anthropologist* 84 (1982).

EISTER, ALLAN. "An Outline of a Structural Theory of Cults," *Journal for the Scientific Study of Religion* 11 (1972).

ELIADE, MIRCEA. *The Myth of Eternal Return: Cosmos and History.* Princeton, N.J.: Princeton University Press, 1954.

———. *The Sacred and the Profane: The Nature of Religion.* New York: Harcourt Brace Jovanovich, 1957.

———. *Rites and Symbols of Initiation: The Mysteries of Birth and Rebirth.* New York: Harper Torchbooks, 1958.

———. *Shamanism: Archaic Techniques of Ecstasy.* Princeton: Princeton University Press, 1972 (1964).

———. *The Quest: History and Meaning in Religion.* Chicago: University of Chicago Press, 1969.

———. *A History of Religious Ideas.* Chicago: University of Chicago Press, 1982.

EMENEAU, M.B. "Dravidian and Indo-Aryan: The Linguistic Area," In A.F. Sjoberg, ed. *Symposium on Dravidian Civilization.* New York: Jenkins Publishing Company, 1971.

EVANS-PRITCHARD, E.E. *Witchcraft, Oracles and Magic Among the Azande.* Oxford: Clarendon Press, 1937.

———. *Nuer Religion.* Oxford: Clarendon Press, 1956.

———. *Theories of Primitive Religion.* Oxford: Clarendon Press, 1965.

FAGAN, BRIAN M. *Clash of Cultures.* New York: W.H. Freeman, 1984.

FARON, LOUIS. *The Mapuche Indians.* New York: Holt, Rinehart and Winston, 1968.

FARQUHAR, JOHN N. *Modern Religious Movements in India.* London: Macmillan, 1929.

FERM, VERGILIUS, ED. *Ancient Religions.* New York: The Citadel Press, 1965.

FERNANDEZ, JAMES W. "The Mission of Metaphor in Expressive Culture," *Current Anthropology* 15 (1974): 119–145.

———. *Persuasions and Performances: The Play of Tropes in Culture.* Bloomington: Indiana University Press, 1986.

FEUCHTWANG, STEPHAN. "Investigating Religion," in M. Bloch, ed. *Marxist Analysis and Social Anthropology.* London: Tavistock Publications, 1984.

FEUERBACH, LUDWIG. *The Essence of Christianity.* New York: Frederick Ungar Publishing Company, 1957.

FIRTH, RAYMOND. *Symbols: Public and Private.* Ithaca, N.Y.: Cornell University Press, 1973.

FORTUNE, REO. *Sorcerers of Dobu.* London: George Routledge and Sons, 1932.

FOX, ROBIN. *The Red Lamp of Incest.* New York: Free Press, 1980.

FRASER, THOMAS M., JR. *Fishermen of South Thailand.* New York: Holt, Rinehart and Winston, 1966.

FRAZER, JAMES. *Totemism and Exogamy* (4 volumes). London: Macmillan, 1910.

———. *The Golden Bough: A Study in Magic and Religion* (12 volumes). London: Macmillan, 1911–1915.

———. *Creation and Evolution in Primitive Societies.* London: Macmillan, 1935.

———. *The Fear of the Dead in Primitive Religion* (3 volumes). London: Macmillan, 1936.

FREEMAN, JAMES M. "Introduction: The Crosscultural Study of Mother Worship," in J.J. Preston, ed. *Mother Worship.* Chapel Hill: University of North Carolina Press, 1982.

FREUD, SIGMUND. *The Future of an Illusion.* New York: Doubleday Anchor Books, n.d. (1927).

———. "Totem and Taboo," in A.A. Brill, ed. *Basic Writings of Sigmund Freud.* New York: Modern Library, 1938.

———. *Moses and Monotheism.* New York: Alfred A. Knopf, 1947 (1939).

FRIEDL, ERNESTINE. *Vasilika.* New York: Holt, Rinehart and Winston, 1962.

FUCHS, STEPHEN. *Rebellious Prophets: A Study of Messianic Movements in Indian Religions.* Bombay: Asia Publishing House, 1965.

FURER-HAIMENDORF, CHRISTOPH VON. *The Konyak Nagas.* New York: Holt, Rinehart and Winston, 1969.

FURST, PETER T., AND MICHAEL D. COE. "Ritual Enemas," *Natural History* 86 (1977).

GEERTZ, CLIFFORD. "Religion as a Cultural System," in M. Banton, ed. *Anthropological Approaches to the Study of Religion.* London: Tavistock Publications, 1966.

———. "Religion: Anthropological Study," *International Encyclopedia of Social Sciences* 13 (1968).

———. *Islam Observed.* Chicago: University of Chicago Press, 1969.

———. *The Interpretation of Cultures.* New York: Basic Books, 1973.

———. *Local Knowledge.* New York: Basic Books, 1983.

GLOCK, C.Y., AND R.N. BELLAH, EDS. *The New Religious Consciousness.* Berkeley: University of California Press, 1976.

GLUCKMAN, MAX. *Rituals of Rebellion in South-East Africa.* Manchester: Manchester University Press, 1954.

GOBLE, FRANK. *The Third Force: The Psychology of Abraham Maslow-A Revolutionary New View of Man.* New York: Pocket Books, 1970.

GOFFMAN, ERVING. *The Presentation of Self in Everyday Life.* New York: Doubleday and Company, 1959.

GOLDSTEIN, LEON J. "The Phenomenological and Naturalistic Approaches to the Social," *Methodos* 14 (1961).

GOODE, WILLIAM J. *Religion Among the Primitives.* Glencoe, Ill.: The Free Press, 1951.

GOODENOUGH, WARD H. "Componential Analysis and the Study of Meaning," *Language* 32 (1956).
――――. *Cultural Anthropology and Linguistics. Report of the Seventh Annual Round Table Meeting on Linguistics and Language Study.* Washington: Georgetown University Monograph No. 9, 1957.
GORDON, HENRY. "The Shirley MacLaine Phenomenon," *Skeptical Inquirer* 13 (1989).
GRANT, MICHAEL. *Roman Myths.* New York: Dorset Press, 1971.
GRAVES, ROBERT. *The White Goddess: A Historical Grammar of Poetic Myth.* New York: Vintage Books, 1948.
GRIMAL, PIERRE. *World Mythology.* New York: Paul Hamlyn, 1969.
GROBSMITH, ELIZABETH S. *Lakota of the Rosebud: A Contemporary Ethnography.* New York: Holt, Rinehart and Winston, 1981.
GROF, STANISLAV. *The Adventure of Self-Discovery.* Albany, N.Y.: State University of New York Press, 1988.
GUTHRIE, STEWART. "A Cognitive Theory of Religion," *Current Anthropology* 21 (1980).
HAMILTON, EDITH. *Mythology.* New York: New American Library, 1958.
HARNER, MICHAEL J., ED. *Hallucinogens and Shamanism.* New York: Oxford University Press, 1973.
――――. *The Way of the Shaman.* New York: Harper & Row, Publishers, 1980.
HARRE, ROM. *Personal Being: A Theory for Individual Psychology.* Cambridge, Mass.: Harvard University Press, 1987.
HARRIS, MARVIN. *The Rise of Anthropological Theory: A History of Theories of Culture.* New York: Thomas Y. Crowell Co., 1968.
――――. *Cows, Pigs, Wars and Witches: The Riddles of Culture.* New York: Random House, 1974.
――――. *Cannibals and Kings: The Origins of Cultures.* New York: Random House, 1977.
――――. *Cultural Materialism: The Struggle for a Science of Culture.* New York: Vintage Books, 1979.
HART, GEORGE. "Women and the Sacred in Ancient Tamilnad," *The Journal of Asian Studies* 32 (1973).
HAWKES, TERENCE. *Structuralism and Semiotics.* Berkeley: University of California Press, 1977.
HEELAS, PAUL. "Semantic Anthropology and Rules," in Peter Collett, ed. *Social Rules and Social Behavior.* Totowa, N.J.: Rowman and Littlefield, 1977.
HILL, W.W. "The Navaho Indians and the Ghost Dance of 1890," *American Anthropologist* 46 (1944).
HITCHCOCK, JOHN T. *The Magars of Banyan Hill.* New York: Holt, Rinehart and Winston, 1966.
HOBSBAWM, E.J. *Primitive Rebels.* Manchester: Manchester University Press, 1959.
HODGEN, MARGARET T. *Early Anthropology in the Sixteenth and Seventeenth Centuries.* Philadelphia: University of Pennsylvania Press, 1964.
HOEBEL, E. ADAMSON. *The Cheyennes: Indians of the Great Plains.* New York: Holt, Rinehart and Winston, 1978.
HOGBIN, IAN. *The Island of Menstruating Men.* Scranton, Pa.: Chandler Publishing Company, 1970.
HONIGMANN, JOHN J. *The Development of Anthropological Ideas.* Homewood, Ill.: The Dorsey Press, 1976.
HOROWITZ, MICHAEL M. *Morne-Paysan.* New York: Holt, Rinehart and Winston, 1967.
HORTON, ROBIN. "Neo-Tylorianism: Sound Sense or Sinister Prejudice," *Man* 3 (1968).

HOSTETLER, JOHN A., AND G.E. HUNTINGTON. *The Hutterites in North America.* New York: Holt, Rinehart and Winston, 1967.

HOWELLS, WILLIAM. *The Heathens: Primitive Man and His Religions.* Salem, Mass.: Sheffield Publishing Company, 1986 (1948).

HSU, FRANCIS L.K. *Under the Ancestors' Shadow: Kinship, Personality and Social Mobility in China.* Stanford, Calif.: Stanford University Press, 1967.

HUGHES, H.S. *Consciousness and Society.* New York: Random House, 1958.

HUME, DAVID. *Dialogues Concerning Natural Religion.* New York: Thomas Nelson and Sons, Ltd., 1947 (1779).

HUTTON, J.H. *Caste in India.* Oxford: Oxford University Press, 1961.

JAMES, WILLIAM. *The Varieties of Religious Experience.* New York: Modern Library, 1937.

JARVIE, I.C. "The Problem of Rationality in Magic," *British Journal of Sociology* 18 (1967).

———. "On the Limits of Symbolic Interpretation in Anthropology," *Current Anthropology* 17 (1976).

JORGENSEN, JOSEPH. *The Sun Dance Religion.* Chicago: University of Chicago Press, 1972.

JUNG, CARL G. *Psychology and Religion.* New Haven: Yale University Press, 1938.

———. *The Undiscovered Self.* New York: New American Library, 1957.

———. *Psyche and Symbol.* New York: Doubleday, 1958.

———. "Psychological Commentary," in W.Y. Evans-Wentz, ed. *The Tibetan Book of the Dead.* New York: Oxford University Press, 1960.

———, ed. *Man and His Symbols.* London: Pan Books, 1964.

KALWEIT, HOLGER. *Dreamtime and Inner Space: The World of the Shaman.* Boston: Shambhala, 1988.

KAMINSKY, H. "The Problem of Explanation," in S. Thrupp, ed. *Millennial Dreams in Action.* The Hague: Mouton and Co., 1962.

KARDINER, ABRAM, AND E. PREBLE. *They Studied Man.* New York: New American Library, 1961.

KING, R. "The Eros Ethos: Cult in the Counter-Culture," *Psychology Today* 6 (1972).

KLUCKHOHN, CLYDE. "Myths and Rituals: A General Theory," *Harvard Theological Review* 35 (1942).

———. *Navaho Witchcraft.* Boston: Beacon Press, 1944.

———. "Foreword," in W.A. Lessa and E.Z. Vogt, eds. *Reader in Comparative Religion* (Third Edition). New York: Harper & Row, Publishers, 1979.

KOLAKOWSKI, LESZEK. *Religion.* New York: Oxford University Press, 1982.

KROEBER, ALFRED L. *Handbook of the Indians of California.* BAE Bulletin 78 (1925).

KUPER, HILDA. *The Swazi: A South African Kingdom.* New York: Holt, Rinehart and Winston, 1986.

KURTZ, PAUL. "The New Age in Perspective," *The Skeptical Inquirer* 13 (1989).

LABARRE, WESTON. *The Peyote Cult.* New York: Schocken Books, 1970.

———. *The Ghost Dance: The Origins of Religion.* New York: Dell Publishing Co., Inc., 1972.

LANTERNARI, VITTORIO. *The Religions of the Oppressed: A Study of Modern Messianic Cults.* New York: Alfred A. Knopf, 1963.

———. "Nativistic and Socio-religious Movements: A Reconsideration," *Comparative Studies in Society and History* 16, 4 (1974).

LAWRENCE, GEORGE M. "Crystals," *The Skeptical Inquirer* 13 (1989).

LEACH, E.R. "Pulleyar and the Lord Buddha: An Aspect of Religious Syncretism in Ceylon," *Psychoanalysis and Psychoanalytic Review* XLIX (1962).

———. "Ritualization in Man in Relation to Conceptual and Social Development," *Philosophical Transactions of the Royal Society of London* 251 (1966).

————. *The Structural Study of Myth and Totemism*. London: Tavistock Publications, 1967.

————. *Claude Levi-Strauss*. New York: Viking Press, 1970.

————. *Culture and Communication*. Cambridge: Cambridge University Press, 1976.

————. "Genesis as Myth," *Discovery*, May 1982.

LEACH, E.R., AND D. ALAN AYCOCK. *Structuralist Interpretations of Biblical Myth*. Cambridge: Cambridge University Press, 1983.

LEACOCK, SETH, AND RUTH LEACOCK. *Spirits of the Deep: A Study of an Afro-Brazilian Cult*. New York: Anchor Books, 1975.

LEHMAN, ARTHUR C., AND J.E. MYERS, EDS. *Magic, Witchcraft, and Religion: An Anthropological Study of the Supernatural*. Palo Alto, Calif.: Mayfield Publishing Company, 1985.

LESSA, WILLIAM A. "Discoverer-of-the-Sun," *Journal of American Folklore* 79 (1966a).

————. *Ulithi*. New York: Holt, Rinehart and Winston, 1966a.

LESSA, WILLIAM A., AND E.Z. VOGT, EDS. *Reader in Comparative Religion*. New York: Harper & Row, Publishers, 1972.

————. *Reader in Comparative Religion* (Fourth Edition). New York: Harper & Row, Publishers, 1979.

LESSON, IDA. *Bibliography of Cargo Cults and Other Nativistic Movements in the South Pacific*. Sydney: South Pacific Commission, Technical Paper No. 30, 1952.

LETT, JAMES. *The Human Enterprise: A Critical Introduction to Anthropological Theory*. Boulder, Co.: Westview Press, 1987.

LEVI-STRAUSS, CLAUDE. "The Structural Study of Myth," *Journal of American Folklore* 67 (1955).

————. *The Savage Mind*. Chicago: University of Chicago Press, 1962.

————. "The Sorcerer and His Magic," in Claude Levi-Strauss. *Structural Anthropology*. New York: Basic Books, 1963a.

————. *Structural Anthropology*. New York: Basic Books, 1963b.

————. *The Raw and the Cooked: Introduction to a Science of Mythology*, 1. New York: Harper & Row, Publishers, 1964.

————. *From Honey to Ashes: Introduction to a Science of Mythology*, 2. New York: Harper & Row, Publishers, 1966.

————. *The Scope of Anthropology*. London: Jonathan Cape Ltd., 1967.

————. *Tristes Tropiques*. New York: Atheneum, 1968.

————. *Totemism*. Middlesex: Penguin Books, 1969.

————. *The View from Afar*. New York: Basic Books, 1984.

LEVY-BRUHL, LUCIEN. *How Natives Think*. New York: Alfred A. Knopf, 1925.

————. *Primitive Mentality*. New York: The Macmillan Co., 1923.

————. *Primitives and the Supernatural*. New York: Haskell House Publishers, 1973.

————. *Primitive Mythology: The Mythic World of the Australian and Papuan Natives*. Brisbane, Australia: University of Queensland Press, 1983.

LIENHARDT, GODFREY. *Divinity and Experience: The Religion of the Dinka*. Oxford: Oxford University Press, 1961.

LINTON, RALPH. "The Comanche Sun Dance," *American Anthropologist* 37, 3 (1935).

————. "Nativistic Movements," *American Anthropologist* 45 (1943).

LITTLETON, C. SCOTT. *The New Comparative Mythology: An Anthropological Assessment of the Theories of Georges Dumezil* (Third Edition). Berkeley: University of California Press, 1982.

LONG, J. *Voyages and Travels of an Indian Interpreter and Trader*. Chicago: University of Chicago Press, 1922 (1791).

LOWIE, ROBERT H. *Primitive Religion*. New York: Boni and Liveright, 1924.

MAIR, L.P. "Independent Religious Movements in Three Continents," *Comparative Studies in Society and History* 1, 2 (1959).

————. *Witchcraft.* New York: McGraw-Hill Publishing Company, 1971 (1969).

MALEFIJT, ANNMARIE DE W. *Religion and Culture: An Introduction to Anthropology of Religion.* New York: Macmillan Publishing Company, 1968.

MALINOWSKI, BRONISLAW. *Myth in Primitive Psychology.* New York: W.W. Norton and Co., 1925.

————. *Magic, Science and Religion.* New York: Doubleday and Co., 1954.

MANDELBAUM, DAVID G. "Form, Variation, and Meaning of a Ceremony," in R.F. Spencer, ed. *Method and Perspective in Anthropology.* Minneapolis: University of Minnesota Press, 1954.

MARETT, ROBERT R. *The Threshold of Religion.* London: Methuen and Co., 1909.

MARRIOTT, MCKIM. "The Feast of Love," in Milton Singer, ed. *Krishna: Myths, Rites and Attitudes.* Honolulu: East–West Center Press, 1966.

MARSELLA, A.J., ET AL., EDS. *Culture and Self: Asian and Western Perspectives.* New York: Tavistock Publications, 1985.

MARTINDALE, DON. *The Nature and Types of Sociological Theory.* Boston: Houghton Mifflin Co., 1960.

MARWICK, MAX, ED. *Witchcraft and Sorcery.* Middlesex: Penguin Books, 1970.

MAUSS, MARCEL. *A General Theory of Magic.* New York: W.W. Norton and Co., 1975.

MCCLELLAND, DAVID C. *The Achieving Society.* Princeton, N.J.: D. Van Nostrand, 1961.

MEAD, GEORGE H. "The Social Self," *The Journal of Philosophy* 10 (1913).

————. *Mind, Self and Society.* Chicago: University of Chicago Press, 1934.

MERTON, DON, AND GARY SCHWARTZ. "Metaphor and Self: Symbolic Process in Everyday Life," *American Anthropologist* 84 (1982): 796–810.

MESSENGER, JOHN C. *Inis Beag.* New York: Holt, Rinehart and Winston, 1969.

METRAUX, ALFRED. *Voodoo in Haiti.* New York: Schocken Books, 1972.

MIDDLETON, JOHN J., ED. *Lugbara Religion.* New York: Holt, Rinehart and Winston, 1965.

————, ed. *Magic, Witchcraft, and Curing.* New York: The Natural History Press, 1967a.

————. *Gods and Rituals: Readings in Religious Beliefs and Practices.* New York: The Natural History Press, 1967b.

————. *Myth and Cosmos: Readings in Mythology and Symbolism.* New York: The Natural History Press, 1967c.

MOERMAN, DANIEL E. "Anthropology of Symbolic Healing," *Current Anthropology* 20, 1 (1979).

MOONEY, JAMES. *The Ghost Dance Religion and the Sioux Outbreak of 1890* (Abridged Edition). Chicago: University of Chicago Press, 1965 (1896).

MOORE, OMAR K. "Divination: A New Perspective," *American Anthropologist* 59 (1957).

MORRIS, BRIAN. *Anthropological Studies of Religion: An Introductory Text.* Cambridge: Cambridge University Press, 1987.

MULLER, MAX. *Lectures on the Science of Language.* New York: C. Scribner and Col., 1870.

MURRAY, MARGARET A. *The Witch-Cult in Western Europe.* Oxford: Clarendon Press, 1921.

NADEL, S.F. "A Study of Shamanism in the Nuba Mountains," *JRAI* 76 (1946).

NEWMAN, PHILIP L. *Knowing the Gururumba.* New York: Holt, Rinehart and Winston, 1965.

NORBECK, EDWARD. *Religion in Primitive Society.* New York: Harper & Row, Publishers, 1961.

———. *Religion in Human Life.* New York: Holt, Rinehart and Winston, 1974.

OBEYESEKERE, GANANATH. *Medusa's Hair: An Essay on Personal Symbols and Religious Experience.* Chicago: University of Chicago Press, 1981.

O'FLAHERTY, W.D. *Siva: The Erotic Ascetic.* New York: Oxford University Press, 1973.

———. *Women, Androgynes, and Other Mythical Beasts.* Chicago and London: University of Chicago Press, 1980.

———. "Origins of Myth-Making Man" (review of Joseph Campbell's Historical Atlas of World Mythology), *The New York Times Book Review,* December 18, 1983.

O'HARA, MAUREEN. "A New Age Reflection in the Magic Mirror of Science," *The Skeptical Inquirer* 13 (1989).

OHNUKI-TIERNEY, EMIKO. *The Ainu of the Northwest Coast of Southern Sakhalin.* New York: Holt, Rinehart and Winston, 1974.

O'KEEFE, D. *The Social Theory of Magic.* Oxford: Clarendon Press, 1982.

OPLER, MORRIS E. "An Interpretation of Ambivalence of Two American Indian Tribes," *Journal of Social Psychology* 7 (1936).

ORTNER, SHERRY B. "On Key Symbols," *American Anthropologist* 75 (1973).

———. "Theory in Anthropology Since the Sixties," *Society for Comparative Study of Society and History* 26 (1984).

PANDIAN, JACOB. "Rituals of Reversal Among the North American Indians," Department of Anthropology, Rice University, Houston, 1970.

———. "The Teaching of the History of Anthropology as a Course on Western Intellectual Tradition," *AAA Newsletter* 20 (1982).

———. "Anthropology in the Humanities," *AAA Newsletter* 25 (1984).

———. *Anthropology and the Western Tradition: Toward an Authentic Anthropology.* Prospect Heights, Ill.: Waveland Press, 1985.

PARKER, SEYMOUR. "Rituals of Gender: A Study of Etiquette, Public Symbols, and Cognition," *American Anthropologist* 90 (1988).

PARSONS, TALCOTT, ET AL. *Toward a General Theory of Action.* New York: Harper & Row, Publishers, 1951.

———. "Religious Perspectives in Sociology and Social Psychology," in W. Lessa and E. Vogt, eds. *Reader in Comparative Religion.* New York: Harper & Row, Publishers, 1972.

PEACOCK, JAMES L. *The Anthropological Lens: Harsh Light, Soft Focus.* New York: Cambridge University Press, 1986.

PEARCE, JOSEPH C. *The Crack in the Cosmic Egg: Challenging Constructs of Mind and Reality.* New York: Julian Press, 1971.

PEIRCE, C.S. "Semiotic and Significs." In C.S. Hardwick, ed. *The Correspondence between Charles S. Peirce and Victoria Lady Welby.* Bloomington, In.: Indiana Univ. Press, 1977.

PERINBANAYAGAM, R.S. *Signifying Acts: Structure and Meaning in Everyday Life.* Carbondale: Southern Illinois University Press, 1985.

PETTIT, PHILIP. *The Concept of Structuralism: A Critical Analysis.* Los Angeles: University of California Press, 1975.

POOLE, ROGER C. "Introduction," in Claude Levi-Strauss. *Totemism.* Middlesex: Penguin Books, 1969.

POSPISIL, LEOPOLD. *The Kapauku Papuans of West New Guinea.* New York: Holt, Rinehart and Winston, 1964.

PRESTON, JAMES J., ED. *Mother Worship: Theme and Variation.* Chapel Hill: University of North Carolina Press, 1982.

RADCLIFFE-BROWN, A.R. *Taboo*. Cambridge: Cambridge University Press, 1972 [1939].

————. *Structure and Function in Primitive Society*. New York: The Free Press, 1952.

RADIN, PAUL. *Primitive Religion: Its Nature and Origin*. New York: Viking Press, 1937.

————. *The Trickster: A Study in American Indian Mythology*. New York: Schocken Books, 1956.

————. *The Autobiography of a Winnebago Indian*. New York: Dover Publications, Inc., 1963.

RAPPAPORT, ROY A. *Pigs for the Ancestors*. New Haven: Yale University Press, 1968.

————. *Ecology, Meaning, and Religion*. Richmond, Va.: North Atlantic Books, 1979.

————. *The Construction of Time and Eternity in Ritual*. Department of Anthropology, Indiana University, Bloomington, 1986.

RAY, BENJAMIN C. *African Religions: Symbol, Ritual, and Community*. Englewood Cliffs, N.J.: Prentice-Hall, Inc., 1976.

REED, GHALAM. "The Psychology of Chanelling," *The Skeptical Inquirer* 13 (1989).

REICHEL-DOLMATOFF, G. *The Shaman and the Janguar: A Study of Narcotic Drugs Among the Indians of Columbia*. Philadelphia: Temple University Press, 1975.

REYNOLDS, V., AND R.E.S. TANNER. *The Biology of Religion*. White Plains, N.Y.: Longman, 1983.

RIGBY, PETER. "Some Gogo Rituals of 'Purification': An Essay of Social and Moral Categories," in E.R. Leach, ed. *Dialectic in Practical Religion*. Cambridge: Cambridge University Press, 1968.

RITZER, GEORGE. *Contemporary Sociological Theory*. New York: Alfred A. Knopf, 1983.

ROSEN, JAY. "Consumer Culture and the New Age," *The Skeptical Inquirer* 13 (1989).

ROSSI, INO, ED. *The Unconscious in Culture: The Structuralism of Claude Levi-Strauss in Perspective*. New York: E.P. Dutton and Co., Inc., 1974.

SCHIEFFELIN, EDWARD L. *The Sorrow of the Lonely and the Burning of the Dancers*. New York: St. Martin's Press, 1976.

SCHULTZ, TED. "The New Age: The Need for Myth in an Age of Science," *The Skeptical Inquirer* 13 (1989).

SCHWARTZ, T. *The Paliau Movement in the Admiralty Islands, 1946–1954*. New York: The American Museum of Natural History, 1962.

SHWEDER, RICHARD A., AND R.A. LEVINE, ED. *Culture Theory: Essays on Mind, Self, and Emotion*. Cambridge: Cambridge University Press, 1984.

SIMPSON, G.E. "The Ras Tafari Movement in Jamaica and Its Millennial Aspects," in S. Thrupp, ed. *Millennial Dreams in Action*. The Hague: Mouton and Co., 1962.

SINGER, MARGARET T. "Coming Out of Cults," *Psychology Today* 12 (1979).

SINGER, MILTON. "Signs of the Self: An Exploration in Semiotic Anthropology," *American Anthropologist* 82 (1980).

SISKIN, EDGAR E. *Washo Shamans and Peyotists*. Salt Lake City: University of Utah Press, 1983.

SKORUPSKI, JOHN. *Symbol and Theory: A Philosophical Study of Theories of Religion in Social Anthropology*. Cambridge: Cambridge University Press, 1983.

SLOTKIN, J.S. *The Peyote Religion: A Study in Indian-White Relations*. Glencoe, Ill.: The Free Press, 1956.

SMITH, W. ROBERTSON. *The Religion of the Semites*. New York: Shocken Books, 1972 (1889).

————. *The Prophets of Israel and Their Place in History to the Close of the Eighth Century B.C.* Edinburgh: A. and C. Black, 1882.

SPINDLER, G.D. "Personality and Peyotism in Menomini Indian Acculturation," *Psychiatry* 15 (1952).

SPIRO, MELFORD E. "Ghosts, Ifaluk, and Teleological Functionalism," *American Anthropologist* 54 (1952).
————. "Religion: Problems of Definition and Explanation," in M. Banton, ed. *Anthropological Approaches to the Study of Religion.* London: Tavistock Publications, 1966.
————. *Burmese Supernaturalism.* Englewood Cliffs, N.J.: Prentice-Hall, Inc., 1967.
SPIRO, MELFORD E., AND ROY D'ANDRADE. "A Cross-Cultural Study of Some Supernatural Beliefs," in Clelland S. Ford, ed. *Cross-Cultural Approaches.* New Haven: HRAF Press, 1967.
STALL, J.F. "Sanskrit and Sanskritization," *The Journal of Asian Studies* 22 (1963).
STANNER, W.E.H. "On the Interpretation of Cargo Cults," *Oceania* 29 (1958).
————. *On Aboriginal Religion.* Sydney: Oceania Monographs 11 (1963).
SUNDKLER, B.G.M. *Bantu Prophets in South Africa.* London: Lutterworth Press, 1948.
SWANSON, GUY E. *The Birth of Gods: The Origin of Primitive Beliefs.* Ann Arbor: University of Michigan Press, 1960.
————. *The Birth of Gods: The Origin of Primitive Beliefs.* New Haven: HRAF Press, 1962.
TALMON, Y. "Pursuit of the Millennium," *Ar. Er. Sociology* 3 (1962).
THRUPP, S.L. *Millennial Dreams in Action.* The Hague: Mouton and Co., 1962.
TREVOR-ROPER, H.R. *The European Witch-Craze of the Sixteenth and Seventeenth Centuries.* New York: Harper & Row, Publishers, 1967.
TRIGGER, BRUCE G. *The Huron.* New York: Holt, Rinehart and Winston, 1969.
TUCHMAN, BARBARA W. *A Distant Mirror: The Calamitous 14th Century.* New York: Ballantine Books, 1979.
TURNER, VICTOR W. *Ndembu Divination.* Manchester: Manchester University Press, 1961.
————. *Chihamba, the White Spirit.* Manchester: Manchester University Press, 1962.
————. *The Forest of Symbols.* Ithaca, N.Y. Cornell University Press, 1967.
————. "Religious Specialists: Anthropological Study," *International Encyclopedia of the Social Sciences* 13 (1968).
————. *The Ritual Process: Structure and Anti-Structure.* Chicago: Aldine Publishing Co., 1969.
————. "Symbols in African Ritual," *Science* 179 (1973).
————. *Dramas, Fields, and Metaphors: Symbolic Action in Society.* Ithaca, N.Y.: Cornell University Press, 1974.
————. "Comments and Conclusions," in B.A. Babcock, ed. *The Reversible World: Symbolic Inversion in Art and Society.* Ithaca, N.Y.: Cornell University Press, 1978.
TYLER, STEPHEN A. *India: An Anthropological View.* Pacific Palisades, Calif.: Goodyear Publishing House, 1973.
TYLOR, EDWARD B. *Primitive Culture* (2 Vols.) London: John Murray, 1957 (1873).
ULIN, ROBERT C. *Understanding Cultures: Perspectives in Anthropology and Social Theory.* Austin: University of Texas Press, 1988.
VAN BAAL, J. *Symbols for Communication: An Introduction to the Anthropological Study of Religion.* Assen, Netherlands: Van Gorcum and Co., 1971.
VAN GENNEP, ARNOLD. *The Rites of Passage.* Chicago: University of Chicago Press, 1960 (1909).
VAYDA, ANTHONY P., ANTHONY LEEDS, AND DAVID SMITH. "The Place of Pigs in Melanesian Subsistence." In Viola E. Garfield, ed. *Proceedings of the American Ethnological Society.* Seattle, Wa.: University of Washington Press, 1961.
VOGT, EVON Z. "Water Witching: An Interpretation of a Ritual Pattern in a Rural American Community," *Scientific Monthly* 75 (1952).
WADLEY, SUSAN SNOW. *Shakti: Power in the Conceptual Structure of Karimpur Religion.* Chicago: University of Chicago Press, 1975.

WALLACE, ANTHONY F.C. "Revitalization Movements," *American Anthropologist* 58 (1956).

―――. *Religion: An Anthropological View.* New York: Random House, 1966.

―――. *The Death and Rebirth of the Seneca.* New York: Random House, 1969.

WALLIS, ROY. "Ideology, Authority and the Development of Cultic Movements," *Social Research* 41 (1974).

―――. "Scientology: Therapeutic Cult to Religious Sect." *Journal of the British Sociological Association* 9 (1975).

―――. *The Road to Total Freedom.* New York: Columbia University Press, 1976.

WARBURG, MARGIT. "William Robertson Smith and the Study of Religion," *Religion* 19 (1989).

WEBER, MAX. *The Theory of Social and Economic Organization.* New York: The Free Press, 1947.

―――. *The Protestant Ethic and the Spirit of Capitalism.* London: George Allen and Unwin, 1958 (1930).

―――. *The Religion of India: The Sociology of Hinduism and Buddhism.* New York: The Free Press, 1958.

―――. *The Sociology of Religion.* Boston: Beacon Press, 1963.

―――. *The Religion of China: Confucianism and Taoism.* New York: The Free Press, 1964 (1951).

WHITE, LESLIE. "Culturological vs. Psychological Interpretations of Human Behavior," *American Sociological Review* 22, 6 (1947).

WHITING, JOHN W.M. "Socialization Process and Personality." In. F.L.K. Hsu, ed. *Psychological Anthropology.* Homewood, Ill.: Dorsey Press, 1961.

WILLIS, R.G. "The Head and the Loins: Levi-Strauss and Beyond," *Man* 2 (1967).

WINCH, PETER. *The Idea of a Social Science and Its Relation to Philosophy.* London: Routledge and Kegan Paul, 1958.

WOLF, ERIC. "The Virgin of Guadalupe: A Mexican National Symbol," *Journal of American Folklore,* 71 (1958).

―――. *Europe and the People Without History.* Berkeley: University of California Press, 1982.

WORSLEY, PETER. *The Trumpet Shall Sound.* London: Macgibbon and Kee, 1957.

―――. "Millenarian Movements in Melanesia," in J. Middleton, ed. *Gods and Rituals.* Garden City, N.Y.: The Natural History Press, 1967.

WUTHNOW, ROBERT, ET AL. *Cultural Analysis.* London: Routledge and Kegan Paul, 1984.

YINGER, MILTON. *Religion, Society and the Individual: An Introduction to the Sociology of Religion* (Part I). New York: Macmillan, 1957.

YOUNG, F.W. *Initiation Ceremonies: A Cross-Cultural Study of Status Dramatization.* Indianapolis, In.: Bobbs-Merrill Co., 1965.

ZNANIECKI, FLORIAN. *Cultural Reality.* Chicago: University of Chicago Press, 1914.

―――. *The Method of Sociology.* New York: Farrar and Rinehart, 1934.

Index

A

Aberle, David, 30, 113–14
Afro-American polytheistic religious
    movements, 125–29
Animism, 9, 40–41

B

Beck, Brenda, 90
Benedict, Ruth, 18, 79
Berger, Peter, 80–81, 118
Bettelheim, Bruno, 174
Boardman, E.P., 120
Brown, Michael, 205

C

Cannon, Walter B., 158
Carstairs, Morris, 57

Cassirer, Ernst, 132
Casteneda, Carlos, 95, 109, 201
Charisma, 59
Cohen, Abner, 87–88
Comte, August, 35–36
Crawford, J.R., 159–61
Culture:
    definitions of, 3, 13–16, 59, 64

D

Divination, 157–58
Douglas, Mary, 26–27, 75–76
Durkheim Emile, 10–11, 22–23, 37,
    45, 47–49

E

Eliade, Mircea, 82, 173–75, 194
Eschatology, 20, 175–76